Some comments about *The* about **Jack Olsen:**

"*The Pitcher's Kid* is a haunting memoir full of laughter and tears that beautifully depicts the ancient inherited shame of fathers and sons." - Joseph Wambaugh

"This book is a treasure. The last of the deep footprints left by the master, and our first insight into his "formative" years, combining that self-deprecating style Jack always used when speaking of himself with information we never expected to see the light of day. Anyone interested in journalism, true-crime reporting, or writing with real narrative force who passes this one up is passing up the entire course for the price of cab fare to the school. And, not for nothing, this one hit me deep in the heart. Hard." - Andrew Vachss

"I'd known for years that Jack Olsen was the preeminent true-crime writer of our time. Now - ten years after his death - I find out he's a gifted memoirist as well. *The Pitcher's Kid* is the best personal account of growing up in the '30s and "40's that I've ever read (and I was there!) - entertaining, insightful, rich in detail, and laugh-out-loud funny. It's a wonderful book!" - Aaron Elkins

"Jack Olsen was the first writer who told me, long before I'd published anything, that I could be a writer. He was one of the most warm, humane, and decent people I ever met, *The Pitcher's Kid* is the story of his early life. I hope you'll read it, I think it's the only thing he ever wrote about himself." - Alan Furst

"With a storyteller's passion for narrative and a forensic investigator's ear for wrong notes, Jack Olsen set the bar for crime journalists. His ultimate goal, he once said, was to learn how and why a child grows up to be a monster. In his best work, Olsen gave us the chilling truth about psychopathic behavior. In *The Pitcher's Kid*, Olsen lovingly writes of a transient childhood where his father, a hustler of dubious reputation and miserable morals, is the ghostly center of the story and the child's measure of manhood. Olsen spent his writing career unveiling the atrocities humans commit. In his own memoir, he shows us the tenacity of a child's love as well as the origin of the author's search for truth." – Zak Mucha, LCSW

"The irascible, quick-witted, and passionately opinionated Jack Olsen lives among us again with the publication of his wonderful and colorful posthumous memoir, *The Pitcher's Kid*, which is at once a window into Jack's soul and a piercing, and telling, emotional and psychological portrait of his younger years. We can now add to the considerable body of his work–33 books–his illuminating self-examination, which sheds light on all the rest even as it stands alone with, in the end, a curious and peculiarly American rough dignity. *The Pitcher's Kid* will prove of value to anyone interested in the art of the memoir, and in the vagaries, too, of paternal love." –David Guterson

Comments for *Salt of the Earth:*

The cold mind of a criminologist, the relentless spirit of an investigative reporter and the searching heart of a poet all combine to produce Jack Olsen — the acknowledged master of American crime journalism.

Comments for *Last Man Standing:*

Jack Olsen, the undisputed King of True Crime, combined dazzling, suspenseful narrative and superb investigative reporting to illuminate one after another dark chapter in American history. His unique blend of surgical logic and lyrical language will never be duplicated. Ever.

The Pitcher's Kid

The Pitcher's Kid

by
Jack Olsen

New York: Aequitas Books

The Pitcher's Kid: A Memoir
by Jack Olsen

ISBN (hardback copy): 978-1-929355-78-5
ISBN (paperback): 978-1-929355-76-1
ISBN (E-Book): 978-1-4657-0632-4
Library of Congress Control Number: 2010905853
Design by Laura Tolkow
Cover by Korum Bischoff
Pleasure Boat Studio (including its imprint, Aequitas Books) is a proud subscriber to the Green Press Initiative. This program encourages the use of 100% post-consumer recycled paper with environmentally friendly inks for all printing projects in an effort to reduce the book industry's economic and social impact. With the cooperation of our printing company, we are pleased to offer this book as a Green Press book.

Aequitas Books is an imprint of Pleasure Boat Studio: A Literary Press
Our books are available through the following:
SPD (Small Press Distribution) Tel. 800-869-7553, Fax 510-524-0852
Partners/West Tel. 425-227-8486, Fax 425-204-2448
Baker & Taylor 800-775-1100, Fax 800-775-7480
Ingram Tel 615-793-5000, Fax 615-287-5429
Amazon.com and **bn.com**

and through
PLEASURE BOAT STUDIO: A LITERARY PRESS
www.pleasureboatstudio.com
201 West 89th Street
New York, NY 10024

Contact **Jack Estes**
Fax; 888-810-5308
Email: pleasboat@nyc.rr.com

Su Su Su Su Su

one
Beginnings

1.

No one in my family expected me to earn my living off murder, mayhem, overtime parking, and other high crimes and misdemeanors. In early photographs I look like a guileless little fellow trying to think of something nice to do for his mommy. Pictures taken with our Kodak Box Brownie show me in droopy socks, short pants, and an oversize cap that could have been worn by a striking miner. In one picture I hold a Bible as a prop, in another a toy car. Family and friends regarded me as a pious and mannerly child. I knew better.

The first victim of my larcenous ways was our bulldog, Jiggs. After Mother put his soaked kibble on the back porch, I nudged him aside and ate his meal. It was the perfect crime. We were both three and a half, but Jiggs couldn't talk.

Our family was vacationing in Atlantic City when I made my next score: a tin of chocolates from Mother's travel case. The brand name was on the little blue box; I couldn't read, but I recognized two X's. We were promenading on the Boardwalk between the frozen custard and Ski-ball when the spasms struck. Before we straggled back to our rented bungalow, I'd paid a call on every public restroom from the Steel Pier to Connecticut Avenue. Daddy promised to enter me in the sprint events at the 1932 Olympics.

The details of my birth in June 1925 have been lost in other events of that portentous month. The country was suffering through a heat wave that took 200 lives. Walter P. Chrysler opened an auto plant. Tennessee schools dismissed the theory of evolution. An earthquake hit Santa Barbara. A man named Schaetzle invented a wireless phone for automobiles. Civil war broke out in China, inflation in Germany, military revolt in Greece. In so much commotion, hardly anyone noticed that a child named John Edward Olsen had been born in St. Vincent's Hospital in Indianapolis, Indiana.

I was never entered in a baby contest, and the old photo albums show why. An uncle told me that Daddy took one look at me and summoned the nurse. Listen, girlie, he said, there's been a big mistake.

When she showed him my I.D. band, he said, Between this here model and a used Hupmobile, I'll take the Hup.

Daddy took his revenge by running out on the hospital bill. He collected me and my nineteen-year-old mother at the back door and drove us non-stop to Detroit. As we passed Navin Field, he reminisced about his triumphs as a Detroit Tiger pitcher. Two or three times he took Mother across the river to Canada to enjoy beverages that were outlawed in the United States. When creditors banged on the door of our furnished room, the landlady would say, They went abroad. Daddy repaid the kindness by sparing her some tedious bookkeeping. We left while owing three months' rent.

After a few weeks in Dallas, we ran up another unpaid bill in a Miami trailer park, then lit out for a low-rent section of Philadelphia. Family history holds that we left Miami just ahead of the 1926 hurricane and that I was napping on our Reo sedan's back seat when a hanging traffic light broke loose and smashed through the rear window. This may or may not be true. Everything concerning my family may or may not be true. As a journalist, I am the only family member trained to tell the whole truth, most of the time.

2.

The human infant has been described as a long tube with a loud noise at one end and a total lack of responsibility at the other. I have no memory of my first few years, but I'm told that I met the description. I recall no moo-cows on the road, no magical timeless summer, no cameras with their shutters open. I wasn't called Ishmael or much of anything except It. When It flung a cupcake against the wall at Its second birthday party, Daddy predicted (mistakenly) that another Olsen was headed for the major leagues.

At three I wobbled around the house in footie pajamas and banged into bureaus and tables. I remember the sting of iodine and the bright red color of Mercurochrome. I squooshed a butterfly to see if there was real butter inside. Mother said I was annoyed at the results.

Early photos show a resemblance to Babe Ruth: the same dark hair, brown eyes, broad face, and upswept nose. Mother later claimed that my looks came from her grandfather Francis Zawadzki, a figure of respect in Jersey City's Polish community and the dominant male in our family tree. The resemblance ended at our personalities. I have tiptoed through life in a state bordering on hysteria, but Great-grandpa Zawadzki feared nothing and no one. He decked a beefy dockworker who referred to him as a greasy Polock. When the man apologized and said he'd meant to say Pole, Francis Zawadzki slammed him against a bulkhead. No Pole, he said. No Polock. Greasy American.

That incident was said to have taken place around 1850, after Great-grandpa and five other members of his family arrived from Gdansk along with mobs of eastern Europeans headed for the coal mines of Appalachia. In three weeks at sea, my ancestors survived on a pig's head and a sack of turnips. Family history holds that Great-grandpa Zawadzki kissed the Hoboken wharf and announced to his wife Balbina Rumienska that they must start speaking American immediately. Overnight, *borscht* became beet soup and *kielbasa* became sausage. Pigs' heads were permanently banished from the menu after he declared, Pig heads for old country.

Apparently Francis Zawadzki was a stern parent whose rules applied in perpetuity. Decades after he died, his daughter Caroline Zawadzki Drecksage sang me a Polish lullaby about a girl who wished for wings like a goose so she could fly to Johnny in Silesia. It was the only time I ever heard my grandmother use the language of her parents. Jackie, she whispered, don't tell nobody.

Great-grandpa Zawadzki was famous in Jersey City for winning a test of strength at the Communipaw Engine Terminal, where he supported his family by chipping slag off locomotive boilers. The roundhouse workers argued over who could move a 4-6-2 Royal Blue Pacific by hand. Great-grandpa's main competitor, a triple-chinned Irishman named Hanlon, shoved and strained, grunted, cursed and gave up. Great-grandpa climbed into the cab, released the brakes, and won handily. Or so I was told by an aunt who died before ethnic jokes were in style. I doubt that she realized she was telling one.

The Zawadzki family remained properly respectful of its patriarch, even in his fading years when he would don a flashy uniform and join in the parades along Ocean Avenue. All spit-and-Polish, the old man would ignore entreaties from his embarrassed children: Pop, it's the Sons of It'ly.... Pop, it's the Spanish-American War Vets....

At intervals along the line of march he would unsheathe his saber and demonstrate some of the techniques that had made the Polish Cavalry the most feared mounted force in north-central eastern Europe.

I hasten to admit that some of these stories may seem short on provenance. Even as a child I didn't believe every word of my family's alleged history. But we had positive proof of one fact (and were quick to show it to doubters): Great-grandfather Zawadzki had served as an officer in the Imperial Polish Army. On our mantelpiece we kept a photo of our aristocratic ancestor in dress uniform, his chest bedecked with embroidery, gloved hand resting on the hilt of his sword, sleeves bearing the four gold stripes that traditionally denote exalted ranks like Navy captain or Supreme Court Chief Justice. Copies of this picture, edged in a frame of simulated gilt, may still be seen in the homes of some of my relatives.

Alas, the photo is not worth a thousand words, or even a dozen. An elderly second cousin informed me that Great-grandpa had posed in the uniform of a Jersey City fraternal order. Before my grandmother died in 1960, she told me that her parents had owned a farm near Warsaw and were run out of Poland by the Cossacks who swept across the country in the 1800s. Sleep well, Field Marshal Zawadzki. I hope you were buried with full military honors.

3.

In 19th-century Denmark, the name Olsen was as common as sprats, but the paternal branch of my family seemed to include no one of that name until certain members decided to reinvent themselves in America. When the soil turned fallow, my ancestors deserted the family farm on Falster Island in the North Sea. My great-grandfather, Ole Kristofferson Moeller, stayed behind with his wife Ane, but their seven sons worked passage to America. By the time of their arrival in the 1850s, they'd recast the family name as Olsen (son of Ole), perhaps to begin a family tradition of eluding bill collectors.

The freshly minted Olsens were met at the Hoboken docks by a Danish-American preacher who guided them to a part of the Wild West where Lutherans were in short supply and had been named after Indians. With one eye out for burning arrows, the brothers helped to build the Danish Lutheran Church in

Indianapolis. My great-aunts Edna and Elva Olsen were the church organists for fifty years.

The immigrant Olsens and their descendants prospered in the New World. Even my raffish father achieved a degree of success. For a few years he earned his living as a juvenile delinquent and newsboy before finding steady work as a baseball pitcher. Daddy claimed that he could curve a baseball around a haystack and through the side of a barn. And if you didn't believe it, he would show you the haystack.

Or so he told eighteen-year-old Florence Mae Drecksage on one of their first meetings. When my sister Carolyn and I were kids, Mother seldom spoke to us about her courtship with Ole Olsen, perhaps because she was never one to dwell on the past. But in her declining years she opened up about the greatest tragedy of her life: her marriage.

4.

My mother and father met in 1924 while he was working in Newark, N.J., as an insurance adjuster, specializing in auto collision. Early photos depict a sternly handsome throwback to the dandyism of a previous century, a bon vivant with the same keen sense of dress style as Zachary Taylor. In the nineteen-twenties and well into the thirties, Daddy's everyday wardrobe included corduroy knickers, flat straw hats, derbies, and high-top shoes. Except when wading, he wore spats. His stiff brown hair was cut about three inches tall, *en brosse*, or what was known in those days as a German haircut. If the pictures in our family albums are any indication, he chain-smoked cigars. His generation seemed to regard the stogy as a mark of distinction.

Flo Drecksage was put off when she first encountered Ole Olsen. He acted fresh and talked out of the side of his mouth.

He told her that "Swede" was his baseball moniker and he didn't care what she called him as long as she didn't call him late for breakfast. Mother had an ear for stale lines and wasn't impressed.

She was equally bored by his baseball credentials. As "Swede" Olsen, he might have pitched in the big leagues, but baseball didn't count for much in the Drecksage family. There were three major-league teams across the bay in New York, and Mother didn't know their names.

She was also put off by his English. His standard greeting amounted to How ya was, Toots? He pronounced the P's in words like *ptomaine* and *pneumonia* on the grounds that the people who invented English had put them there for a reason. *Ain't* and *youse* were staples of his vocabulary, along with double and triple negatives. At first, the lovely young Flo wasn't sure if he was serious or playing the fool. By the time she found out, it was too late.

Somehow this specimen had talked himself into a white-collar job with the New Amsterdam Insurance Company of Newark. At the time Mother was working as a steno for Bristol-Meyers and dating an accounting major at Syracuse University. She was a high school honors graduate, chestnut-haired, hazel-eyed, bright and pretty – and naive, as it turned out. Her friend Mary Martin introduced them. Mother forgave her after fifteen or twenty years.

One Sunday after church, Mary had informed Mother that Ole was smitten with her. Mother said, Doesn't he know that you and I are best friends?

Mary confessed that her own romance with the insurance man was over. He talks about you all the time, Flo. Why don't you go out with him? He doesn't bite.

5.

The ex-pitcher arrived at the Drecksage's first-floor flat on Claremont Avenue in Jersey City in a sputtering car that sent the family beagle diving under a bed. Mother's younger brothers Bob and Sonny stood googoo-eyed as the gentleman caller unlatched the hood to show off the engine. Look here, sport, he said. Twenty horses! Four cylinders. You couldn't buy no better for a thousand clams.

Mother waved a nervous farewell to her family as Ole headed toward the waterfront in a cloud of fumes and dust. He told her he'd written a poem about his car and recited it on the way. Mother was sure the poem was stolen but didn't challenge him. Every man she'd ever met had tried to impress her with little white lies. She asked Ole if he liked Browning. He said he didn't cook.

They parked at the Jersey Central Terminal and took the ferry to Manhattan, where a ten-cent jitney delivered them to a vaudeville theater off Broadway. After the opening number, Ole whispered, That jane can step. Mother gathered that *jane* meant girl and *step* meant dance. If I see this guy again, she said to herself, I hope he brings a translator.

After weeks of persistent attention, Ole arrived at the family residence on foot. Mother asked what happened to his car. He gave a long answer that she didn't understand, as the word *repossess* was not yet in her vocabulary. That night they returned to Broadway for *The Cat and the Canary* with Henry Hull (later to star as the Werewolf of London), and Ole autographed the ticket stubs before handing them to her as souvenirs. She showed them to a friend at Bristol-Meyers. Those are Annie Oakleys, Mother was told. They punch 'em twice so you can't use 'em again. He ain't going broke on ya.

When Mother inquired, Ole explained that the New Amsterdam Company awarded incentives to its top adjusters. She asked what an insurance adjuster did for a living, and he explained that after every car wreck, the customer always demanded too much and the company offered too little. I adjust the difference, he explained. It's a living. Keeps me in walking-around money. He flashed a roll of bills.

Walking-around money. Mother shook her head.

After some polite conversation on her stoop, he told her he had to return to Newark for his beauty sleep. Night, Flo, he said. It's twenty-three skidoo for me.

Mother said, Pardon?

Gotta take it on the lam.

He pecked her on the cheek and left.

6.

On a hot July weekend the courting couple rode the subway to Yankee Stadium. Ole pointed to the sidelines and said, That's Meuse! He don't signify. See that there fat guy? That's the Babe. Swings like a rusty gate. That's Gehrig over there. I got his number. Don't tell nobody....

If he knows so much about baseball, Mother said to herself, why isn't he on the field? She still hadn't learned his age, but he looked to be in his late twenties and seemed healthy enough. When she asked why he'd quit pitching, he said, The old soup bone went bad. Then he changed the subject.

The next weekend he showed up in a 1916 Reo touring car, charcoal black, with side curtains, spoke wheels and two little vases for flowers. It was shaped like a bar of laundry soap. He told her he was test-driving it for a friend. (He test-drove it for years; it was the car that was hit by the falling traffic light in the 1926 hurricane.) En route to Bear Mountain he stopped at a roadhouse speakeasy where he seemed to be known. He ordered an ale for himself and a sarsaparilla for Mother. As they strolled across a meadow, he broke into song:

Although the Kaiser is a friend of Budweiser
Budweiser's a friend of mine....

Mother wondered why he was so backward about music. Hadn't he heard of Paul Whiteman and the Rhythm Boys? Rudy Vallee? Laura La Plante? Some of his selections were from the 1800s. Her German father and Polish grandfather had sung musical tributes to beer, giggling over lines like, If you don't want to drink it, they force it on you....

On the return drive Ole described his riverside home in Indianapolis and other holdings, including a Locomobile racecar and a racehorse. He said he didn't expect to be stuck in Jersey much longer; New Amsterdam Insurance had big plans for him. He said, Stick wit' me, Flo, and you'll wear diamonds.

After a few more dates he bought her a friendship ring. He held it up to a lamp and said, Chick, ain't it? Stimulated rhinestones. Them's the rage this year.

Mother accepted the gift even though something told her she might be making a mistake. Her Syracuse boyfriend hadn't written in weeks, and she'd begun to find him a little dull, with all his talk about double-entry bookkeeping and vertical integration in the ladies' hose industry. Ole was a study in words and music. He waltzed like a professional and performed an energetic buck and wing. He taught her a tango variation that he said he'd worked out on his own.

What do you call it? Mother asked.

The Tapioca, he said. It's registered with the Patent Office.

He offered to do a sand dance if Mother supplied the sand. She asked if he'd ever considered vaudeville and he said he didn't want to put Jolson out of business. He said, Al's the sole support of a aging mother. I went into baseball instead.

7.

En route with Ole to see her favorite movie actor, Francis X. Bushman, Mother admitted to herself that her fiancé was becoming more interesting with each date. He talked about catching sailfish off Miami, racing a car up Pike's Peak and shaking hands with Mr. Pike himself, wrestling a crocodile for Ringling Bros. He said, Take my word, Flo. Them crocs can bite!

Mother had never been south of Bayonne, west of Newark, or north of Hoboken. When they were out on the town, Ole seemed on a first-name basis with everyone. If he ordered two items from a menu, he would instruct the waitress, One must be good, girlie. After the main course, he would ask, What's on the desert? Afterwards he would request the total incurred indemnity. He never failed to tip. There you be, girlie, he would say as he dropped a dime in the waitress's hand. Don't spend it all in one place.

He drank his share of bootleg beer and bathtub gin but never seemed tipsy. He addressed men as cap, old top, or old-timer, depending on their age. Mother marveled at the clever phrases that poured from his mouth: It takes all kinda people to make a world.... Never trust a guy that wears a funny hat.... You can't fool me; I'm too ignorant... There's more than one way to skin a cat.... Not for all the tea in China.... It just shows to go you.... More than you can shake a stick at....

When Mother invited him to the annual rummage sale at St. Anthony's Roman Catholic Church, he said, No, thanks. I already got plenty of rummage.

When her friend Bette Jane Holder said that she intended to have lots of children, Ole warned her to stop at three.

Why?

Jeez, ain't you heard? Every fourth kid born on earth is Chinese.

On a thoughtful evening of conversation on a bench overlooking the Hudson, Mother's new boyfriend explained how to tell the races apart. Eyetalians like music and spaghetti, he told her. Swedes are quiet and dumb from eating too much herring. Germans are bullheaded. Chinks eat rice, wash clothes, and can't speak English. Jews are clever with a buck but don't turn your back. The colored can step and do good work on shoes. Englishmen are all pansies.

What about Poles? Mother asked him.

Polocks? he said. What about 'em?

Mother informed him that she was half Polish. A few days later he warned a mutual friend, Don't knock Polocks. You'll hurt half of Flo's feelings.

Sometimes Mother wondered if English was his second tongue, or maybe his third. If he was in a hurry, he would tell her to shake a leg. He never seemed to call anything by its correct name. Eyeglasses were *cheaters*, clothes were *rags*, trains *rattlers*, restaurants *hash houses*, bums *palookas*, matches *lucifers*, cigarettes *coffin nails*. He called money everything except money – *dough, cabbage, lettuce, spondulix, sugar, simoleons, mazooma, geetus*. A five-dollar bill was a *fin*, a ten a *sawbuck*, and a twenty a *double-saw-buck*. He called the $100 bill a *C-note* and told her, I ain't holding one at the present time, but I got a few back in my wall safe.

On an evening stroll to a dime moviehouse on Ocean Avenue, the couple encountered some men kneeling along the curb. Ole stopped as though he'd walked into a wall. This is my game, he whispered. I wrote the book.

He dropped to his knees and slapped down a dollar bill. Gimme them rats and mice, he ordered. Mother grimaced when he spat on the dice and exclaimed about Big Dick from Boston and eight the hard way. His dollar bill grew to two, then four, then eight, then disappeared.

He led Mother away by the arm. Out of the players' earshot, he said, They musta rung in some crooked dice.

8.

They were married in the office of the Manhattan borough clerk. It was 1924; Mother was eighteen and Daddy was thirty-four. The newlyweds had barely settled into his two-room furnished flat in Newark when a private detective arrived to ask the bride if she knew the bridegroom's whereabouts. It appeared that he'd made a midnight requisition of two thousand dollars from his company's cash reserve. When Ole got home, he explained, I didn't steal that dough, Flo. I borrowed it. Is that a crime?

Mother thought it was an odd comment. Shortly after midnight they were chugging west in the old Reo on U. S. 40, the Lincoln Highway. Everything they owned was in the trunk.

In Indianapolis the teen bride discovered that her husband's riverside mansion was a sagging frame house near a stagnant creek that the locals called the White River. The house belonged to the estate of his first wife, Margaret Pine. When Mother asked why he hadn't mentioned the marriage, he said that Margaret had died in childbirth and he didn't like to talk about it.

A day or two later Florence learned from his organist cousins that there'd been a second wife, a "fast" Philadelphia woman named Josephine, whom he'd divorced on grounds of adultery. In between wives, he'd dated a long string of flappers. By the time Mother realized that she might have made a terrible mistake, John Edward Olsen was on his way.

9.

Up to the day I dined on that serving of sun-dried dog food in Philadelphia, my life is a fuzzy memory of long drives in the dark, being shushed, being hoisted in the air, and dining on pabulum and zwieback. When I learned to walk, I would toddle into Mother's closet, rub her beaver coat, and marvel at the way it turned from dark to light brown. Our household was an infant's paradise, with songs like "Japanese Sandman" and "Poor Butterfly" tinkling out of the kitchen radio and the scent of baby powder and *eau de cologne* in the air.

Then something alien arrived on the scene. It was called a sister. It yelled in the night and burped. I was glad I'd never acted like that. Mother explained that the noisebox came from a cabbage patch. She refused my request to put her back.

A few months later Mother's story changed. In response to shrill questioning, she admitted that Carolyn Louise hadn't come from a cabbage patch. She'd come from Lit Brothers Department Store.

I was relieved. I said, Then you *can* take her back.

Mother said, You can't return sale items.

A captioned lithograph summed up the relationship between my sister and me. It hung on the wall of the row house we rented in the Overbrook section of Philadelphia and showed two children seated at table with their parents.

Is that big piece for Sister?

No, son. That's for you.

Oh, what a little bit of a piece!

A single document survives from my fourth year. It is printed in red crayon on a cardboard shirt stiffener:

> I LoVe MY MoTHeR.
> LoVe
> JACK
> SISYISMeNe

From our earliest years, Carolyn and I turned the back seat of our Reo into the Battle of the Marne.

Sissy's on my side....

Jackie touched me with his foot....

She's....

He's....

Decades before the expression would enter the culture, my parents were imploring, Can't we just get along?

Eventually Daddy would say, If youse don't stop fighting, I'm taking youse straight home.

Sis would say, He fighted on me first!

I would whisper, Tattletale.

Sis would start to cry and I would tell her to shut up.

Jackie said me to shut up!

That's a false lie![1]

One Sunday our trench warfare grew so loud that Daddy made good on his threat. On the drive home, Sis and I wailed and sobbed and begged him to reconsider. Will youse shud-dup? he yelled. He lit a fresh Bayuk Phillies cigar and puffed hard. His hoarse whisper reached the big ears in the back seat. Florence, he said, I'm gonna install two belts back there, good strong webbing with a goddamn snap in the middle. That'll keep them little buggers in their place.

Luckily nothing came of his idea.

10.

Our dark-haired young mother didn't seem bothered by the war between my sister and me or any other kinds of dissension. When controversial subjects like Herbert Hoover or the prohibition laws came up, she would smile agreeably and say, I wouldn't be surprised. Or: That's one point of view. Or: Some would say so, some would disagree.

Mother's child-raising techniques came straight from her own mother, Caroline Zawadzki Drecksage, who'd raised two sons and three daughters in an era when a parent's main job was

---

1 Carolyn was a competitor and always got her way. At the table she always got the largest portions. She still does.

to produce kids who survived. Nanny taught Mother that children should be seen and not heard, fed on schedule, put to bed at the same time, and awakened at the same time, never hugged (because it would spoil them), never praised (it would make them braggarts), and never exposed to nudity (it would turn the males into sex fiends and the females into unwed mothers).

I'm sure Mother loved Sis and me, but she took pains to keep it a secret. This seemed to be the parenting style of the era. Hugs and kisses were out; dedication and hard work were in. Mother stayed up late making me a pirate costume and decorating my trike for a Fourth of July parade. She would spend days preparing for our birthday parties – selecting games, buying prizes, making up guest lists, sending out invitations. On party day, she would get up at dawn to prepare cakes and pies, cut out favors, and drape the house and yard with swags of Dennison's crepe paper. Later she would collect the favors and birthday cards and paste them into scrapbooks. Sometimes the entries included planted items from the neighborhood newspaper:

For his fifth birthday, Master Jackie Olsen of Diamond Street, Overbrook, entertained....

Every night she tucked us in and read us stories 'til we learned to read them back: Tim is sad. The fat pig is bad. Tim ran and ran....

I became an early but wildly imprecise reader and speaker. Mother patiently corrected my mispronunciations: *corpsuckle, Sir Lank-a-lot, org* for *ogre, Alsop's Fables, fantackus.* Her own English was simple and direct, with a preference for well-worn expressions and an occasional indulgence in our family tradition of getting things a little wrong. She might refer to shooting fish in a barrow, as calm as a clam, as Polish as Paddy's pig. She was the first person I ever heard who said *Perish forbid.* But she was also the first to open my eyes to the rich possibilities of English, correct or incorrect. Mother taught lessons that couldn't be learned in school.

On the other hand, Daddy's English was just plain confusing. One of his pet phrases was I'm from Missouri. I figured he'd had plenty of years to find out he came from Indiana. He didn't seem sure about his own son's birthplace. When I sneezed and sent a few drops of grape juice across the kitchen table, he asked, Where'd you come from? The city dump?

I came from Lit Brothers.

Who learned you that?

Mother.

Your mother ain't worldly. You come from the same place I come from.

Missouri?

I once heard him claim he was free, white, and twenty-one; at the time he was forty. He would open a door and say, After you, dear Alphonse. Once he called me Lucky Pierre. If I spilled food, he would say, Sloppy Joe, the bartender's kid! But I was *Jack*, the *pitcher's kid*. Didn't he know that?

In my first five or six years of life I spent half my time laughing at Daddy and the other half trying to figure out what language he was speaking. Why did he say, A stopped clock is right twice a day, ain't it? Why did he order Mother to tell it to the Maureens? Why did he let friends call him Swede? He was half Danish and half German. Why didn't they call him Dane, or German?

When I wasn't trying to understand Daddy, I was trying to make sense of other words and expressions. I was baffled by the pledge of allegiance and the phrase One nation invisible, and the Fourth of July ceremonies when people sang about My country tizzifee. Who was this man named Franklin Rose Velvet and what was a prez-dent? Why was a playmate nicknamed Reds when there was only one of him? Why did Mother tell me not to cut off my nose despite my face? Who would want to idolize salt? Why did Daddy call our mayor the lesser of two weevils? Why did that huge gray animal at the zoo use his long tail to pick things up, and where was he stuffing those cabbages?

For a time, a flasher operated on our block, and we kids didn't understand why we were ordered to stay away from such a friendly man. Usually he showed his wee-wee, but when he exposed his belly button to Margaret Stine, she inquired as to why his went out and hers went in. He just giggled and gave her a kiss. How could you dislike a guy like that?

Daddy yelled, Do not ever! – bring him! – home! – again!

No one would have guessed that someday I would write books about sex criminals.

11.

Our family's love of pets probably came from Mother's side. Drecksage females kept their kids at arm's length but slobbered over pets. If my grandmother was in a hugging mood, she reached for Laddie, the dog she'd raised from a yearling. Laddie combined German shepherd and pointer in unknown proportions. He was a dark brown animal with a black muzzle, eyes like Ronald Colman's, and teeth from a Pepsodent ad. In his middle years, Laddie pointed only small birds and Norwegians, or so Nanny explained on one of our visits to Jersey City. When my Aunt Ronnie brought her fiancé over to meet Nanny, Laddie went on point. To make matters worse, he followed Bill Johnson down the hall and pointed him through the bathroom door, then dogged him to his car. Bill Johnson never returned, even after he married Aunt Ronnie and became my Uncle Bill. As he explained to my aunt, I'm not gonna be pointed by no goddamn dog.

In the Olsen family, pets were loved to death. Daddy

backed the Reo over my angora rabbit, and when he was rushing to Fluffy's rescue he stepped on my frog Rivet. Our angelfish Teddy expired after too much kissing by my sister. Our pug Jiggs[2] died of distemper that he caught from a nasty bill collector, or so my father explained. The innards of Frosty, our snow-white Samoyed, began to leak out of her orifices from too much squeezing and she had to be put to sleep before she disappeared.

A chow named Chan was our only success story. He was a one-man dog, and the one man was my mother. He enjoyed sitting at her feet, his purple tongue rolling around and dripping. Anyone who got between Chan and Mother risked a nip. He turned two or three circles before flopping on our rug. Mother explained that chows and Tasmanian devils had developed this habit to avoid sitting on snakes, but Daddy said he was from Missouri. He would take the dog's muzzle in both hands, stare into his brown eyes and say, There's no goddamn snakes in our house! No! Snakes! Understand? Then he would turn to Mother and mutter, He don't listen.

Chan would pad to his corner, circle two or three times, and sit. That don't phrase me, Daddy would say. Then he would resume the lesson.

The infighting between the dominant males lasted three years, until our chow caught the ague from a shot of blackberry brandy that Daddy gave him to cure diarrhea. Full of remorse, he held Channie on his lap all night, stroking his head and instructing him not to die. Just after dawn, the dog batted his

---

2   In those days male dogs were named Rex, Prince, Laddie, Blackie, King, Duke, Spot, Fido or Rags in much the same manner that male Frenchmen and Italians were named after saints. The list applied to all male dogs except Pekingese, which were named Ching, Ling, Ping, Ming or Sing; and chow-chows, which were named Chan. In later years, of course, these names went out of style and dogs were named Cadwallader's Tsetse Fly of Westport or Peter B. Collins Jr., or something similar. I knew a family that had a dog named William and a son named Prince.

eyes, gave Daddy's hand a purple lick, and stopped breathing.

I can't understand it, Daddy said. I thought he didn't like me. Whattaya think, Flo? Did he really like me?

Mother said it was a language problem.

After we presided over the deaths of a small zoo of animals, including guinea pigs, white rats and canaries, we decided to try cats. Pearl, a calico, slept in her litter box and meowed until someone picked her up and petted her. Then she returned to the litter box. Gemini, a half-Persian with a contralto purr, dragged her kills into the house and suffered from permanent mouse breath. Daddy's attempt to rinse her mouth with Listerine resulted in a call to the fire department to remove her from a locust tree. The fireman who handed her to Mother said, That cat has some breath!

Our twin toms Mike and Ike began a campaign to beat up every cat in Philadelphia. When they didn't come home one night, Daddy explained that they'd tangled with a border collie and were herded to death.

We tried to turn an angora kitten named Blossom into a watchcat, but she just wanted to lick our hands with her No. 3 sandpaper tongue. Mother worked for two hours cleaning up a set of prints that Blossom left after I dipped her front paws into a bottle of black ink for my J. Edgar Hoover Fingerprint Kit. I never understood Blossom's choice of escape route: across the rug, over the sofa, up the curtains, down the curtains, back across the rug, and out the front door. You could tell she was moving fast because she left one pawprint on the ceiling. Mother hadn't been so annoyed since Sis and I tied cantaloupe rinds to our shoes and turned the kitchen floor into a skating rink.

12.

Our house wasn't far enough from civilization to have wild animal problems, but one thieving visitor couldn't resist adding our property to his beat. He would rattle the lid off our garbage pail and scatter cans, meat wrappers, and bones. Most suburbanites would have tried to snap his picture, but Daddy took the intrusions as a personal insult.

One night he grabbed his flashlight and his war surplus single-action Webley revolver and padded out the front door. Neither adversary acknowledged the other for several seconds. Then Daddy sighted down the flashlight beam and fired. The raccoon took another bite of drumstick. Daddy had neglected to pull back the hammer.

Fumbling and cursing, he cocked the pistol while the animal ambled around the corner of the house. Daddy followed, and so they went, around and around, with Daddy firing three shots, all wild. His ammo exhausted, he flung the gun at the coon, picked up a rock, missed again, and put a dent in the neighbors' Moon cabriolet. It took a while to explain to the police, but we had a good record in the neighborhood and he was released on his own recognizance.

13.

Jesus Christ entered my life when I was four. I'd heard his name around the house and noticed that it was usually yelled. Our cleaning lady, Amanda May Johnson, crossed herself frequently and referred to Jesus, Mary and Joseph. That made me wonder if Jesus was a family man, but somebody told me that he was an only child and his parents had passed away.

The six-year-old boy next door said he thought Jesus's middle name might be Herbert, as he'd heard his father mention

Jesus H. Christ. He also claimed that he'd seen a sign: Jesus Saves. We were pretty sure that Jesus was in banking.

One morning our milkman dropped a bottle and exclaimed, Christ on a crutch!

I thought, How unfair! Not only is Jesus an orphan, but he's crippled. I asked Mother if we could buy him a sympathy card, but she couldn't find his address.

I learned more about Jesus from a Sunday School teacher who gave me the impression that God was an old man with a beard, Jesus was his son, Mary was his mother, and they lived in a riding stable. Once a year three wise guys brought them franks and incense. People in trouble asked Jesus for advice. Daddy always said, Tell your troubles to Jesus.

One night I tried to find out where the wholly family lived. Daddy pointed into the sky and said, Up there, just behind the Dipper. I scrooched up my eyes but couldn't see anything. Daddy said, They must of went out for the evening.

Even though I couldn't read, I began to comprehend the stories in my illustrated book, "Minute Stories From the Bible." The Bible itself just confused me. Our Sunday Kinder-School teacher made us recite the Twenty-third Psalm, but I couldn't get past the first line: The Lord is my shepherd, I shall not want.... I thought, What kid wouldn't want a nice guy like Jesus?

I heard about the parable of the Five Talents and asked Mother, What're these five talents anyway? Singing? Dancing? One of my friends said the Bible must be about baseball as there was something about a sermon on the mound.[3]

My father, Rudolph Olaf Olsen, didn't attend regular church services and had to be reminded about all holy occa-

3   Years later, when I blundered into the newspaper business, I realized that the Bible was a good book that needed work. A tough editor should have been called in: Hey, Moses, let's brighten this up. Cut some of the begats and hype the leads....

sions except Christmas and Easter. He had one foot in the 19th Century and the other in the mythology of his ancestors, so when he announced that our family would celebrate Christmas in the Scandinavian tradition, Sis and I rejoiced. That meant we could stay up late on Christmas Eve to greet the Danish Santa.

I was prone on the living room floor trying to read the comics in the *Evening Public Ledger* when a fat bearded man in a red suit burst into the room yelling Ho ho ho!

Carolyn screamed and I jumped into Mother's lap.

He won't hurt you, she said, patting me between the shoulder blades.

When the racket subsided, I said, Are you Jesus?

I'm Santa, the fat man said. Ho ho ho!

Why din't you come down the chimbley?

I did. You musta just missed me, Sonny.

He spoke in a strained voice, as though a reindeer had gored him in his wee-wee. I asked myself, Is this Jesus, Santa, ... or Daddy? I decided it had to be Daddy. Jesus wouldn't smoke cigars and Santa wouldn't smell like bay rum.

After everybody went to bed, Mother put out milk and almonds for our night visitor's return. When Daddy woke me up on Christmas morning, he had almonds on his breath. Who did he think he was fooling? He must have thought Mother and I were stupid.

two

Highland Park

1.

When I was six we moved to a two-story stucco house on Fairview Avenue in Highland Park, a leafy suburb in the historic township of Upper Darby, first settled by English and Dutch explorers who paddled up Darby Creek from the Delaware River in the 17th Century. About 50,000 exiles from the crowded streets of Philadelphia lived in relaxed communities with names like Bywood, Stonehurst, Beverly Hills, Drexel Hill, and Highland Park. Thick canopies of maples, oaks, and sycamores muffled sound. A neighbor lady told us that in the old days a squirrel could walk across Pennsylvania without touching the ground. When I repeated this at the dinner table, Daddy said, Why?

Why what? I asked.

Why would a squirrel wanna walk across Pennsylvania?

Mother said, The boy was just making a point.

That must of been a pretty dumb squirrel, Daddy said.

He ordered me to eat my peas. They'll put lead in your pencil, he said.

I told him I didn't know about the lead, but the peas kept rolling off my fork. Here, Mother said, reaching across the table. She mixed the peas in my mashed potatoes. See? she said. It's as easy as giving candy to a baby. Now two of my dishes were ruined. I decided to just shut up and eat.

Highland Park husbands took the Red Arrow trolleys and the Market Street El to work in town, but a few drove off in the mornings in Chevies, Fords and Plymouths. Buicks were the accepted sign of success. Anything more expensive was regarded as bad taste. A family that could afford a Lincoln or Cadillac was expected to move to Bala-Cynwyd or Bryn Mawr and not make the rest of us feel inferior.

Our mothers stayed home to pursue their occupations of homemaking, childraising, and worrying, on duty twenty-four hours a day. We kids knew that whatever was happening in the outside world, Mother would be home to greet us after school and Daddy would arrive for supper. Highland Park mothers were accessible to all the neighborhood kids, not just their own. If a child was upset or frightened, he knocked on the nearest door and a nice lady came out and comforted him.

In all of suburban Philadelphia there were rigid customs. Kids wore sneakers (called *sneaks*). Adults never went out without a hat. Women didn't smoke, drive, or cuss. Only the oldest friends called one another by their first names. Mr. Boone and his wife socialized with my parents for three years and none of them ever graduated beyond "Mr." and "Mrs." When I asked Mrs. Boone's first name, Mother said she thought it was Doris.

Boys were addressed as Master 'til they were in long pants. Druggists were called Doc. If a hearse or ambulance passed, we stared at the ground. Kids were instructed not to take the Lord's name in vain or say a bad word about the dead. When adults mentioned the departed, they added God rest his soul or She was a good wife and mother. There was a church every few blocks, but no synagogues. If atheists, agnostics, or Jews lived in our neighborhood, they kept a low profile. The sun never set on a black face. Our household retainers boarded the trolley to Philadelphia at dusk. Families held the personal details of their lives as tightly as their door keys. I once asked my friend John Tanner if they had a canary. He replied, That's our business.

Gossiping went on but only face-to-face. The few phones on our block were off-limits to children since they were powered by something treacherous called current. In the 1930s everyone suffered a hair-straightening shock now and then, if not from a phone, then from a wall socket or lamp. Every week or two we blew a fuse, and Daddy almost burned the house down when he substituted a penny and forgot to replace it with a regular fuse 'til a wire overheated and ignited my sister's doll collection. We had to give Raggedy Ann a Christian burial in the yard and Mother made wigs for the other three.

I admired a neighbor boy named Billy Glossop because he and his family ignored the neighborhood customs and regulations. Billy lived in an unpainted frame house with three older sisters and a baby brother. It seemed that everything the Glossops had ever owned remained in sight on their property: tires, washing machines, broken toys, old trellises, fencing material, rolls of "bob wire," stacks of newspapers and magazines, curtain material, torn rugs, shredded clothing, stuffed animals. Strange drivers would pull to the curb and ask when the sale started. Mother said the Glossops acted as though they were just passing through the neighborhood even though they'd lived here for twenty years. Later in life I caught on to a fundamental truth: there is a Glossop family on almost every block of almost every neighborhood. They are the human equivalent of magpies and no doubt perform an important function. I just wish I knew what it was.

2.

To a child from the city, living in Highland Park almost seemed like camping out. Everything happened under trees or next to bushes. An artist who tried to capture the scene would need an extra supply of green. There was almost no traffic. Most of the houses stood back from the street and had porches, driveways and detached garages. Horse-drawn wagons delivered bread, milk, vegetables, even meat. The iceman sang to his horse:

Horsey, keep your tail up.
Keep the sun out of my eyes ...
And if you want to look real smart
Raise your tail before you f-f-f-start ....

Once a year we would hear the bell that signaled the arrival of the tinker's wagon, pulled by a one-eyed mare that was kept muzzled. We kids were told that her favorite foods were oats, barley, and ears.

A Gypsy wagon rolled along on wobbly wooden wheels as Mother shooed us into the house. A man in a bandana and an eye-patch shouted, Feex you' pot! Sharp' you' knife!

Mother held her index finger to her lips. Everyone on Fairview Avenue knew that Gypsies kidnapped children, cooked them over open fires, and ate their livers with paprika. After the Lindbergh baby was kidnapped in nearby New Jersey, Daddy wrote to the head of the state police in Flemington and told him to arrest every Gypsy in sight. He was enraged when Colonel Norman Schwarzkopf failed to acknowledge his suggestion. Daddy was even angrier when G-men killed a fellow Hoosier outside a Chicago movie house. He insisted it wasn't a fair fight.

Our deliverymen were friendly. A neighborhood marriage broke up after the husband read his wife's note to the milkman: – 2 qts milk, 1 pt cream, all my love, Alice.

Was it fair when this Dillinger robbed banks? Mother asked.

Daddy said, You wouldn't understand, Flo. You ain't worldly.

My Highland Park turf extended to a polluted brook in a woodland valley where boys caught frogs and salamanders to put down girls' dresses. I'd read about Martin and Osa Johnson and used the area to refine exploring techniques like fording treacherous streams three or four inches deep and fending off man-eating squirrels. Life in suburbia made me wonder how I'd ever managed to live without treehouses, tire swings, stray dogs to stone, cats to zing with my slingshot. I'd never seen so many birds – robins, cardinals, wrens, song sparrows, blue jays, bluebirds, hawks, buzzards, finches, crows, and at least one Baltimore Oriole. He's a hundred miles off course, my father said.

Daddy was born and raised in a city, and he had odd ideas

about natural history. When a Sunday drive took us past the Rose Tree Hunt Club, Mother said, That's where they hunt foxes.

Daddy said, Fox is stringy and tough. Them rich people'll eat anything. They eat frog eggs, for Chrissakes.

The rest of us knew better than to comment.

Our neighborhood crawled with bugs, from grasshoppers and praying mantises to gnats and no-see-ums that tried to set up housekeeping in our eyeballs. Highland Park kids didn't romanticize insects; we hunted them down and put them to death. We trapped the hated Japanese beetles in kerosene. Cicadas frustrated us because they lived too high in the trees to be smushed underfoot. We kept lightning bugs in jars until their lanterns flickered and died, then flushed them down the toilet. Our policy was Death to bugs.

They weren't called fireflies in Upper Darby Township until they became the official state insect decades later.

Every day brought new and wondrous discoveries. Red bayberries were the perfect caliber for my peashooter. Buttonwood balls exploded against windshields. Maple keys spun to the ground like autogyros. Our trees were big enough for swings or ropes. The leaves of a certain weed turned bright silver in water. Another sent up bubbles. Some weeds curled up and slept at night. You could blow on a willow leaf and produce a screechy sound that made girls jump and show their underpants. Sassafras root tasted like root beer, Queen Ann's lace like sweet carrots, watercress like mild pepper, nasturtiums like radishes, peppergrass like horseradish. May apples burned the tongue and were useful in abusing little kids. Pie cherry trees grew in every other backyard; we would gorge ourselves and throw up and scare our mothers half to death. Don't worry, I told Mother in my fledgling Philadelphia accent, it's only churries.

Violets, buttercups, and dandelions dotted our lawns, and every house had a garden. When I was six I hit on the idea of selling flowers door to door. Mrs. Parks, who was half-bald and wore a slash of pink lipstick for a moustache, became my best customer. I picked bouquets from her garden and sold them to her for a dime, always including a hand-drawn card with a kid's idea of a clever slogan:

Focus on the crocus. Thissis narcissus. Pansys is dandy....

These sales may have been an early step on the road to crime, but the crime was victimless. The widow Parks wasn't sure what planet she lived on and seldom called me by the same name twice. It wouldn't have occurred to her to harvest her flowers and arrange them in neat little sprays. She was especially fond of violets but probably didn't know that a lush crop grew on her front lawn.

One day she complained that my bouquets were beginning to look a little tired – "peak-ed" was the word she used, a new one on me. Well, Mrs. Parks, I advised, you might try a little fertilizer.

Yes, she said after a thoughtful pause. I should do that. Thanks for reminding me, Tom.

3.

Most of our Highland Park neighbors were middle-class citizens who'd moved to the suburbs in the late '20s and lived in constant dread of being forced back to town. The Tanners lived across the street, and Daddy emphatically told me that they were Catholic, an abstraction that I couldn't grasp, even though the maternal side of my family had belonged to St. Anthony's Catholic Church in Jersey City before Mother converted to Lutheranism for a man who wouldn't have known a chalice from a sprinkling can. Daddy tried to tell me the difference between Lutherans and Catholics, but I didn't get it. How do you snap a mackerel? And who would want to?

Catholic or not, the Tanners seemed like nice people. There were a half-dozen children and each had a nickname. Mary was Mary the Fairy. Little Sally was Pally Sally, or Pally for short. Joe was Yard Bird. Michael was Bigs Bag.

Bigs and I became pals after I learned to adjust to a peculiar habit. If I angered him, he would press the back of his freckled hand against his teeth and rush headlong at me while he bit himself. He knocked me down several times before I learned to step aside.

All Tanner children had been taught to be polite to elders. Sometimes three-year-old Pally Sally would drop by our house and announce, I gotta sit on. After Mother lifted her to the seat, Pally would say Oh, sank you! When the littlest Tanner was finished, she would take tiny ballerina steps toward the door and say, Sanks again, Mrs. O-sen. Toodle-oo.

When our cat killed a grackle, six-year-old Mary the Fairy Tanner made an X in the air with her finger and said, He's with our Lord now.

I remarked that it was a long flight for a grackle.

No, no, Jackie, Pete the Neat explained. The whole bird don't go to heaven, just his soul.

Pete the Neat was eight and already an authority on church law. He held up a clump of black feathers and a beak and said we had to give the remains a proper burial.

After the ceremony, I ran home to ask Mother where my soul was. She was busy cleaning up a mess in the attic. We'd had a week of ninety-degree weather, and a case of her homemade root beer had exploded, leading a neighbor to comment that ours was the only house on Fairview Avenue with a head on it.

Mother ducked my question and told me to ask Daddy. That's how I know that the soul is an inch to the right of the pancreas.

The Saroyans, Anna and Aram and their parents, lived a few doors away and appeared content and well nourished despite their horror stories about the starving Armenians and how lucky their ancestors had been to escape the no-good rotten sumbeetching Turks. Hey, tell your troubles to Jesus, my father told Mr. Saroyan over thimbles of plum wine.

Mr. Saroyan operated a tailor shop and also did dry cleaning and pressing, and Mother wondered why he hung six or eight pairs of white flannel pants on his backyard line at night. I think he's working wet, Mother commented.

She insisted that Daddy stop referring to the Saroyans as "those damn rug merchants." She said, Just between you and I, Ole, Persians make rugs.

Daddy corrected her. Any idiot knows that Persians make cats.

Nothing would dissuade him. When Daddy was right he was right.

4.

By the winter of 1931 Highland Park was beginning to fall on hard times, and we heard talk of mortgage foreclosures, trips to the poorhouse, and families ripped asunder. Some of our neighbors bent under the strain, and a few broke. Mr. Wilkes, four houses down, staggered home from the saloon night after night, trying to get up the courage to tell his wife that he'd been laid off. Mrs. Wilkes warned him that the next time he came home drunk she would lock him out. Two nights later, he fell asleep on his icy front steps and froze to death.

Mr. Wilson lived directly across Fairview Avenue. One morning Mother told me that he'd passed away from a heart attack.

You mean he died? I asked.

She shook her head. Jiggs died, she said. Mr. Wilson passed away.

The truth came out a little at a time. Mrs. Wilson had opened the door to her basement and spotted the dangling feet. Her husband was alive when she cut him down, but he died before she could run for help.

Several other neighbors disappeared without explanation. Men in white drove Mrs. Braun away in a Dodge ambulance, her eyes rolling like a wild mare's. Where's old lady Braun going? I asked my 25-year-old mother.

Away, she said.

To Heaven?

I wouldn't be surprised.

I was already fearful enough without the help of adults. I followed the bouncing ball at the Tower Theater's Saturday sing-along and then watched a serial featuring the villainous Mudmen, who oozed from the walls of caves, to murder the innocent. This made me deathly afraid of walls, caves and mud. Daddy told me that bats tangled up little boys' hair and dragonflies sewed their lips. This made me deathly afraid of flying objects. He advised me to avoid outhouses as ticks crawled up your wee-wee. This made me deathly afraid of outhouses. A playmate claimed that snakes slithered under moviehouse seats and struck at children's feet. This made me sit with my feet scrunched up on the chair. By the end of a movie, I was half-paralyzed.

For years I was afraid of cobs. I'd seen webs under the cellar stairs and asked Mother what was making them.

Cobs, she'd said.

Where do they come from?

They just come.

Mother, they gotta come from somewhere.

That's one point of view.

I went on cob patrol under the basement steps but gave up at bedtime. In the morning there was a new web. I checked it after school and found a strange bug in the center. That night I asked Daddy, Is this a cob?

No, he said. That's an earwig. The only cob I knew was Ty.

That was one of the times I wished my father had learned English.

The scariest of my demons was Blackbeard, also known as Edward Teach. In my book of famous pirates, he had the body hair of a gorilla, a tangle of greasy pigtails, and a nose like a vulture's. Even when he was asleep he clutched a razor-sharp cutlass that could separate your head from your shoulders faster than you could say Yo-ho-ho and a bottle of rum. He dressed in black, never changed clothes, set off firecrackers in his hair, carried six cocked pistols in a bandolier across his chest, took pot shots at his deckhands for sport, and enjoyed barbecuing children and basting them with their own baby fat. When he was beheaded and thrown in the sea, his corpse swam around the victor's sloop three times before vanishing in a trail of blood.

I read the Blackbeard story over and over, and he became as vivid as my own family. I would wake up screaming, and Mother would come running into my bedroom saying, Blackbeard's dead! He was killed a hundred years ago.

I still don't believe her.

5.

For my first day in Highland Park Elementary School, Mother dressed me in clothes that were twenty years behind the times, a compromise between my parents' attitudes about style. Left entirely to Daddy, I would have gone to school resembling Abraham Lincoln, probably including the stovepipe hat. After a heated discussion, Mother had managed to convince him that boys no longer wore derbies or high-top shoes. They settled on a sailor hat and a squeaky new pair of Buster Browns.

That night I told my parents what I'd learned in first grade. Primary colors are red, yellow, and blue. Miss Mary Jones is our principal. If you dig straight through the earth you'll reach China, but it will take a long time. George Washington was the father of our country and never told a lie. His regular job was land surveying.

Daddy said, Ain't no money in that.

For the first few weeks of school, both my parents saw me off in the mornings, and both were over-protective. If a drop of rain had fallen overnight, I had to wear rubbers or galoshes because wet feet caused pneumonia, consumption, flux, and the ague. On cold days my divine head was shielded by a genuine aviator's cap with fleece-lined earflaps, isinglass goggles, and a chinstrap. When I complained that my classmates wore wool hats and ball caps, Mother advised me not to look a gift horse in the face.

I wore short pants, and my toothpick legs were protected by brown cotton stockings that were attached to garters that in turn were held up by something high on my legs, perhaps my scrotum. Friends said they sometimes heard screams from our house in the morning. Later I graduated to corduroy knickers that squeaked, but in a lower key than my Buster Brown shoes. I never had a problem with rodents.

6.

Something pre-sexual must have been festering in my brain in the first grade, even though I wouldn't have understood sex even with schematics and voice narration. None of us boys were sure what girls had between their legs, if anything. From fleeting glimpses at my sister it looked as though God hadn't finished the job. Tom Clyster, a nurse's son, tried to enlighten us, but we boys just scrooched up our noses at words like *bagina* and *public area* and told him he was volgar.

A classmate and I had a discussion along the lines of you show me yours and I'll show you mine, but it foundered when she asked, Show you my what?

In second grade, my friend Louisa Lucretia Abernethy revived the subject as we were walking home from school. Lulu was my Valentine, a headstrong girl with dirty-blonde curls and a snippy little nose. She'd created a scene at our Christmas pageant. The choir director had borrowed Lulu's doll cradle for the crèche. When the passion play was over, Lulu dumped Jesus on the floor, grabbed her cradle and ran. The sexton tried to stop her, and she bit him on the arm.

Lulu and I admired Orphan Annie, used expressions like Leapin' Lizards and Jumpin' Jehoshaphat, and wrote notes in Radio Orphan Annie's Secret Code. We already had a romantic history. During nap time at kindergarten, she'd rolled over on our rubber mat and asked for a kiss. I pecked her on the cheek and she slapped me hard. When I asked why, she said, That's what they do in the movies.

On a cool spring day a year later she steered me behind a row of bayberry bushes and said, Now that we're Valentines, I getta see your heinie.

I said, You mean, uh – bare?

Yep, she said. I show you mine and you show me yours. That's how it's done.

I asked if I had to show my entire heinie or just a portion.

She said, Uh, just your oringinal.

I asked why she wanted to see the oringinal, and she explained, I'll give you a nickel. In 1932, a nickel bought a bag of jawbreakers or a Hershey Bar and a penny change. Any normal boy would have accepted the deal. Lulu handed over the coin and lowered and raised her white bloomers with the speed of a camera shutter. I glimpsed enough flesh to tell that her basic design was the same as mine, at least from the rear.[4] A month or so later I received an invitation to Lulu's birthday party. As I was climbing her front steps, her mother met me and said, I understand you, uh ... you did something, um, nasty to my daughter.

Nasty?

I said to myself, It was Lulu's idea!

Mrs. Abernethy said, Suppose you tell me what happened.

I said, I really couldn't say.

She ushered me inside where the party-goers were playing pin the tail on the donkey. As she leaned over to tie my blindfold, she whispered, I'll discuss this with your mother. I left after the cake and ran all the way home.

A few days later I was playing in our backyard when I spotted Mrs. Abernethy striding up our walk. Mother was at the grocery store and Daddy was at work. I ducked behind a hydrangea bush and watched her through the big blue flowers. Mrs. Abernethy knocked at our front door a few times, peeked in a window, then left. I was sure she'd be back.

I remembered Daddy's advice about telling your troubles to Jesus and ran four blocks to the Church of the Holy Sacrament. I knocked on the big wooden door. The wood made a hollow sound. I knocked harder. I was about to seek out anoth-

---

4 I doubted that the experience had added anything to my growing store of knowledge, but in a way, it had. As a student of criminal behavior in later years, I evolved a simple theory about the origin of pedophilia that was based on this childhood incident. I considered these sub-humans to be simple cases of arrested development. At six, I wanted to see Lulu Abernethy's undraped backside, but later I became interested in attractions like stamps, coins, baseball, and fishing. I moved on. Pedophiles didn't.

er church when a voice called from an adjoining house, Hello? May I help you?

Yes, I said. Is Jesus home?

Well, uh yes. This is the house of God.[5]

I recognized Dr. George Barnes, the Episcopal preacher. His church had been my parents' second choice since there was no Lutheran Church in our neighborhood. I remembered him because he was both a minister and a doctor, although I was pretty sure he didn't do tonsils.

He walked over and said, What did you want to talk about, son?

I said, I gotta see Jesus.

He started talking about the Holy Trinity, but I barely listened. The way I saw it, Jesus was home or he wasn't.

I said, Daddy says tell your troubles to Jesus. He didn't mention no Holy Trinity. The preacher squatted so our eyes were at the same level. Maybe I can help, he said. Can you give me an idea what it's all about?

Nope. It's my business.

He tried to draw me out, but I refused to give up my secret. He asked if I knew how to pray. I told him we recited the Lord's Prayer every morning at school, and at bedtime I asked God to bless my family and the poor people of the world and protect me and Sis from cobs and infantile paralysis.

He patted me on the head and said, Go home and pray.

That night I told my troubles to Jesus, and it turned out that Daddy and Dr. Barnes were right. Mrs. Abernethy never returned.

It wasn't long before I came under the spell of another female without even seeing her heinie. Bigs Bag Tanner and

---

5   It was a relief to learn later in life that I wasn't the only boy of my era to endure such an ordeal. At 10, the author and journalist Roger Angell wrote a letter: Dear Sarah, I am sorry I took your pants off and threw them down the sewer. Love. Roger. (At least Lulu kept her pants.)

I were playing territory with his new penknife when a pretty girl of about ten strolled down Cedar Lane with an armload of books. She wore a red sweater, pleated skirt, white socks, and saddle shoes. Her short brown hair swung from side to side. From a distance she resembled Buck Rogers' girlfriend Wilma Deering.

As I watched, a girl across the street yelled, Hey, Jessie, you coming over?

Jessie hardly broke stride. In a haughty voice, she called out, In due time.

In due time! I'd never heard anything so neat in my life. I found out that her name was Jessie Willis, and every day for a week I waited for her to walk down Cedar Lane. I never saw her again, but I still haven't given up hope that she'll reenter my life in due time.

7.

In those early years I was a firestorm of energy. Even though I was undersized compared to my playmates, I went up and down stairs two or three steps at a time. I hopped, jumped, skipped, slid, and cartwheeled more than I walked. If I went somewhere, I could hardly wait 'til I arrived. When I arrived, I couldn't wait to get back. I skipped all the way to school, avoided cracks to protect my mother, sloshed through puddles, slid down snowbanks, and launched myself headlong into piles of leaves. In class, I drummed finger paradiddles on my desk top, aggravating my teachers. Sometimes I used both hands and clenched my toes to the same beat. I kept busy.

After school I would run home, meet up with my pals, and say, C'mon, let's go!

Where?

I didn't know, but I had to get there fast.

Daddy would say, Take it easy, you'll live longer. That was a big help.

For some reason, Fairview Avenue seemed to spawn mouthy little kids who were full of opinions, usually their parents'. Never in our lives would it be so important to be right. No subject was too petty for a screaming argument. We were obsessed with records: the biggest, tallest, fastest. Billy Glossop claimed that the PSFS Building in Philadelphia was the tallest building in the world, and I said that the tallest was the Umpire State Building. My father settled that one. He said he knew a little about buildings, and the tallest was in India. I was sure he'd been there as everybody knew that Daddy was the worldliest man on our block.

One summer day we looked up and saw a dirigible floating overhead. Bigs Bag and I began a hot discussion. I said the biggest airship in the world was the Graph Zeppelin. Bigs was sure it was the Hinden Bird. I got so angry I went home in tears. Daddy said we were both wrong; the biggest was the Akron.

We boys also argued over the biggest transport plane. I was sure it was the Ford Trimotor. Billy was the only boy I knew who had a complete vocabulary of cuss words, learned at his father's knee (and his mother's), and he told me that the Fokker was the biggest but you couldn't say the name in polite company.

Daddy settled that argument, too. He said that the world's biggest transport plane wasn't the Fokker or the Ford but the Douglas Airliner. I hadn't seen one yet, but I'd read about it in *Popular Science*. The neatest thing was its color: silver. Who could imagine a silver airplane?

At age six going on seven, it was my expert opinion that Big Bill Tilden had a better serve than Ellsworth Vines, but Vines was superior at the net. At the time I'd never laid eyes on a tennis court.

We kids were suspicious of the great athlete Babe Didrikson. Billy said she was a man masquerading as a lady so he could set new records. Danny Mackin said that Babe had male and female genitals, but Billy said she used the same clubs as the other golfers.

Some of us half-pint experts were positive that Gene Tunney was a better fighter than Jack Dempsey, even after Dempsey regained his championship. The giant Primo Carnera was hyped as the next heavyweight champion, but he proved to have a glass chin. No surprise to us short-pants sophisticates.

In those years professional wrestling was still a respected sport and almost as popular as boxing. When Danno O'Mahoney won the championship belt, we marched up and down Fairview Avenue chanting:

Ta-rah-rah boom-dee-ay
Mahoney's champ today!

We were impressed by Rudy and Ernie Dusek, Jim Londos, Ed Strangler Lewis, Battling Nelson, and the Canadian champ, Yvon Robert, with his patented rolling shortarm scissors. It was exciting when a wrestler named Cliff Olsen put the great Robert in a leglock and threatened to break his leg. Robert refused to give up, and Olsen snapped his leg like a matchstick.

I assured the other boys that he was my uncle.

8.

I was six when Daddy took me to the fifth game of the 1931 World Series, between the Philadelphia A's and St. Louis Cardinals. About all I noticed was that the home team lost and a man named Pepper hit a ball into the grandstands and the kid who caught it didn't have to give it back. The players had nicknames like the Tanners': Ducky, Bing, Dib, Flint, Ripper, Mule, Doc.

After the game Daddy and I were making our way along a dingy runway and ran into Mickey Cochrane, the A's star catcher. How you doin', Swede? Iron Mike called out.

Daddy said, Still breathing, Mike.

I said to myself, Didja hear that? Daddy called him Mike! The newspapers call him Mickey, but Daddy calls him Mike. And he calls Daddy Swede!

I wished they'd said more, but the best catcher in baseball was gone, his spikes clattering on the cement.[6]

Sometimes Daddy took us to the ballroom of the Broadwood Hotel to watch Eddie Gottlieb's SPHAS and their ladykiller forward, Cy Kaselman, who held the world's record of 25 straight free throws in competition and 125 in practice. My eyes bugged out as the players took the court in their underwear and practiced shooting baskets from mid-court. They missed some two-hand set shots but never missed a lay-up. They lined up for a drill and dribbled faster than I could run.

Kaselman was a darkly handsome specimen, with a spare muscular physique, a Dick Tracy nose, and kinky brownish hair that he slicked back. One night as we were leaving the hotel, Daddy and I walked past a group of young women elbowing one another in the lobby. Them's Cy's janes, Daddy said. Most guys would settle for his leftovers.

It was the first time I realized that women sometimes chased men.

---

6 It turned out that Mickey Cochrane wasn't the only Philadelphia sportsman who knew my father. Daddy was friendly with Connie Mack, owner-manager of the A's, and Gerry Nugent, owner of the Phillies, as well as players and coaches from both teams. We had season passes to Shibe Park (later Connie Mack Stadium) and Baker Bowl, the Phillies' snakepit also known as the Toilet Bowl. As a member of the local sporting establishment, Daddy had passes to the Arena, the indoor sport center on Market Street, where we watched everything from wrestling to hockey to roller derby.

SPHAS (pronounced Spaws) stood for South Philadelphia Hebrew Association, the hottest, fastest, slickest and most successful basketball team on earth. In an era of open anti-Semitism, they flaunted their religion. Ikey, Chickie, Shikey, Ossie, Inky, Cy, Gotty and Mockie pranced onto the court wearing Hebrew initials and the Star of David. The racial aspects went over my head even though the SPHAS' biggest rival was a black team, the New York Renaissance. Old-timers in the grandstands called these matches the Yids vs. the Niggers – which also went over my head. There was never an empty seat. Daddy explained why: They come to see the Hebes get killed.

I thought, That's Daddy – always joking.[7]

9.

In the Philadelphia suburbs of the thirties, we kids wore the same clothes every day. After school we changed into play clothes, usually patched, darned, handed down, shortened and re-shortened year after year. Used toys and even wagons and sleds were available at the Salvation Army, but we suburban plutocrats would never think of shopping with the lower classes. We didn't know that some of us would soon be lower classes ourselves.

Since Highland Park boys were short on fancy toys and playthings, we fell back on dirt – the plain old kind that abounded in empty lots. Mother kept a spotless house and tried to raise

---

7   Racial stereotyping fanned the flames, and spectators threw beer bottles and jabbed enemy players with hatpins. The Rens were considered stupid and the SPHAS sly and pushy. When the novelist and literateur Paul Gallico was sports editor of the New York *Daily News*, he explained to his readers: "The reason, I suspect, that basketball appeals to the Hebrew, with his Oriental background, is that the game places a premium on an alert, scheming mind, flashy trickiness, artful dodging and general smartaleckness." My father put it more simply: Them Hebes can shoot. (Hitler was just coming into power.)

spotless children, an impossibility in a world whose raw earth hadn't yet been paved over. Every kid on our block had filthy scabby knees from kneeling and playing in dirt. Unlike city boys, we had all the vacant lots we needed for a rich, exciting, dirty life. You could pat dirt, shape it, throw it, roll in it, make mud pies, dig tunnels, fashion miniature truckyards and race-tracks, plant seeds, play territory and mumbly-peg and marbles. At night you could water a patch of dirt and wait 'til the tip of a worm appeared. If you pulled nice and easy, you might get a foot-long night crawler. If you pulled hard, you got two.

There was just no downside to dirt. One day a teaspoon of mercury bubbled up in Georgie Henneke's backyard, and we put it on his kitchen table and banged it with hammers. When the last little globule had mysteriously disappeared, Georgie's big brother Albert said, Don't worry about it. Quicksilver never hurt nobody.

We unearthed a rich deposit of Pennsylvania lignite in a vacant lot and set it afire with kerosene from Billy Glossop's porch. This attracted the attention of a cop who told us it would burn itself out. It did, in three weeks, leaving a gaping hole the size of a house and a neighborhood reeking of foul gases. My pal Tommy Sevlin ate teaspoons of dirt and later became a Cordon Bleu chef in Pittsburgh, where I heard he mixed traces in his steak tartare. At the end of each day, our heels and Achilles tendons would be caked with dirt. As my mother scrubbed away with a brush and a cake of Fels-Naphtha, I winced and said, Why bother, Mother? It don't show.

You never know who'll see it, she said. I knew what was going through her mind:

Scene. A Hospital room.

Doctor: The boy has a fractured ankle.

Nurse: I'll take off his socks.

Doctor: Ugh. Get me his mother!

I had so much confidence in the high quality of our Highland Park dirt that I planted an egg in it and watered it for a week. Nothing came up, but by way of consolation Mother brought home a packet of radish seeds from Woolworth's Five-and-Dime and suggested that I start a vegetable patch.

I was almost seven at the time and looking for a more rewarding diversion than Lulu Abernethy's heinie. Behind our one-car garage I dug a bed about four feet square and a foot deep. I borrowed Mother's sifter and set about refining my dirt into the consistency of her Pond's talcum powder. I'd just popped my first seeds into the earth when Daddy arrived in our Reo. Stand back, Sonny! he yelled. That wall's gonna fall!

Mother heard him and ran outside. She argued that a shallow trench couldn't possibly undermine a garage wall.

I know a little bit about walls, Daddy said. I seen it happen.

That was always his fallback position: *I seen it happen.* For emphasis, he would add that he'd seen it with his own eyes, which always made me wonder who else's eyes he could have used. On long drives, my sister and I liked to kneel backwards on the rear seat of our Reo and make faces at the drivers who were behind us. Cut it out! Daddy warned. If I hit the brake, youse'll go through the back window. When Mother tried to argue, he insisted that he'd seen it happen. With my own eyes.

It wasn't long before shoots began poking through my manicured patch of dirt, and in no time I was harvesting skinny radishes the color of Mercurochrome. I sowed another crop and then another, expanding my growing area and my agricultural savvy each time.

Our next-door neighbor Mr. Saroyan tipped me off to a secret ingredient that was readily available on our streets and would make my radishes as big as turnips. He said, In old country, people live on rainwater and radish.

With so many horses clopping up and down Fairview Avenue, there was no shortage of Mr. Saroyan's special ingredient. The secret, he advised me, was freshness. I followed the delivery wagons and collected the round balls while they were still steaming. I patted and shaped them along the sides of the radish holes and sometimes remembered to wash my hands before meals.

By mid-July I'd produced a crop of fat radishes with snow-white cores and a snappy taste that puckered your mouth and shriveled your tongue and made their presence known all the way to your large intestine and sometimes beyond. By late August, I'd grown two more crops. I produced so many radishes that I abandoned my flower business and began to sell radishes door to door.

Old Mrs. Pond became my best customer. She was famous on Fairview Avenue for a story that Mother insisted wasn't even true. It was said that she'd had her husband's two pet monkeys put to sleep after his death, and when the veterinarian asked if she wanted them mounted, Mrs. Pond replied, No. Just holding hands. Daddy said he didn't care if it didn't happen. It *shoulda* happened.

I assured the addled old lady that she was looking at home-grown radishes available exclusively to Fairview Avenue residents at a penny apiece, fifteen cents the dozen. Some guys on Lynn Boulevard had been trying to buy into my business, I told her, but I would never sell.

As she fished in her purse, Mrs. Pond observed that she'd read in the *Evening Public Ledger* that H. J. Heinz started his career by peddling horseradish roots from his home garden. I told her that I liked his ketchup, but it needed more snap.

Word of my red thumb spread. I was the radish king of Fairview Avenue. When people saw me coming, they burped. With a little help from Daddy, I sent thank-you notes to my customers to encourage repeat business:

Dear Mrs. _____,
I would like to take this oportunity to thank you again
for your busines. It was my pleasure indeed to have
your busines. You are most considered.
Jackie Olsen, age 8

Toward the end of September I decided to retail my product to a local store, but the pharmacist wasn't interested. I was
sorry to learn that there was no such thing as winter radishes. I
earned a little money shoveling snow, but my only other source
of income was the nickel or dime that Daddy gave me when he
was in a generous mood. He would say, Don't spend it all in one
place heh heh heh.... He seemed relieved that winter was here
and our garage was still intact.

10.

I mailed in a coupon from *Boys Life* and the postman delivered
twenty-four packets of seeds on consignment from a mail order
company. I sold them in a month and won $1.20 cash plus a di-
ary with a genuine leatherette binding. On the strength of my
record the company sent me four gross of packets and a prize
catalogue that made it seem impossible for me not to win a bicycle, if not a Buick or a Chris-Craft or the state of Delaware.
Daddy said there were enough seeds in the box to re-forest the
Alleghenies and part of the Poconos.

I gave it a try, but I'd already saturated the local market and
now was calling on householders who didn't know me, didn't
think I was cute, and had better things to do than buy seeds
from a kid.

I stored the big box of packets in the garage while I tried to
decide what to do. Three months later I was still thinking. Then
I got a letter from the seed company. It opened with a friendly

Hi! and pointed out that they hadn't heard anything for a while and were just wondering, gee willikers, how things were going with that last shipment, by golly. Then came a letter beginning, Dear Salesman, We'll bet you're just too darn busy selling our seeds, but we couldn't help wondering if you would drop us a line and let us know how sales are going....

I appreciated their notes but since Highland Park was now covered with ice and snow I just pushed the packets deeper into the garage.

My incoming mail hotted up. Dear Salesman: We cannot believe that you would deliberately ignore this problem. We have a substantial investment in you and your integrity.... And finally: You leave us no choice but to communicate directly with your parents or guardian if we have not heard from you in ten days.

I slid the box behind the furnace. A week later I found that the Spring Green Lettuce and River Valley Snap Beans were germinating. Was this good or bad? I consulted with the eminent agriculturists Billy Glossop and Bigs Bag Tanner, and we decided on a 3-0 vote that it was bad. I marked the ten days off on my calendar. On the ninth day I filled my canteen with soup and made plans to hitchhike to Greenland. On the tenth day I received a letter addressed to Master Jack Olsen. It began with Hi! and went on to say that the company hadn't heard anything and was just wondering, gee willikers, how things were going, by golly. The dreary sequence of letters began all over again and ended a month later with another threat to contact my parents. Soon came a letter addressed to R. O. Olsen.

I intercepted it and replied:

Gentleman:

My son Jackie has proven hisself to be a kid of real en

terprize. You will need have no fears that, when

he gets home from the hospital he will go out and sell

your seeds in ernest.

My father,

Mr. Olsen

That was the end of our communications. I planted some of the seeds in the spring and put the rest in our bird feeder.

Having learned nothing, I sent a coupon to the *Open Road for Boys* and received a magazine subscription sales kit. Most of the neighbors turned me down. Mrs. Baynard, usually an easy mark, told me that she would soon be leaving for Florida and had all the magazines she could read.

A trip? I said. Well, then, just between you and I, you'll need road maps and stuff. That's where *Open Road for Boys* comes in.

She signed up for a year, which entitled me to a keyring from the subscription department's catalogue. With nine more sales, I would qualify for an electro-energized Rogers Hornsby bat.

Thus encouraged, I decided to branch out and offer *Bluebook*, *Liberty* and *Colliers*. I pounded the sidewalks but couldn't give the subscriptions away. Ditto with *Saturday Evening Post*, *Ladies Home Journal*, *Boys Life*, and *Women's Home Companion*. I discussed my problem with Daddy and he told me I was on the right track. There's tax advantages, he informed me, in being a non-profit corporation.

11.

Toward the end of second grade I'd stopped short of becoming known as a teacher's pet, but I campaigned hard to make the teachers think of me as a good little boy, and then as a big boy, as in, Oh, what a big boy!

At the slightest hint I took our blackboard erasers outside and clapped them together, stumbling back into class coughing and choking. Once a week the teacher would let me slosh water on the blackboards and squeegee them dry. I emptied wastebaskets, collected crayon stubs, and raised and lowered the upper windows with long poles that the other students weren't allowed to touch. I called our teachers Miss and Mrs. – we had no Misters – and thus stood out from kids like Billy G, who usually called them Hey or Teach. On the playground, I perfected a dying swan act in which I would pretend to fall down. This would earn me a trip to the infirmary, where the school nurse kept a jar of goodies for good little boys and big boys.

In English class I memorized a poem, getting it a little wrong in the Olsen style:

Fee fie foe fun
I smell the blood of a Englishman
Be him alive or be him dead
He'll grind my bones to bake his bread.

For a class project I wrote a fan letter to the poet Edgar A. Guest and in return received an inscribed copy of "It Takes a Heap o' Livin' to Make a House a Home." Our principal tacked it to the bulletin board while my teacher beamed and the other students seethed with envy.

I memorized a poem about a cow and claimed it as my own, neglecting to mention that I'd found it in a book of verse by somebody named Gelett Burgess. In front of the class I recited the opening line – "I never seen a purple cow" – but forgot the rest and said I had to go to the boys' room. I still didn't seem fated for literary success.

By third grade I began to use my PR skills on other adults, including my parents. Every Saturday afternoon I would huddle in front of our upright Philco and pretend to enjoy (and understand) the Metropolitan Opera from New York. I couldn't tell the sopranos from the announcer or the contra-bassoons from a penny whistle, but neither could anyone else in my family. Look at Jackie, Mother would whisper to friends. He loves ballroom music.

Sometimes I tuned into the screeches and howls and crashes of WOR, the Bamberger Broadcasting System, coming to you from Newark, New Jersey. The war had been over for years, but WOR still featured songs like "Mademoiselle from Armentieres," "Over There," and "How You Gonna Keep 'Em Down on the Farm (After They've Seen Paree)." I tuned to "Music by Gershwin" over WJZ, New York, 'til I learned that it was sponsored by Feenamint, a laxative that masqueraded as chewing gum. I disapproved of this practice as a result of my traumatic experience with Ex-Lax on the Boardwalk at Atlantic City.

I was almost eight when I first heard Jack Benny on the air for Canada Dry, Daddy's preferred highball mix. A few months later I heard the sandpapery tones of Fred Allen on his Bath Club Review, sponsored by Linit, a clothes starch. After I listened to Amos 'n' Andy, I asked our black cleaning lady Amanda what 'regusted' meant. She said she'd never heard the word in her neighborhood but promised to ask one of her white-trash friends. My favorite show was Ed Wynn's Fire Chief program for Texaco, since it opened with a siren that sent our cat up the drapes. Every Philadelphia kid listened to Uncle Wip on station WIP, 610 on your radio dial. Announcer Wayne Cody, who claimed to be descended from Buffalo Bill, conducted a radio talent show that I intended to use as our staircase to fame. All I lacked was talent.

I continued upgrading my personal image by putting on a pious look and turning the pages of the family Bible while seated in the sofa in our living room. I couldn't tell the verilys from the yeas and untos, but it didn't matter since I wasn't reading to learn. I was reading to impress.[8]

---

8   I also became aware that sick boys received close attention and even got hugged, not an everyday occurrence in our family. One day when I was recovering from measles and reading the Boy Scout Handbook in bed, I heard footsteps and

By the time I reached the half-century mark of life, my mother was still telling friends that her son had read the Bible from cover to cover four times before he was ten. In fact, I never managed to get through Genesis, let alone the whole Bible, and I'm still not sure who ate the snake.

Done your duties today? she asked.

Uh, no, I managed to squeak. I knew what was coming. It was Nanny who'd introduced the enema to our household. If she overheard me complaining that I couldn't go to school because my stomach hurt, she would suggest a warm soapy enema. Daddy insisted that Nanny had inspired the old hospital joke, Who goes there? Friend or enema? which he repeated whenever we were within sight of a hospital, including veterinary and lying-in.

I don't need no enema, I told Nanny as she stood over my bed.

Yes, you do, she said, rolling up her sleeves.

12.

Largely because of illnesses, enemas, and other adversities, the graph of my grammar school career became a study in descending spikes. I'd got off to a misleadingly fast start. In first and second grade I scored As and Bs despite missing 123 school

---

saw my chance for a *grand tableau* entitled Lovable Little Boy. I grabbed my miniature American flag, laid it across one shoulder, draped the open handbook over my other shoulder, composed my face in a gentle smile and shut my eyes. Soon I heard a soft ahhh and felt a lingering kiss on my forehead.

I waited 'til I heard Mother's receding steps, sat up and opened my eyes, and spotted my grandmother at the foot of the bed. We all loved Nanny, and Nanny loved us, but she didn't go out of her way to show affection any more than Mother or the rest of the Drecksage clan. If you can imagine Gertrude Stein wearing a short gray boyish bob in the style of the 'twenties, you have a fair picture of my grandmother. Not only was Nan wise to me and my act, she was onto my father and every male alive, including cats, dogs, and circus animals.

days due to mumps, chickenpox, measles, German measles, and enemas. Nevertheless, Miss M. Ruth Taylor, my nice second-grade teacher, reported that I was Preparing Work Neatly, Gets Along Well With Others, and weighed 58 pounds.

In third grade I carefully printed the obligatory message on my book jackets:

Jackie Olsen
Highland Park Grammer School
Pennsylvannia
United States
The World
The Univers

The ink was hardly dry before the principal and my parents conspired in a tragedy of errors. On October 7, 1933, when I was entering the second month of third grade, my mother received a note from our principal, Mary F. Jones, a nice old woman who'd started teaching in the Upper Darby School System in 1911. In her clear hand she'd written, "Jack made a very high score in the recent test given in the third grade. Miss Lukens suggests promoting him to fourth grade." The note added, "Jacqueline's eyes tested 20-20 which means normal."

For years that ambiguous message was the subject of several theories, none of them comforting. Was this battlefield promotion intended to apply to me? Or had the overworked Miss Jones meant to honor a student named Jacqueline and sent the note to the parents of Jack by mistake?

My parents asked no questions. They also failed to discuss the matter with the party of the first part. One day I was an average kid in the front row of my third-grade classroom with easygoing Miss Lukens and two dozen friendly faces, and the next day I was the shortest kid in the rear of a fourth-grade classroom with an icicle named Miss Moore and a bunch of hard-eyed strangers who wanted to know who invited the midget.

I muddled through the rest of the school year, but the leap from third to fourth grade had come smack in the middle of the multiplication tables, and I never got them straight.[9]

13.

Doomed to middling grades, I flung myself into the social life of my classroom and fell in with some wiseguys in knickers. Our password was "rotten rabbit guts," and if you forgot, you were subjected to bumps and bruises.

Armageddon, one of my pals would say. Spell it.

Before I could answer, he would say, I-T.

Then: Constantinople. Spell it.

I-T.

No, sucker. I-S-T-A-N-B-U-L.

Someone would ask, What bus crosses the ocean?

The correct answer was Colum-bus. If you got it wrong, you were thumped.

At heart we were cruel little demons with sharp tongues. We divided politicians into Republi-CANS and Democ-RATS and echoed our parents' wisecracks. Someone would say, Calvin Coolidge died, and someone else would say, He was already dead! Or: How could they tell?

The Roosevelts were favorite targets. Billy Glossop said, You heard about that guy Roosevelt Penis? He changed his name. Now he's Joe Penis.

Bigs Bag Tanner asked if I knew FDR's real name. Frank? I said. Francis?

Naw. He looked around and whispered, It's ... Frankie. Frankie Rosenfeld.

---

9   Decades later, I am still under the impression that eight times nine is 72.

Are you cereal? I said. That was one of our wiseguy expressions.

Bigs gave the proper response: Yeah, I'm Corn Flakes.

I said, Why would he change Rosenfeld to Roosevelt?

How the heck would I know? My dad told me.

The next day Bigs Bag informed me that Rosenfeld was a Jewish name. He said, That's why he changed it.

I asked him what Jewish meant. He said he would check, but he never brought up the subject again. Race prejudice was alive and well in the Philadelphia suburbs, but we weren't old enough to recognize it. My father knocked every race, including Danes and Poles. In a different era, he would have been called an equal-opportunity racist. In the first half of the 1930s, you didn't take such matters seriously. Unless you were Jewish or black or living in Germany.

Two sisters were on the faculty at Highland Park Elementary School: Miss Eppeheimer and Miss Eppeheimer. The younger sister, Miss Eppeheimer, had soft brown hair, a face like Clare Trevor's, and a figure that even an eight-year-old could appreciate. Her first name was Diane. Her sister, whom we called Miss Eggie-heinie, was a bleached blonde and I forget her first name. I'd seen her entering the Adobe of Beauty, so-named by a hairdresser who probably thought she was spelling "abode."

Miss Eggie-Heinie put a lifelong curse on me in the fourth grade. She was prone to headaches and sometimes asked students to stand up in front and tell stories while she sat at her desk trying to recover.

When it was my turn, I launched into an exciting yarn about chocolate. My hero coincidentally named Jackie – had his own LaSalle limousine, an electric runabout, a birchbark canoe, personal valet, three maids, a barber, and other servants, but he was miserable because he'd eaten all his chocolate and his parents refused to buy more. So he searched the world for Hershey's chocolate bars, Supplee chocolate milk, and Breyer's chocolate ice cream with sprinkles. His goal was to build up a reserve so huge that it would never run out. My words were inspired: ... Lo and behold! As our hero was climbing a mountain in Rangoon, Burma, he came around a corner and seen a wise man with chocolate syrup dripping from his moustache and running down his samovar....

As I skillfully led up to my smash ending, I saw that the girls were following closely and the boys were leaning so far forward that Chris Brays lost his balance and fell on his face. I glanced sideways and saw that Miss Eppeheimer had raised her head a few inches off the desk. It felt good to be making our poor teacher feel better.

I raised my voice for the dramatic conclusion.

And the wise man waved to the little boy and led him up the mountain to a eNORmious cave. Inside Jackie seen a pile of chocolate the size of a, the size of a, a − ... − Buick ....

My listeners gasped.

And every time he took a bite, more chocolate syrup bubbled up from the ground. Jackie had discovered − a chocolate spring! He got a big bucket and....

Oh, Jackie, Miss Eppeheimer cried out, why don't you just sit down? Up to that second I'd thought I was a hit. I'd thought my teacher would give me an A, rumple my hair, and send a note to my parents that some day my name would be in lights at the Erlanger Theater. What did I do wrong?

As I slouched back to my seat, a wave of shame swept over me. My throat hurt from holding back tears. Several days passed before I found out from a teacher's pet that Miss Eggie-Heinie had been tested for allergies, and chocolate was her worst.

Lucky for me, most of my other teachers were more tolerant of the creative mind. Miss Blondel, our nature studies teacher, showed me how to press weeds in the pages of books (but neglected to tell me how to identify poison ivy). My English teacher, Mr. Burton, spoke for the principle of "I before E except after C" until I brought in a Hairbreadth Harry comic strip and pointed to "seize."

Well, that's an exception, he said.

What's a exception?

An exception, not *a* exception,

An exception.

An exception is something that proves the rule.

I thought about this for a while, but it didn't make sense. A few days later, I dropped a copy of *Weird Comics* on Mr. Burton's desk. And this proves exactly what? he asked. It proves that I before E except after C is a false lie. He sighed and said, I don't make the rules, Jackie. When I returned to school the next year, Mr. Burton had retired and gone into roofing.

It wasn't long before I became a rapid reader, no thanks to Highland Park Elementary School. In the fourth grade a teacher almost convinced me that English was a foreign language by assigning *The Adventures of Huckleberry Finn*. After I spent a weekend trying to decipher Chapter One, I scribbled a few questions:

How come Huck can say ain't but we can't?

How come Huck can say I never seen nobody when my daddy says, I didn't see nobody?

What's a awful sight of money?

How could gold fetch something?

Shouldn't sivilize be spelt sivilise?

How much is a sugar-hogshead?

What kind of foods is victuals?

The teacher crumpled my list and reminded me that *Huckleberry Finn* was Mark Twain's greatest work. Stick with it, she told me. It'll come to you. So I took another stab and got as far as Chapter Two:

Say, who is you? Whar is you? Dog my cats ef I didn' hear
sumfn. Well, I know what I's gwyne to do ....

I knew what I was gwyne to do. I put the book aside and explained to my teacher that I could only understand Amurrican.
The experience put me off Mark Twain until college. I learned
later that his popularity was hardly affected.

14.

The rest of my early childhood reading consisted of *Big Little
Books*, dime magazines like *Good Housekeeping* and the *Saturday
Evening Post*, an occasional hard-cover work like *Aesop's Fables*
or *Hans Brinker and the Silver Skates*, and dozens upon dozens of comic strips. In Disney's earliest work, Mickey Mouse
was little more than a stick figure, but as soon as Minnie and
Donald Duck came on the scene, the characters jumped into
life. Lying on my stomach on the living room rug, I would lose
myself in *Bringing up Father, Ella Cinders, Smiling Jack* and his
curvy De-icers, *Terry and the Pirates* with the exotic Dragon
Lady, *Blondie* and her bumbling husband Dagwood, *Gasoline
Alley, Maggie & Jiggs, 'tilie the Toiler* (who later re-entered my
life doing tricks with a Great Dane in obscene comic books),
Joe Palooka and his con-man manager, Knobby Walsh.

My big hero was the space traveler Buck Rogers, who lived
in the 25th Century with his mentor Dr. Huer, the beautiful co-
pilot Wilma Deering, the evil Killer Kane, the seductive Ardala,
and swarms of foot-high Asterites who came from asteroids
and weighed as much as full-grown humans. With his Electro-
cosmic Spectrometer, Super Radiating Protonoformer, Atomic
Bomb, and Thermic Radiation Projector, Buck could wipe out
an enemy galaxy with a single word in the balloon above the

action: ZAP! Flash Gordon, a polo-playing Yalie before he was shanghaied into space by the lunatic Zarkov, was a feeble imitation. When Buck went on the air for Cocomalt, I couldn't wait to send for his free map of the planets and his cardboard space helmet. Thus protected, I zapped neighborhood evildoers with my copper-colored Disintegrator ray gun, which emitted the same buzz as Buck's own weapon on the radio.

By the mid-thirties a dozen of my comic strip heroes were on the air. I listened to Bobby Benson, the all-American boy, and Jack Armstrong, who waved the flag for Hudson High and never tired of Wheaties, "the best breakfast food in the land." Neither did I. If there had been a Church of Wheaties, I would have been ordained. I liked the flavor, but I was also influenced by a publicity campaign aimed at making boys ignore oatmeal, Wheatena, and Cream of Wheat. Radio announcers asked, Have you tried Wheaties? Sportscasters pushed Wheaties; on the rare occasions when a Philadelphia A's batter hit a home run,[10] play-by-play announcer Bill Dyer would yell in his high-pitched voice, He's just won – a case of Wheaties! Babe Ruth endorsed the Breakfast of Champions and so did Lou Gehrig, Jack Dempsey, Bob Feller, Sonja Henie, Johnnie Weissmuller, Hank Greenberg, and just about every great athlete except Swede Olsen.[11]

In those days, America had no obesity problem. Most of us went to bed hungry, even in the suburbs. We salivated as we listened to the radio:

I love Bosco, it's rich and chocolaty.

Chocolate-flavored Bosco is mighty good for me ....

We were reminded every day that Tastykakes were "the cake that made Mother stop baking" and Tastyeast was "tempt-

---

10 The sound effects man used a Schick razor.

11 In Des Moines, Iowa, Wheaties awarded an all-expense paid trip to Hollywood to a young sportscaster named Ronald "Dutch" Reagan.

ing to the appetite."Tom Mix told us that "Ralston cereal can't be beat." Food commercials were as popular as radio programs. Sometimes they were the only food in the house.

After I wolfed down my morning Wheaties, Mother would hand me a dime to buy lunch in the school cafeteria. My favorite entree was shepherd's pie, a blending of mystery meat and mashed potatoes. Our celery soup came in many delicious flavors, none tasting like celery. SOS hadn't been invented yet – it was another horror of World War Two – but the cook at Highland Park Elementary School concocted a version that was almost as tasty as the sunbaked dog food I'd eaten as a toddler. Thursday lunch was calves' liver, which made me wonder why someone didn't strangle the nutritionist. Why not pancakes with Log Cabin syrup? Bacon, sausage, even scrapple[12]? Why not something kids would eat?

On Friday our cafeteria served fish, and by 11:00 a.m. the school smelled like the inside of a flounder. In the early 'thirties, refrigeration came from iceboxes; electric models with white honeycomb fins on top were a year or two away. In those days, fish were fish. Pedestrians walked faster as they passed seafood restaurants. My Catholic friend Bigs Bag Tanner told me I would burn in hell if I insisted on eating meat on Friday. I'm still running the risk, and I'm still worrying about it.

Twice a year our teachers escorted us on field trips. Our little in-crowd would sit in the back of the school bus and sing our favorite travel song:

> Suck suck suck your toes
> All the way to Mexico.
> While you're there
> Cut your hair
> And stick it in your underwear.

On the tour of the Breyer's Ice Cream Company, our snack

---

12   A Philadelphia speciality: a deep-fried loaf made of unmentionable pork parts.

was a Dixie Cup containing four or five salted pecans, the same nuts that went into their smoothly delicious butter pecan ice cream, as a tour guide informed us in a short lecture. Billy Glossop nudged me and said, They make ice cream, so they hand out ... nuts?

At the Hershey's plant we received miniature chocolate bars. Supplee-Wills-Jones Dairy treated us to straight shots of milk, a substance which most of us regarded as every bit as delicious as fish juice. The Bond Baking Company opened the doors of its safe and doled out an oatmeal cookie for each child.

We looked forward to visiting the McGinley farm in Conshohocken because the farmer fed us sausages, hard-boiled eggs, and apple pie with whipped cream. On one trip we arrived just as a farm hand was castrating hogs. Walt Hannon pointed to several hairy whitish objects lying on the ground and asked, What do you do with them?

The bags? the man said. We don't waste nothing.

We watched as he tossed one to a big sow who snuffled it down with a snort.

Billy Glossop jumped up and down and said, Wasn't that neat?

This was our introduction to recycling. The farmer laid out his usual nice spread, but none of us ate much.

On another field trip, to the Franklin Institute in Philadelphia, I got into a big argument with my friend Carter Harrison. Cartie hated to admit that he didn't know everything, and if he didn't know an answer, he would make one up. I found this annoying as I used the same technique and thought I had a patent on it, inherited in a straight line from my father.

Cartie told me that the Franklin Institute was named after President Benjamin Franklin, and I said, Why're you telling me? Any fool knows that.

We were walking past the stainless steel seaplane in front of the Institute when Cartie asked if I knew the most important tool in the plane's cockpit. Before I could answer, he said, A can opener!

I said, Ha ha, very funny.

He said he'd been to the Franklin Institute twice and his favorite exhibit was the one that turned water into wine. He led me straight to the big glass case and I read the description on a little brass plate. Oxygen and hydrogen would be introduced into the chamber and an electrical current would make them combine into water. I pushed the button; a bluish-white spark danced, and drops of H_20 formed before our eyes.

I said, Where's the wine, Cartie?

He said, You didn't see it?

It don't say nothing about wine.

You didn't see the drops?

That was water.

That was white wine, ya dope. I was here with my pop. He knows more about wine than you.

That night I described the exhibit to Daddy. All he said was, That's a hard way to make water.

15.

In those early years of my life I wasn't sure what my father did for a living, except that he drove all over Philadelphia and suburbs and sometimes disappeared under cars. I found out later that he was inspecting damaged automobiles and working out insurance settlements with the clients, a procedure that was known as adjusting.

Sometimes he took me along. Our car always reeked of smoke from his Bayuk Philly cigars (five cents, three for a dime, one dollar the box), but to me it was just the smell of

Daddy. He would spin the radio dial 'til he found music that sounded as though every member of the orchestra was playing his instrument at top volume and the first player to finish would win a prize.

Whattaya think of that there Wang-Wang Blues, Sonny boy? he asked, neglecting to notice that I was holding my ears. At eight I preferred classical themes like "Yankee Doodle" and "There's Something About a Soldier."

We drove all over the dirty old town, to Frankford and Manaynnk, to Germantown and Overbrook and South Philly, past rows of rabbit-hutch houses with postage-stamp lawns or no lawns at all, while he peered through his glasses for the right address. If he got lost, he would pull out his little red street directory and squint at the tiny type. Unlike most males, he didn't hesitate to ask for help.

Hey, Cap, where's Silver Street come in at?

Not every answer satisfied his critical standards. No, no, that ain't right, he told an elderly black man on South Street. You ain't from this neighborhood, are ya? I didn't think so.

At our destination we would find a damaged car and a surly owner. Daddy would start his inspection by lifting the hood and peering inside. Then he'd frown and circle the car, finally sliding out of sight on his back. I panicked the first time I saw this, but it turned out he was riding a wooden "creeper" that he kept in our trunk. Then he would pull out his pencil, wet the point with his tongue, and start arguing with the owner.

My sister and I had always been taught that there was only one good driver on earth, and we were lucky to have him for a father. As a former race driver he was a terror behind the wheel and I would of won twice at Indianapolis if my pit crew hadn't been Eye-talian.

Daddy was a one-man driving clinic. If a vehicle didn't make room when we attempted to pass, he would yell, Get over, ya jerk ya! He accused errant motorists of only needing half the road: the middle half! His all-purpose insults were Sunday driver, cowboy, and clown. Once in a while he would yell, Farmer!, an odd choice for someone from Indiana. If a car cut him off, he would shout, That's how they make angels! If someone started to back toward us in a parking lot, he would holler, Keep coming 'til you hear glass! If the other driver had the audacity to reply, Daddy would invite him to kiss his tuckus. If someone beeped at us, he would advise, Blow your nose, you'll get more out of it! Or: Your horn works. Now try your lights! He knew how to make our car backfire, and he used the explosion to emphasize his points. If enemy vehicles pulled away from traffic signals too slowly, Daddy would yell, The light'll never get any greener! Or: milk it or move it!

Sometimes he was challenged to fights, but we always sped away in time. I remember one night when Daddy climbed out of our car and made the other driver say uncle. Then the white-haired old man went back to his Olds sedan, stowed his crutches, and drove away.

Daddy's territory included South Jersey and its famous traffic circles, which always seemed to confuse him. There would be six or eight exits marked with black letters on a dull gray background, not easy to distinguish while in motion. An elderly friend once spent twenty minutes in the Haddonfield circle before running out of gas.

Daddy would drive around the circle two or three times, squinting and complaining and peering through the two-bit glasses he bought from the bin at McCrory's Five-and-Dime. Finally he would peel off at the exit marked Vineland, but only if we were headed for Cape May. If we were headed for Vineland, he would turn off at the exit marked Perth Amboy. Now and then he took the exit marked Camden, which meant, of course, that we were headed back to Philadelphia, a mistake that he would correct after we passed Monsanto's mound of raw yellow sulphur a few miles east of the Delaware River Bridge. It wasn't hard to identity the mound since we'd have passed it a short time before.

In all such endeavors it never occurred to me that Daddy could be in the wrong, not even the night we sideswiped the streetcar. There was the screech of metal and Daddy jumped from our car and started yelling at the motorman. I can't believe you done that, he said. What're you, cap? A Sunday driver?

The case ended up before a magistrate, with Daddy insisting on representing himself. I'm more worldlier than them other shysters, he explained to Mother.

In court he clung to his position that the streetcar had sideswiped us. His only witness was an engineer from the Budd Company who testified that yes, there was a little play in the streetcar's suspension, perhaps an inch. Daddy worked and reworked this slim testimony, created a reasonable doubt, and won the case. On the way home he told me and Sis that we'd just seen the greatness of the American judicial system. Always remember, he told us. The truth will out. Ain't that a fact, Flo?

Mother said she wouldn't be surprised.

16.

In the 1930s, grocery shopping was usually done on foot. Few of our Fairview Avenue neighbors owned cars, and if they were lucky enough to have a Ford Model A or Plymouth roadster or an elderly Marmon, it disappeared into the city each morning with the man of the house. About one in five kids had a bike. Most of us got around on roller skates, the kind you clamped to your shoes and tightened up with skate keys that were always lost. When worn skates became too old to repair, we nailed them to the bottoms of orange crates to make skatemobiles, a constant hazard to foot traffic, sanity, and eardrums in our quiet neighborhood.

The shortage of motor vehicles meant that we were constantly running errands for our parents. Get me a half-dozen of eggs... A pack of Luckies... I need a cube of butter... Get this prescription filled....

I didn't have a bike 'til my junior year in high school, when a neighbor sold us a girls' model for five dollars. It was on its last wheels, a 24-incher, smaller than the standard 26 or 28, and it was designed so that a female wouldn't have to show her bloomers when she climbed on. For a long time I rode only after dark.

We kids had an inside joke: I'm going down to the A&P. Sis didn't laugh. She was at an age when urination was a serious matter. I didn't bother to add that the Daring Young Man on the Flying Trapeze. She would just tell Mother, and then I would have to look at two long faces.

Most of my pals saw our errands as a continuing burden, but with my sly nature I saw them as opportunity. As Mother told me, if you run out of lemons, make lemonade.

Like all criminal types, I looked for an angle.

Self-service was still eight or ten years away, and white-aproned grocery clerks assembled your purchases and collected your money: thirty cents for a dozen eggs, sugar at a nickel a pound, potatoes at two cents, onions at three. The markets smelled like molasses, coffee, and sawdust. Items like Wheaties were stacked ten feet up the wall; clerks grabbed them with long poles with big tweezers at the end, sometimes making circus catches behind their backs. They wore celluloid armbands on their forearms[13] and made notes on them in pencil. Customers were allowed to bag their own cookies from bins in front.

---

13   Perhaps the origin of the expression "on the arm" for credit purchases.

When I was seven, our neighborhood A&P streamlined the operation. Instead of collecting your money at the grocery counter, the clerk bagged your purchases and handed you a chit listing your Total Incurred Indemnity, as Daddy would have described it. On the way out of the store, you paid a mean-looking woman in a metal cell. It didn't take me long to figure out how to beat the system – or so I thought. I would buy the grocery items on Mother's list and accept my chit. Then I would linger around the cookie bins as though mulling important matters. Should it be the gingerbread or the vanilla wafers? After a suitable pause, I would bag up a dozen chocolate-covered Grahams and request a second ticket for the cookies. I would wander around the store for a few more minutes before paying the first chit and swallowing the second (they had a faint lemony flavor).

After three or four scores, I figured I was set for life. This scam was too good to keep to myself. I told Billy G all about it and he said I was stupid. He said, Don't you know them tickets is numbered? Every time you walk out without paying, they know it.

My father's old teammate Ed Turk was at our house that night, talking about his new job as a guard at Eastern State Penitentiary. From what I overheard, prisoners were held in solitary confinement, never fed cake or pie, and saw the sun for an hour a day if they behaved. I decided that chocolate-covered Grahams weren't worth the risk. The next time Mother sent me to the A&P I was trembling in my knickers. My favorite clerk didn't return my smile. Another looked away. I'd just paid the bill when Officer Napolitano appeared at the door. In those days Upper Darby cops wore leather puttees from ankle to knee, as though ready to ride into battle in the Crimea. He fingered a polished black club.

I looked around, but there was no back door. I decided to plead for mercy. Please don't put me in jail, Officer Napolitano,

I said. I'll never do it again. Honest.

Never do what? he said.

Why did he ask? I said, Om, uh – you know.

As I tried to control my bladder, I heard the words of the Shadow: The weed of crime bears bitter fruit. He was right.

Officer Napolitano looked puzzled and then annoyed. He was a rangy middle-aged man with a thick black moustache and little black eyes. My father had taught me how to tell one race from another, but he didn't look as though he ate much spaghetti.

How old're you, young fella?

Uh, seven. No, eight. Yeah, I think I'm eight. My mother knows for sure.

I didn't want to be charged with lying on top of wholesale cookie thefts.

He clamped a bony hand on my shoulder. Eight years old, huh? How'd you get so fresh?

I, uh….

He squeezed 'til I let out a little gasp. Beat it, smarty-pants, he said. Next time I'll run ya in.

After a fifty-yard speedwalk, I looked back. Officer Napolitano and one of the clerks were looking at me and grinning.

It would have been better if I'd been caught.

17.

Two or three times a year Daddy would come home with a pocketful of cash and announce that he'd hit the number. As I understood it, the odds against hitting the number were 999 to one and the pay-off was 500 to one, which seemed more than fair to Daddy, or, as he said, It's a steal. Even with my limited arithmetical skills I could see that the odds over a long series of bets were hopelessly in favor of the bookie, but that didn't keep Daddy from placing his bets every week, sometimes losing money that was intended to put food on our table.

On the rare occasions when he won, he turned festive and generous. He might drive us to Hap's Ice Creamery on Market Street – twenty-five cents the quart, fifteen flavors including banana and cantaloupe – and Mother would dish it out when we got back home, making sure to give Sissy the most. Or he might take us to a restaurant called Henri's in the 69th Street shopping area. He enjoyed these dinners so much that he seemed to want to drag them out, even if he had to be unpleasant about it. While Mother hid behind her napkin, he would demand a full description of every menu item, haggle over what was "on the dinner" and return dishes that weren't precisely to his taste.

When the waiter asked if he liked soup or salad, Daddy would answer yes. The subsequent dialogue was as formal as a Broadway script:

Sir, I asked if you like soup or salad.

Yes, my good man, and I said yes. I do like soup or salad. If you're asking which do I want right now, I'll be only too glad to tell you.

Yes, sir. Which may I bring you now?

What's the *soup du jour* of the day?

After the waiter answered, Daddy would say, Okay, just gimme *soup du jour*, cap. That's always good.

If you asked for extra butter at Henri's you got a bowl of ice water with a dozen or so pats floating on top. Daddy would spread them on bread, then demand more. If a waiter so much as raised an eyebrow, he was in trouble. Daddy was no more hesitant about insulting waiters and other diners than he was about insulting drivers. His pet aggravation was parents who showed off their kids. Oh, what a cute child, Daddy would say.

Should his ears be sticking out like that?

On a trip to the Horn & Hardart Automat, Daddy stopped at the cage near the front door and bought two dollars worth of nickels. He walked up and down the long line of treats, stopped at a slab of meat loaf and tapped on the glass.

Can I get that with *au jus*? he called out. A disembodied voice replied, Uh, yes, sir.

Is that on the dinner?

The meat loaf? Sir, meat loaf is the dinner.

Having taken a deep sniff at the coin slot and satisfied himself in all other particulars, Daddy risked his three nickels. I myself had the shepherd's pie. It didn't come with *au jus*.

18.

In the 1930s semi-pro baseball flourished in the eastern cities, and it was enthusiastically covered in Philadelphia's five daily newspapers. For a quarter, fans could watch talented young amateurs and washed-up old pros cavort around in a reasonable facsimile of the national game. The A's and Phillies charged $1.25, didn't play much better ball, and usually lost.

Most of the semipro fields were near factories or railroad yards. Spectators showed up in overalls (locally "overhauls"), lumber jackets and work-boots. Factory walls loomed over the outfields. Spectators stood in foul territory, edging toward the baselines and ducking hard-hit foul balls, sometimes successfully. A few fields featured rickety grandstands made of sagging wooden planks held up by pipes. Sit-down fans risked splinters. Small boys crept below the stands conducting field studies of ladies' underwear.

My father achieved a small degree of local fame as player-er-manager of a succession of sandlot teams, starting with the

Columbia Turners Athletic Club. Turners was short for Turn-verein, a sweaty smelly gym and social club where members could work out with medicine balls, horses, parallel bars, rings and weights, and cool down over pool, poker, pinochle, and pilsner. Steins of beer cost a dime, refills five cents. Women weren't served, but male children of members in good standing were allowed to nibble at the free lunch pig's knuckles, Limburger cheese, onion slices, and other treats that no self-respecting kid would dream of putting in his mouth.

Daddy also managed baseball teams from the Trevose (N.J.) Athletic Club and the Media (Pennsylvania) A.C. before using his runaway imagination to create a couple of novelty teams that helped to destroy semipro baseball in Philadelphia. An early photo shows the two of us in the black uniforms of the Trevose team. I remember how confused I was when he gave me my first pair of baseball socks. Daddy, I said, they left out the toes! And they left out the heels!

Our Trevose shirts and caps were edged in orange to simulate Princeton's school colors, but the orange doesn't show in the pictures. Nor does the pitcher's toe-plate on my right shoe. In the history of baseball, no half-pint ballplayer ever needed a toe-plate. But Daddy and I convinced ourselves that I was the exception. I was the pitcher's kid.

I'd hardly started school before sweaty men in baseball uniforms began trooping into our house on Fairview Avenue. They would hand Mother their dirty clothes, line up to use our shower, and loll around our living room in bathrobes and BVDs discussing batting averages, how to hit the screwball, the poor vision of umpires and other inside subjects.

Even as a little kid it struck me as odd that blind men would be hired to call balls and strikes.

At first Mother balked at the idea of serving as washer-woman for a bunch of unshaven men who spat tobacco juice and filled their pockets with sticky resins and grease.

This isn't a clubhouse, she told my father. Washington freed the slaves.

But her general policy remained peace at any price, and Daddy's wishes, unreasonable as they might be, usually prevailed. An hour or two after each game, Mother would station herself at our front door to head off the players who forgot to take off their spikes, but one day a third-baseman named Greasy John Middleton slipped by and made a line of punctuation marks across our living room floor.

Was he raised in a barn? Mother asked.

I never seen nobody wear no spikes in a barn, Daddy said. It was his typical answer. It sounded reasonable and logical but ignored the question.

For two seasons, Mother washed the ballplayers' uniforms and hung them on the backyard clothesline to dry, but she refused to change her position about the garments known as jock straps. At first my father insisted that they were thigh braces, but Mother reminded him that she had two little brothers. She said, Do you think I don't know where you wear those things?

I wanted to ask, Where?

Daddy tried to kid her along. Say, Flo, are you a Phillies' rooter or an Athletic supporter? But she didn't get the joke and wouldn't respond to off-color remarks anyway as she said they were against her original religion. She may have converted to Lutheranism for Daddy, but she still didn't countenance blasphemies about the mother church. There was a row the night the Kellys were over for mah-jongg and in the course of the conversation Daddy asked the rhetorical questions, Does the Pope poop in the woods? Is a bear Catholic?

To make Mother's job as team washerwoman easier, Daddy bought her a Maytag washing machine with the new electrically operated power rollers for squeezing out water. The first time she used it, she squeeze-dried her arm up to the elbow. By the time our neighbor Mr. Saroyan came to the rescue, Mother's arm was black, blue, and yellow, and I was screaming as though I'd been shot.

From then on, the players laundered their own clothes, jock straps included.

Looking back, I don't think that my father had a particular talent for managing baseball teams or any other group – he was too stubborn and impatient – but it gave him an excuse to give his favorite old pro a second chance at greatness: Rudolph Olaf "Swede" Olsen.

A 1931 article from the Philadelphia *Evening Bulletin* ("In Philadelphia, nearly everybody reads the *Bulletin*") hailed the tenth straight victory of Swede Olsen's Columbia Turners. The sportswriter paid tribute to the "former Detroit Tigers' hurler" and concluded: Olsen pitched both games over the weekend, working four innings against Coatesville ... while he hurled three frames against Media.

Crumbling clippings confirm Daddy's attendance at a 1932 baseball banquet along with Connie Mack, legendary manager of the Athletics, and other baseball luminaries. In an article in the *Public Ledger*, "Ole Olsen" was described as a former big-league ballplayer "now active in independent circles in this city...." At the first annual banquet of the Philadelphia Baseball League, an organization of semipro teams, Daddy was listed alongside honored guests like A's stars Mickey Cochrane, Jimmy Dykes, and Jimmy Foxx.

I snipped out each article and showed them in class. The teachers said I must be proud of my father.

I couldn't tell them how exciting it was to sit on the wooden bench alongside sweaty tobacco-spitting grown-ups and watch my old man fool the batters. I was so proud when the announcer would shout through his megaphone, "Now pitching for the Columbia Turners – and formerly of the DEE-troit Taggers – Swede OL-sen!" Daddy was a giant in my eyes, and the pitcher's mound only made him taller. In my mind, he added two or three inches to my own height. The paying customers must have tired of hearing the uniformed little punk babbling, That's my dad! Hey, look! Daddy's pitching!

19.

My career as a performing musician began in the first week of June, 1932, at the junior piano recital of the Delaware County School of Music. I sat nervously as Danny O'Dell announced that he would play "Medication from Thais," and Cindy Hogue followed with a song about a waterbird named Clare. In the middle of "The Fairy Waltz," Lulu Abernethy got up from the piano and strode back to her seat. I'm bored of this, she explained.

Next on the program came "Little Jack Horner. Jack Olsen (6 yrs old). Folk song." I thought I played well, but rave reviews failed to materialize in the Philadelphia press. I was treated to a short critique by my parents. After six months of lessons, Daddy said, shouldn't you know a chord?

I said my fingers weren't shaped right for piano but I would probably excel on snare drum if Santa brought me one. Mother said we would cross that bridge when we went over it.

In my second recital, at the Upper Darby Art Museum, I performed Adair's "Playing Soldiers" to a loud smattering of applause. For encore, I sang a modern version of "Abdul el Bulbul Emir," as taught to me by my neighbor Aram Saroyan, who'd learned it at Boy Scout Camp. I opened up in my bold soprano:

> In the harems of Egypt it's good to behold
> The fairest of harlots appear...

The audience stirred, but I attributed this to excitement over hearing real music instead of sissy stuff like "Sleep Baby Sleep" and "Where Are You Going, My Pretty Maid."

Certainly none of the women in the audience could be offended by a neat word like *harlots*. Aram had told me that it was Egyptian for pretty ladies. I continued *fortissimo*, or as *fortissimo* as my small voicebox could produce:

A traveling brothel came into the town

Run by a pimp from afar...

I saw a few mouths snap open but carried on without fear. Brothels were caravans and pimps were camel drivers. Aram would never lie to me. I continued:

Abdul the Bulbul arrived with his bride

A prize whose eyes shone like a star... when somebody's pet cat let out a yowl from backstage and my old-maid music teacher Miss Rosalie Murray arose from her seat in the front row, thanked me enthusiastically, and announced that the next number would be "Wee Son John," performed by Selma Siosberg. I didn't understand why I was getting the hook as there were six more verses.

Over dinner Mother observed that my weekly lessons didn't appear to be leading toward a concert career. She said it wasn't wise to chase bad money after good, and the two dollars plus carfare could be put to better use. Wasn't that what I'd been telling her?

Daddy said, At least the cat was on key.

20.

By July of 1932, I was recovering from my musical failures when my friend Warren Wigo came running across Fairview Avenue waving a piece of newsprint. Jackie! he yelled. Your father's in the paper!

I wondered if Daddy had sideswiped another streetcar.

Your old man's famous! Wig said.

At the top of page one of the *Bulletin*'s sports section was a picture of four men in baseball uniforms, headlined "Old Friends Meet Again in Night Baseball Game." The men were identified as Howard Ehmke, Joe Bush, Whitey Witt, and Swede Olsen, all former major leaguers. A caption noted that my father's semipro team was scheduled to play the bearded stars of the House of David, managed by Grover Cleveland Alexander. I'd never heard of Ehmke, Bush, Alexander, or Witt. I'd heard of Swede Olsen, of course, but I knew little or nothing about his major league pitching career, as modesty prevented Daddy from discussing his greatness in front of us kids.

Who're these other guys? I asked my friend Warren.[14]

That one use to be president, he said, pointing to Grover Cleveland Alexander.

Yeah, I said, right after John Clancy Adams. What's he doing playing baseball with my dad?

Wig said he had no idea.

When Mother got home from an afternoon Cootie game, I said, Daddy's famous, huh?

Some would say so, she replied. Some would disagree.

---

14 At the time, Howard Ehmke held the World Series strikeout record. Whitey Witt had been a major league outfielder for ten years and achieved notoriety as Babe Ruth's drinking companion. Grover Cleveland "Pete" Alexander won 373 games in a twenty-year career. Fireballer "Bullet" Joe Bush won 195. In the 1960s, when I became baseball editor of *Sports Illustrated*, I informed my colleague Robert Creamer that I'd known Witt and Bush personally. Yeah, sure, my friend remarked. And you taught Babe Ruth how to mix martinis, right? Despite his cynical attitude, Creamer went on to become Ruth's most respected biographer.

21.

When Daddy wasn't driving all over southeastern Pennsylvania inspecting wrecked cars, he was assembling a ragtag team called the All-Phillies and scheduling a slate of games at a gritty old field that was squeezed between the Pennsylvania Railroad freight yards and the nine-thousand acre Fairmount Park, where Philadelphians assembled on hot nights to wriggle around on blankets.

At first his club had gone unmentioned in the local press, but after Daddy inveigled several sports entrepreneurs into putting up money for floodlights, the reporters came to life. Night baseball had never been tried in Philadelphia. Cynics predicted that the lights would illuminate the top half of the ball, grounders would jump up and hit infielders in the crotch, and fly balls would descend on the outfielders' heads. No game could start without an ambulance in readiness.

Always a visionary, Daddy accepted the challenge. He hired electricians to install four banks of lights, and for the first time in the long history of Philadelphia baseball, the cry of Play ball! rang out after sundown.

Some of the dire predictions came true. Outfielders ran through puddles of light and into one another, and fly balls flitted in and out of sight like lightning bugs. There he is! fans yelled when our five-foot centerfielder chased a routine drive.

Where? someone else shouted.

There! came the reply.

Naw, he's gone again.

At inopportune moments, cinders and smoke from Pennsy locomotives and switch engines curled across the field. Spectators watched through a scrim of oily haze. Players coughed, sneezed, and rubbed their eyes but refused to quit, in the highest traditions of the theater. Buddy Wishart, Daddy's first baseman, caught a pop fly on his head and lay flat on his face until the last canary flew away and he wobbled back into action, only to be conked by a low line drive. After Buck Weaver's nose was broken by a screwball that he mistook for a curve, the ump started calling time at the first sound of locomotives. Under these conditions, Daddy stole three bases. It didn't surprise me. Nothing about Daddy surprised me.

The All-Phillies' upcoming game against the colorful House of David was expected to push the new venture into the black. Daddy drove Sis, Mother, and me all over town to tack signs on telephone poles: Whiskers! Whiskers! The Bearded Ballplayers!! The most unique attraction in Baseball!!!

An item in the *Philadelphia Daily News* hinted that a few major leaguers had been known to don fake beards and play for the House of David. Daddy picked up on the cue and composed an ad:

> Do not miss this grand event! Tris Speaker might be
> playing right field! Rogers Hornsby could be
> playing second. A lady might play short.[15]

Seated in the front row at the game, Mother and I were fascinated by the House of David nicknames, as listed in the program, and we made up double-play combinations to surpass the famous Tinker-to-Evers-to-Chance. My favorite was Eggs-to-Goober-to-Beaus. Mother preferred Ug-to-Slick-to-Smoke. My four-year-old sister and I were enjoying infield practice when a player named Woody swaggered over to make friends. Carolyn let out a shriek.

I tried to calm her as the bearded monster took her hand and dragged her tiny fingers across his beard. See? he said. It's peach fuzz.

I thought, How neat! I wish he'd do that to me!

When my sister refused to stop crying, Woody ran back on

---

15 Eventually two females, Babe Didrikson and Beatrice Mitchell, played for the House of David, though without beards.

the diamond. It's okay, Sis, I said, giving her a rare squeeze. The bad man's gone.

She bawled 'til the bottom of the second inning.

The final score has faded from memory, but the barnstormers from Michigan won easily. Daddy, then forty-two, called the umpire a goddamn blind hunky and got ejected.

He signaled the electrician and the lights went out like snuffed candles. After a few minutes of arbitration, the field lit up and Daddy returned to action.

After the game Woody signed our scorecard. When we got home, Carolyn ripped it up and flushed it.

Daddy's All-Phillies were soon challenged by other traveling clubs, including a few black teams. The Pittsburgh Crawfords' battery consisted of Josh Gibson, the Babe Ruth of the Negro leagues, and Satchel Paige, perhaps the best pitcher in history.[16] In one of the games at the grimy old field at 44th and Parkside, Gibson hit a ball that cleared the center field fence and landed in the coal tender of a locomotive bound for the North Philadelphia yards, thus becoming the longest home run in history.

When attendance fell off, Daddy and his backers realized that they had to liven up their act to compete with other Depression-era attractions like dance marathons, six-day bike races, cock fights, dog fights, bank nights, dish nights at moviehouses, dollar days at department stores, carnivals, and flagpole sitters. Daddy's first move was to hire a midget umpire, but fans claimed that it was depressing to watch someone who was not only blind but short. He hired an ump with tumbling experience and taught him to call balls and strikes in a showy manner, including slapping strikeout victims between the shoulder blades and doing an occasional backflip.

Fans seemed to enjoy the performance, but the gymnast

16 He was still mowing down major league hitters at 50.

quit after he slapped one of the Baltimore Black Giants and the player chased him into the stands, yelling, You don't touch me! You don't know me well enough! You do not touch me!

22.

With the 1932 season coming to a close, Daddy arranged a game with the Detroit Stars, a team of clowns who played in flap-toed shoes, foot-long gloves, isinglass goggles and dunce caps with propellers and lights. Before the game, five or six of the Stars got into a vigorous game of pepper, standing in a little group, taking hard-hit batted balls at a range of eight or ten feet, winding up to throw in one direction and throwing in another, grabbing at crotches and performing other magic tricks that had Sis and me squealing with delight.

In the second inning, the Stars' shortstop took the field, sat down and read a newspaper. The catcher, comfortably seated in a rocking chair, picked off one of our runners.

Desperate to recoup, Daddy scheduled a game of donkey-ball, usually a hit with kids. Players would swat the ball with a broom, mount a burro, and try to circle the bases. Sometimes the trained animals wouldn't budge, and sometimes they threw riders. The donkeys seldom moved faster than walking speed and almost never in a straight line. That was part of their charm.

After an hour of action, one of the animals collapsed during a rundown and was carried to the parking lot by sweating players. I could swear he winked as he passed Sis and me, so we gave him a round of applause. Mother said that perhaps the event hadn't been as pleasurable as the donkey had anticipated. Spectators demanded their money back and someone threatened to call the ASPCA. Donkey baseball didn't return that year, thus disappointing its dozen of fans.

A few nights after this latest setback, Daddy and his backers regrouped around our dining room table. Sports impresario Eddie Gottlieb, owner-coach of the champion Philadelphia SPHAS and later the founder of the Philadelphia Warriors basketball team, ordered Daddy to ditch gimmicks like donkey-ball and get back to real sport. Daddy nodded agreement. In public he was always respectful of Mr. Gottlieb and grateful for his financial backing, but privately he complained that Eddie squeezed a nickel 'til the Indian rode the buffalo.

Daddy outlined a surefire idea that would outdraw the Phillies and the A's combined. He would assemble a semipro team made up of foreigners, and they would take the field as "The All-Nations." Every ethnic neighborhood in town would have its own hero. There'll be a Polock for the Polocks, Daddy said. A Chink for the Chinks, a Catholic for the Catholics....

Catholic isn't a nation, Gottlieb put in.

Daddy said, On this team Catholic is a nation. I got Ziggy Horowitz lined up to play shortstop. You gonna tell me Jewish ain't a nation?

Gottlieb suggested that Horowitz could wear a yarmulke, but Daddy said he would have to wear a uniform just like the others.

When he was asked about concessions, Daddy said, We won't sell no hot dogs, we'll sell foreigner food.

Like Blintzes? Matzoth balls?

Blintzes maybe, Daddy said. Your Gentiles won't eat matzo balls.

Neither will your Jews, said Gottlieb.

They tried to think of exotic foods that might go over with the crowd, but all they could come up with were hot tamales, and Gottlieb said he wasn't sure whether they were Spanish or Mexican. Daddy explained that they came from Peru and there weren't enough Peruvians in Philadelphia to justify making a batch.

Before the All-Nations' opening game, Daddy papered the city with free passes, "compliments of Swede Olsen," but Philadelphia sportswriters refused to take the team seriously. A few scattered fans stood on the sidelines as my father, an American citizen of German and Danish extraction, took the mound with the blue-and-gold flag of Sweden sewn to his back. His old teammate Buddy Wishart appeared at first base in the role of the Arabian star Aziz Azul and wore a turban that Mother had spun from a bedsheet.

Our South African outfielder, a welder from Germantown, played in khaki shorts, a pith helmet, and boots that laced to his knees, and he tipped off the other team that he would never bunt or steal a base. Our Chinese third baseman Ernie McGovern had been instructed to smile and show his buckteeth. He wore a horsehair pigtail that was pinned to the underside of his baseball hat and hit him in the face every time he struck out. Our left fielder was a Canadian machinist representing Mexico; Daddy said he didn't look Canadian enough. Our right fielder described himself as a Jewish pants presser, which made Eddie Gottlieb ask if he only pressed Jewish pants. Daddy agreed to let him represent Poland under the name Francis Zawadzki.

Mercifully, the All-Nations went out of business after three straight losses. Philadelphians weren't as obsessed by nationality as Daddy. The final game was witnessed by a few dozen spectators, half of them French sailors from a destroyer that had put in at the Philadelphia Navy Yard. They thought they were watching cricket.

I was proud of my father. He showed imagination. He showed style. He wasn't afraid to try something new. I never saw Mr. Gottlieb at our house again.

23.

I turned nine in the summer of 1934 and began to expand my range beyond our neighborhood. On a hazy summer day I wandered up to West Chester Pike, crossed the interurban railroad tracks and peered through a gate marked "Flower Observatory." Inside the landscaped grounds I saw a building that resembled a squat brick silo with a rounded lid. A vertical band ran down the side of the lid. If I'd made a thousand guesses about the strange structure, I wouldn't have come close.

I was still interested in plants and flowers, especially the kind that produced pocket money. On Fairview Avenue I was the kid to see for radishes, and I maintained a businesslike interest in the health of the pansies and violets that I sold to my elderly clientele. Standing outside this locked gate, I thought how neat it was that someone had built an observatory for flowers.

As I peeked through the fence, a man of about forty in a seersucker suit parked his car in front and opened the gate. He'd just stepped inside when he turned and asked, Say, young man, haven't I seen you around here?

I told him that I was a graduate of the fourth grade at Highland Park Elementary School and was interested in flowers. Flowers? he said, and smiled as though I'd said something funny.

I asked if boys were allowed to come inside the observatory and take a peek. I grow flowers myself, I said, lying a little.

I don't see why not, he said, opening the gate for me.

As we crunched down the path toward the silo, I asked if he studied violets in the observatory. Uh, no, he said, still wearing an amused look.

Radishes? I asked.

Out of my line, I'm afraid.

I'm in the radish business myself, I said. The man nodded.

Soon I was crouched inside a dark circular room and watching while he cranked some cranks and pushed some buttons until the tubular barrel that was the room's centerpiece pointed out the side of the circular roof. He did some fine tuning and then said, Look in here.

I peered through an eyepiece in the side of the barrel and saw an explosion of light brighter and more colorful than any flower I'd seen. The colors seemed to flicker and change as I watched.

Man oh man! I said as I yanked away. What a neat plant!

The man said that I was looking at Arcturus.

Arcturus? I said. What's a Arcturus?

The man said it was a star, a hundred times brighter than the sun. The name meant Bear Guard because it was near the Sky Bears, Ursa Major and Ursa Minor. Arcturus was even mentioned in the Bible.

My head swam. Bear Guard? Sky Bears? In the Bible?

The man sat me down at a wooden desk and explained that we were in an astronomical observatory and he was a University of Pennsylvania professor. He told me that the Flower Observatory was named after Mrs. Reese Flower, who donated the land for the university's project. At the moment the observatory's telescope was reserved for teaching and research; in fact, one of his students had used this very telescope to find a new star.

I walked home in a daze. At that age, I wouldn't have known the correct name for my condition, but it came close to coma. I knew that I might never again be permitted inside the Flower Observatory, but nothing could keep me from becoming an astronomer, maybe even enrolling in Penn and discovering new stars: Jackie major, Olsenium, Rudolph minor, Sissyphus. I might even name a new galaxy after Mother: The Florence System.

That night I broke the news to Daddy that I'd changed my plans about becoming a major league pitcher.

Astronomer? he said after I'd rattled on for several minutes. Ain't no money in that.

Yes there is, I said. They look through this tube 'til they find a star.

Tell 'em to come around tonight. I'll show 'em a coupla hundred.

I mean they look for new stars.

How much dough do they make?

I had to admit that I didn't know. I said I thought that maybe some astronomers found new stars for the honor.

Honor, huh? Daddy said. How's that go with mustard?

I had to laugh. My old man was a funny guy.

The next day I described my experience to a new friend, a genius who was barely nine years old but already knew more science than most of our teachers. In my fourth-grade class, he was the only other shrimp, a shy little fellow with a big name: Thomas North Jackson Jr. At Tommy's big frame house, his mother and I got off to a shaky start. In all frankness, I had to tell her that I was puzzled by her son's middle name. Edward's a name, I told her. Jackie's a name. But ... North is a direction.

In Thomas's case, Mrs. Jackson said coolly, it's a family name.

I still couldn't understand why a mother would name her son after a point of the compass.

After a discussion with Tommy about stars, I looked through my dog-eared Johnson Smith novelty catalog[17] and

---

17 A boy's garden of delights, including fake dog mess, fish-flavored candy, the world's smallest harmonica, hand buzzer, X-ray vision glasses, midget camera, dribble glass, whoopie cushion, fart alarm, exploding matches and bloody mouth chewing gum, as well as books on *How to Throw Your Voice*, *How to Impress Women*, and *How to Love and Be Loved*. A Johnson Smith book called *How to Kiss a Girl* suggested practice sessions on the back of the hand, advice that I found useful when I reached my twenties.

found what we needed. I taped some coins to a strip of cardboard and sent away for their genuine pocket spy telescope. Tommy had a book that showed where to look for Orion, the Pleiades, both Dippers, and other heavenly bodies. He seemed to understand every word, including c-o-n-s-t-e-l-l-a-t-i-o-n. As I told Mother, Tommy is a amazing boy.

All summer we did field research in his yard. One of us future Nobel Prize winners would study the stars and planets through my telescope while the other kept an eye out for comets, meteors, the northern lights, and the evening mail plane on its way to Newark. Then we would switch. Within a few days Tommy had taught me the order of the planets from the sun, but I was a little dubious since we couldn't see Uranus, Neptune, or Pluto.

I said, How do we know they're there if we can't see 'em?

Tommy said they might show up if we could get a little closer. After dark we climbed to the top of a tree in the vacant lot next to his house. We swayed in the evening breeze like lemurs as we passed the telescope back and forth. We never caught sight of the missing planets, but our enterprise paid off big. Before we'd begun our project, I was under the impression that the stars marched across the sky from left to right, or east to west, as anyone could see by watching for an hour or two. But my brilliant friend Thomas North Jackson explained that the stars only seemed to move in a straight line. In actuality they circled the North Star as though it were the hub of a wheel.

Tommy had made an important discovery! I couldn't wait to tell my parents that both of us would be famous.

Mother's response was that she wouldn't be surprised. Daddy said he was from Missouri. He added that he'd checked with a few friends downtown and learned that astronomers didn't get paid for finding stars or moons or anything else in the sky. Everything's free up there, he explained. Stick with pitching.

I couldn't bear to report their reaction to Tommy. He'd made one of the neatest discoveries in the history of astronomy, and my parents weren't even interested.

A few months later I was running an errand when I caught sight of the man from the Flower Observatory in a drugstore near Highland Park School. Here was someone who would take Tommy's discovery seriously. I was shaking with excitement as I described my friend's theory.

The University of Pennsylvania astronomer ran his hand along his chin, then pulled a small notebook from his pocket. He licked the point of his automatic pencil and said, Thanks, son. I'll make a note of that.

24.

One day that summer a gray-haired man approached me on the sidewalk as I was leaving home to build an Apache stockade with Billy Glossop. His pants were shiny, his high-topped shoes rounded at the heels. The buttons on his double-breasted suit coat had been replaced by knots and his steel-rimmed glasses were patched with adhesive tape. He needed a shave.

May I inquire? he asked me. Is the lady of the house at home?

You mean ... my mother? I said. Sis and I were under orders to call her Mother, never Mom, Ma, Mama or Mommy or The Lady of the House. "Mother" was her badge of dignity and pride and she wanted the world to know it.

Yeah, I said. She's sitting on the toilet.

After an afternoon of construction work, I went home for dinner. As Mother sliced a tomato she said, Did you see that poor man today? Wasn't that sad?

I said the guy looked okay to me, just kind of dirty.

Mother said, Don't judge a book by its color. He's our third hobo this week.

I asked if she meant bums. Our cleaning lady Amanda was always talking about the white-trash bums that littered Sixtieth Street in West Philadelphia.

No, I don't mean bums, Mother said emphatically. Bums want handouts. Hoboes want work. That man did such a nice job in our yard; I made him a tomato sandwich. He's been living off ketchup and hot water.

Why don't he get a job?

Where? There's no jobs.

Why not?

Mother paused. It's the Depression.

What's a depression?

Lately I'd been hearing the word in hushed conversations that trailed away when I came into earshot. She started to respond but stopped. She said, Never mind. A depression's not for boys to worry about.

One boy worried about it anyway. I began noticing all the magazine ads about money and the lack of it. Vicks Vapo-rub advertised, Nobody can afford a cold this year. Gillette portrayed an unshaven man reporting to his wife: I didn't get the job. Another ad showed a smiling woman saying, The quarters I save on Colgate's help me weather the storm.

On radio the Kingfish told Lightnin': I is flat as a pancake. I got about fifteen cents.... Da butcher done tighten up on me. I gotta git a couple o' po'k chops in dat house some way. You can't ast people comin' to supper to eat gravy all de time ....

The situation began to trouble my sleep. Mother bought some Ovaltine to soothe my nerves just before bedtime. On the back of the package a man tossed and turned in bed. A caption said, If I could only sleep. Will they cut salaries? ...

Songs of false hope and encouragement only made me

more nervous:

> Just around the corner
> There's a rainbow in the sky
> So let's have another cup of coffee
> And let's have another piece of pie....

Another radio song claimed that happy days were here again. I didn't believe a word of it. I wondered when the moving van would pull up in front of our house.

Shoals of hobos began passing through our neighborhood with cloth bags on their shoulders. Some looked like schoolteachers in old clothes and some looked like ax murderers or Democrats. I wondered if Daddy might become a hobo. What about me? Or Sis? Did they have girl hobos? If the worst happened, I would quit school and sell violets and radishes full-time to save our family. It was a recurring fantasy.

I thought about Mr. Wilson, hanging from a pipe in his basement. I asked Mother if he died because of the depression. No, no! she said. Mr. Wilson just ... he just danced to a different drummer.

Later I learned that Mr. Wilson had lost his job a few days before his suicide. He'd probably quit on himself after his job quit on him. It was a heavy load of thought for a kid.

Some of our resident hobos wandered up from the Pennsylvania RR spur in the woods where I explored, studied nature, and peed on tree trunks. That spur was the start of a lifelong obsession with tracks. Even now I will see a set of tracks and wonder where they start and where they end. What's around the next bend? If I keep walking, will I get there?

As a child I developed the first law of railroad tracks: they never end. You can walk a track 'til your legs fall off and you will never get there.

After I turned nine, I began to spend more time at the Pennsy spur, waiting for trains to flatten my pennies. The tracks ran along a stream called Naylor's Run, a ten-minute downhill hike from our house. Naylor's was the first creek I'd ever known personally, and I spent hours peering into pools looking for sunfish and swordfish and splashing in the water.

Eventually I would get bored and turn my attention back to the old railroad spur. Sometimes I had to step aside as a train of two or three cars came ghosting along, the engine clanking and emitting wisps of steam that smelled faintly of oil and warmed my bare legs. After the red lantern on the caboose disappeared, I would stand on the cinder ballast and sniff the smoke. My favorite smell was still my mother's Evening in Paris cologne that came in the cobalt blue bottle with the silver filigree wrapping, but locomotive smoke moved into second place ahead of gasoline.

25.

By the fall of 1934 the Depression was too widespread to conceal, even from children who didn't understand bank closings and dust bowls and stock market crashes. For a long time our family life went unchanged, at least on the surface. Daddy disappeared under cars, managed baseball teams, and gambled on horses, numbers, and how long a fly would remain on the plateglass window in the front of the Columbia Turners. Our living room was still a forum of ballplayers and hangers-on who sat around smoking cigars, drinking highballs and Esslinger's beer, and chattering about how far they would have gone if the manager hadn't favored his old cronies.

Sometimes Daddy would get me out of bed and parade me in front of his guests. I'd already met sports entrepreneurs like Eddie Gottlieb, but names like Whitey Witt, Howard Ehmke, and Buck Weaver still didn't register. After I shook hands with a pleasant man named Herb Pennock, white-haired Harry Davis asked me, Do you know who Mr. Pennock is, Peanut? Mr. Davis was in his seventies then, a turn-of-the-century superstar who was renowned for hitting home runs and stealing signs.

Peanut confessed that he didn't know Mr. Pennock.

Well, Herb here is a pitcher. He's what we call a crooked arm.

I thought I'd heard Daddy use that phrase, but I had no idea what it meant.

A crooked arm is a southpaw, Mr. Davis explained. A portsider.

I must have looked baffled, because he added, A left-hander, son. There's two different kinds of lefties. There's the kind that's born left-handed. And there's the kind that think left-handed. Like your old man here. Swede bats right-handed and throws right-handed, but he thinks left-handed.

Even at nine years of age I understood.

Someone asked Mr. Pennock how his horses were coming along, and I began to wonder if every retired ballplayer on earth had the gambling bug. But it turned out that he came from fox-hunting country and was a master of hounds. He raised silver foxes and his nickname was The Squire of Kennett Square.

After a few more beers, big George "Moose" Earnshaw launched into a poem about the Yankees:

Where's Babe Ruth, the king of swat,

Who rocked the heavens with his blows?

Grabowski, Pennock and Malone.

Lord a mercy, where are those ...?

I smiled as though I knew the words, but the curtain dropped on my precocious-kid act when Mother called me up to bed. After she'd made her usual comment about bedbugs, I sneaked back to my listening post at the top of the stairs. I gathered from the conversation that Mr. Ehmke had struck out a mess of Chicago Cubs for a World Series record. Someone asked why Connie Mack had chosen Mr. Ehmke over his two great starters, Lefty Grove and Mr. Earnshaw, and Mr. Ehmke explained in a soft voice, Nobody knows this, but Connie sent me to scout the Cubs for two weeks before the Series. When I got back, I knew every Cub's weakness.

I thought, What a great secret to tell the kids!

Someone brought up the time a St. Louis Browns' fan threw a soda bottle that knocked Whitey Witt unconscious. Two days later, his head still bandaged, Witt knocked in the runs that beat the Browns 3-2 in the ninth inning and won the pennant. Now this baseball hero was sitting in our living room. It made my heart thump just to hear him talk.

I couldn't wait to see Billy Glossop the next day. Whitey Witt was at our house last night, I told Bill and his father.

Is that right? Mr. Glossop said. We would of came over, but we was entertaining J. Edgar Hoover.

I just clammed up. I didn't want to show my ignorance by asking who J. Edgar Hoover played for.

A week or two later Daddy's baseball friends reassembled in our living room and I learned that Ty Cobb sharpened his spikes to slash second basemen, Babe Ruth was a clown with a mean streak, and five minutes with Shoeless Joe Jackson would put a cocker spaniel to sleep. Daddy was quiet, as usual, and I was as proud of his modesty as I was of his record.

I perked up when I heard Whitey Witt say, Hey, Ole, didn't I see you throw the screwball? '23? '24?

Daddy said, That damn pitch was hard on the old soup bone.

One of the others said, Swede, you weren't around long enough to matter!

All the ballplayers laughed. Later I learned that they used insults and wisecracks for compliments. If you called your teammate a goddamn no-good son-of-a-bitch who stole from the blind, his proper response would be, Gee, thanks!

After another round of drinks, the ex-major leaguers started discussing spitballs and spitters. Mother caught me listening and marched me into my room. I asked what a spitter was, and she told me that it was everyone who ever played baseball. I said, Jeez, Mother, you're turning into a regular Groucho Marks.

After she tucked me in, I thought of an excuse to keep her around for a minute or two. Mother, I said, who's Amy Simple McPherson?

A lady preacher. Why?

Billy Glossop told me a joke about her.

For heaven's sake, Jackie, don't repeat what you hear from the Glossops.

This joke's okay, I said.

Tell me in the morning.

My room went dark and she started down the hall. I called out, What's the difference between Amy Simple McPherson and Eleanor Roosevelt in the bathtub? Amy Simple McPherson has hope in her soul!

The overhead light made me blink. Mother stood there frowning, then broke into giggles. She said, You don't get it, do you, Jackie?

I said, Whattaya expec'? I barely started Sunday School.

One airless summer night an elongated man in a dark suit, high black shoes, and a straw hat visited our living room accompanied by his teen-aged son. The man was so tall and skinny that he seemed to sit down in sections. His kneecaps strained the crease in his pants.

Whatever business the legendary A's manager Connie Mack had at our house didn't take long, but he stayed under our roof long enough for me to hear him call my father Swede, as if they were old friends.

When I told Billy G at school the next day, he said, Connie Mack, huh? Did you tell him a few things about managing? Like don't sell your goddamn stars after you win the goddamn pennant?

That's what Mr. Mack had done in the early thirties, and it was still a sore point with Philadelphians. Billy and I discussed Mr. Mack and the A's for a while, and he asked if I knew that the skinny old man had been a star catcher. I told him Billy he was nuts. He said, Wanna bet a nickel?

I said I didn't want to take his money. I said, My old man pitched for the Detroit Tigers and I forgot more about baseball than you'll learn in the next six centuries. Stick that in your pipe and smoke it.

Billy said, You wanna put your money where your mouth is?

I told him he was a dope.

He told me to put up or shut up.

We extended pinkies to make the bet official. I yanked my hand back and said, J'ever get a lemon?

He grabbed at my crotch and said, J'ever get it squeezed?

Billy won the nickel. He always did.

26.

Three seasons after the collapse of the All-Phillies and All-Nations, Daddy was still managing sandlot teams around Philadelphia and pitching a few innings of his own, either as a starter or in short relief. Mother and Carolyn stayed home, but I seldom missed a game, even on the road. Sometimes I would see Mr. Ehmke or Mr. Earnshaw or one of our other living-room visitors on the sidelines, cheering Daddy's team. It was good to see the old major leaguers sticking together.

I wasn't surprised that Swede Olsen could hold his own on

the playing field, even though it was only semipro. My old man hadn't made it to the major leagues on a fluke. I basked in his glory. I never paid for a hot dog, pop, or candy – the attendant would say, You're the pitcher's kid, ain'tcha?

I would nod modestly and accept his gift. In a game at Norristown, I signed an autograph.

Sonny, Daddy told me as he drove us home from a doubleheader sweep in Smyrna, Delaware, this pitching racket is duck soup. Ya don't need steam. Me, I'm a spotball pitcher. Hitters look inside and I give it to 'em outside. They expect it high and I throw it low. Ruins their balance. Lemme tell you, Sonny boy, a smart pitcher can lose his arm and keep on going for years.

Lose his arm? I was shocked.

Daddy explained that he didn't mean amputation.

Alas, his glory days on the Philadelphia sandlots lasted only a few weeks after the Delaware games. On a steaming August afternoon, a South Jersey meatcutter with the build of a stud bull drove a screaming line drive into Daddy's groin. Sitting on the bench, I could almost feel the crunch.[18]

I knew that ballplayers were superstitious, and I wasn't totally surprised when Daddy came home from the hospital three days later and explained, I brung this on myself, Sonny. I stepped on the foul line.

Avoiding the foul line when he went out to pitch was one of his oldest superstitions. But I was pleased that Billy Glossop's prediction didn't pan out. Daddy was still a baritone.

He groused and bitched and stayed in bed for a week, then hobbled around on crutches. One evening when I brought him his *Public Ledger*, I noticed a strange gadget hanging over the back of his bedside chair. It looked like two leather pads con-

---

18   Later I did some research and learned that only one pitcher in history had duplicated Daddy's feat of making a baseball curve in two directions. His name was Frank Merriwell.

nected by a band of metal and some brownish straps. I asked what it was, and he said I wouldn't understand. Something in his voice made me drop the subject. In our family, the area between waist and kneecaps was never discussed. It was as if nothing of significance happened there. If we could have figured out a way to pee out our ears, we'd have been happier.

Two months after the injury, Daddy was back in uniform as playing manager, but he was just going through the motions. The leg kick that had put one sportswriter in mind of the great Tiger pitcher Schoolboy Rowe was gone. Daddy wasn't pushing off or using his back and leg muscles; he was throwing like a catcher: short-armed, snapping the ball from behind his neck. At the plate, he swung with a lazy motion, and if he hit the ball, he struggled toward first base and often quit halfway. After taking three called strikes in a game against Wentz-Olney, he came back to the bench and told me apologetically, Pitchers don't get paid for hitting.

I didn't tell him what I was thinking. Pitchers got paid for pitching, and the old pro had given up a shower of runs in the first two innings and had to take himself out.

Daddy suited up but didn't pitch in the next game or the next. Our team lost four straight, and the boo-birds began to yell. A foghorn voice bellowed, When we wanna see bums, we'll watch the Phillies! A man named John Q. Public wrote Daddy that it was time to hang up his spikes, but Daddy said he'd checked and the signature was probably fake.

Before the season was over, he was sitting in the grandstands with me and sometimes Sis. I never knew whether he quit the club or the club quit him, and we didn't dare ask. Whatever happened, I was convinced it had something to do with that other subject he didn't want to discuss. In the mornings when he slept late, I would see the ugly brown thing dangling from the chair next to the bed. It looked like the skeletal remains of a large cockroach. He never explained what it was, how it worked or why he wore it, and he never pitched another inning.

27.

By 1935 the great American Depression was pressing hard on Highland Park. Every month or two another neighbor lost his job. Salaries were low and headed down. Sis and I didn't understand economics, but we could tell from the dinner table conversations that we were running out of money. This didn't keep Daddy's eyes from gleaming as he read us the ads for the new Plymouth PJ sedan with its all-steel body, X-frame, mola steel springs, and miserly gas consumption.

It looks big ... it is big! You've never had a ride like this before! I wouldn't buy any car without hydraulic brakes!

The final enticement was a full-page ad that was made up to resemble the front page of a newspaper. Under the headline 56 MORE POLICE DEPARTMENTS PICK THIS RUGGED PLYMOUTH, two uniformed cops were shown climbing into the PJ sedan.

When Daddy came into the kitchen, unfurled the ad, and said, Look at this here beauty. We all knew it was just a matter of time.

He ended up getting a deal from a South Jersey Plymouth dealer who was going out of business and agreed to waive the fifty-dollar down payment. Daddy had always believed that installment purchases were essentially free. He was above such matters, incapable of planning his life two days in advance, let alone two years. Other heads of family would have checked the bank account before committing to such a purchase. We had no bank account to check. Daddy's money was in his wallet, available for poker, baseball bets, and impromptu crap games.

How much did the car cost? Mother asked.

Nothing, Daddy answered. I just got in and drove it away.

Did you sign any papers?

Just license stuff. We can pay later.

How much, Ole?

Oh, five hundred, give or take. I jewed him down from seven hundred.

When do we have to pay up?

Sooner or later.

Where do we send the payments? Hither and yon?

Take it easy, Flo. You'll live longer ….

That was the way my parents talked.

Somehow or other, the sharp new car didn't seem to improve our situation or Daddy's spirits. *The Philadelphia Record* reported that the average family was living on $1,600 a year, which made us below average. We had to let our part-time cleaning lady go. I started to give her a hug but remembered that I was an Olsen. Don't worry, Amanda said as she gathered me in her arms, it don't rub off. Her husband Thaymon picked her up in his old Dodge sedan. He didn't acknowledge my wave.

Mother's closet had a leftover smell of cedar and camphor, but her full-length beaver coat disappeared along with her muskrat jacket and a fox stole that snapped together like a clothespin and was useful for pinching Sis. When I asked about the missing furs, Mother said, They're on loan.

To who?

Never mind. That's water under the dam.

Our parents constantly reminded Carolyn and me to turn out lights, save our good shoes for Sundays, shut windows and doors, eat every bite. When I sent away for a gewgaw or a comic book, I had to use penny postcards or three-cent stamps. Six-cent airmail, Daddy said, is for the Smiths. The Smiths were family friends from nearby Springfield, and they were held up to me and Sis as paragons of thrift and enterprise until Mr. Smith's brokerage went under and they moved back into the city.

The man from Koppers' Coal Company usually backed his truck into our driveway, poked a metal chute through the open basement window, pulled a lever in the side of his truck, and a ton of coke would thunder into our coal bin. But these days he hand-delivered burlap sacks of nut coal. We cut the milkman to a quart a day and discontinued the chocolate milk, which had been one of my reasons for living. Hap's ice cream became a memory. The merry-go-round man's hurdy-gurdy disappeared from Fairview Avenue. It now took the ice cream truck only a few minutes to serve our block. Kids lined the curb and gawked, but their parents weren't buying.

28.

One Saturday afternoon I watched as a middle-aged man in worn overalls and Army shoes chalked a smiling face with strands of long hair next to the number on our curb. As Daddy was rubbing it out, he explained that the symbol meant "good eats here." He added, Them goddamn grifters got more dough'n we'll ever see.

Mother opened a letter and reported that her brothers and sisters were out of work and Nanny had gone on widow's relief. Her husband, Robert Drecksage, the quiet grandfather I'd hardly known, had died of lung disease from thirty years of inhaling lead dust at American Type Founders in Jersey City. He left me a copy of The Lord's Prayer engraved on the end of a piece of type. You could make out the letters with my Johnson Smith super-magnifying glass.

Daddy wrapped ten dimes in cellophane and mailed them

to Jersey City, but my grandmother sent them back. Mom would rather starve, Mother explained.

What's she want? Daddy asked. Sympathy or spuds?

People said cruel things in those days. Daddy and Nanny never got along, but he probably wouldn't have let her starve.

The times turned tough for us kids. The bottom dropped out of the radish market. Mrs. Parks and my other regulars slashed their budgets for flowers even though I'd improved my product by scenting them with Daddy's Lilac Vegetal. Nobody hired boys to distribute circulars anymore. Too many had turned up in storm drains.

At school we were asked to contribute pennies for starving children, and it took a month to fill the jar. Our fifth-grade class made a field trip to the bank to change the coins into dollars for the nice Red Cross lady who sat in the corner of the lobby in a gray outfit and a funny hat. Billy G asked, What're you? A goddamn nun? When he was ordered to the principal's office, I told him, You better bring your tent. You're gonna be awhile.

He was there all day.

Placards began appearing in store windows: red-white-and-blue eagles with lightning bolts in their talons, signs with stark black combinations of letters like NRA, CCC, PWA, WPA. I couldn't get my tongue around such crazy words. All's I know, my classmate Carter Harrison told me, they got something to do with the Depression.

I said, Cartie, what the heck don't?

Every day Daddy looked more anxious. Drivers were putting their cars up on blocks or storing them in garages. They weren't crashing into one another as often, which meant less work for an insurance adjuster. Our income was cut and cut again, and Daddy took a part-time job selling tickets at the Arena, the indoor sports emporium on Market Street. Every night he came home smelling of mustard and onions.

After he went to bed, I would tiptoe downstairs and pour myself a bowl of Wheaties with a blizzard of sugar. I seemed to have an infinite capacity for sweets, and Mother predicted that I would come down with sugar diabetes. Well, I said to myself, everybody has to die of something. One thing I would never die of. Asparagus.

Our hot stove league petered out, and the only ex-major leaguer who came to call was Mr. Ehmke, who hadn't been paid for our new front-porch awnings. The newspapers carried stories about the low attendance at Shibe Park and Baker Bowl, where the A's and Phillies remained in the cellar. One evening in June, Daddy reported a rare occurrence: both Philadelphia teams had won that day. Daddy said, The mayor's gonna have a parade up Broad! We may never live to see this again!

Late at night I was awakened by gloomy conversations in the living room. Sometimes my parents whispered, as though they didn't want Sissy or me to hear, and sometimes they snapped and snarled as though they didn't care.

One night I went to the bathroom and found Daddy patting Mother's eye with a damp washcloth. Get to bed, Sonny, he said. Your mother's got the allergy. The allergy always made me sneeze. Why did it make Mother cry?

Daddy hit a number for $50 and unhocked Mother's beaver coat, hocked it again, then unhocked it, and finally sold it to the pawnbroker. We continued to have regular desserts, and we didn't skip meals or borrow food from the neighbors, but I noticed that our portions were growing smaller. One night I overheard Daddy say, Flo, we're going bust against a knife and a fork. His tone suggested that it wasn't his fault. Maybe it wasn't.

Mother had always kept treats in our kitchen: walnut fudge left over from her weekly game of Cootie, a bag of broken oatmeal cookies from a church bazaar, a saucer of the delicious new Toll House cookies that fired bursts of chocolate into your mouth. But nowadays our Frigidaire and breadbox were mostly empty space. Our worn-out clothes weren't being replaced; I worried that I would end up wearing embarrassing clothes like Carter Harrison's holy pants or Billy Glossop's Salvation Army shoes that he said were three goddamn sizes too big or Bigs Bag Tanner's old lumber jacket that had been passed down from his two older brothers and would probably end up on Pally Sally even though she was a girl.

29.

One night I overheard Daddy tell Mother that he was sorry about her ring. He said, I'll buy you a better one when our ship comes in.

Mother said, Little pitchers have ears.

So that was it: we were waiting for a ship. I wondered if it would dock at the foot of Market Street, and if Sis and I could watch. Later I heard Mother whisper, How could they sell it? When she came into the bedroom to tuck me in, her eyes were red. The next morning her blue velveteen ring box was missing from its usual place on the dresser.

My worst fear wasn't of running out of food or attending school with my heinie exposed or standing on the corner shaking a tin cup. My terror was that we would wind up in a shotgun flat in the rowhouse slums of Philadelphia. On Daddy's inspection trips, I'd been inside a few of those places. They were close, dark, clammy: hot in summer, cold in winter, always smelly. We walked into a rowhouse on Race Street and encountered a stink so bad I almost threw up. The owner kept a flock of Rhode Island Reds in his basement. When Daddy asked if this wasn't against the law, the man said, It's the onliest way we get any meat. He took us into the kitchen, opened a brown wooden icebox and offered us each a drumstick.

Thanks, Daddy said as he gnawed away. That's white of you. I took a furtive glance at our host. Maybe he didn't hear.

I couldn't imagine how city kids passed their time. They had no trees for watching stars, no cardinals or Baltimore orioles, no sour cherries to throw up, no Naylor's Run to skip stones across, no railroad tracks to walk or trains to flatten pennies, no ball fields and sled runs and playgrounds, no buddies like Bigs Bag and Billy G. As far I knew, they didn't have any girls like Lulu Abernethy and Jessie Willis, pretty girls who were soft, smelled nice and didn't pass gas, and made intriguing remarks like, In due time. City girls were hard, like city boys. How could they be dainty and feminine in all that tar and concrete and dust and car fumes and horns and racket? Every night I prayed, Please, God, make people get into more accidents....

We held on 'til the spring of 1935 and didn't end up in the Philadelphia slums. Our fate was worse.

30.

On a misty May night Mother packed bags for Sissy and me. Where're we going? I asked. Atlantic City?

Never mind, Mother said. Maybe ... nowhere. She turned away.

At dinner she served portions of stew that would hardly fill a soupspoon. Daddy stared at his plate, and when Mother asked why he wasn't eating, he just kept staring.

After we finished a vegetable course that consisted of a couple of string beans each, Sis and I waited for Daddy to ask what was on the desert, but he just shuffled into the living room and slumped into his chair. Mother cleared the dishes and sent us to bed.

I awoke after a few hours and tiptoed downstairs to collect my just dessert. Our suitcases were stacked next to the
front door. Mother's favorite picture, September Morn, leaned
against an overflowing Boston bag, and there was a bare spot
on the wall. The Frigidaire door was open and the plug lay on
the floor.

I'd just gone back to sleep when Daddy shook me awake.
By the radium dial on my Ingersoll, it was three minutes after
three. He touched his lips with his finger and told me to get
dressed.

I followed Mother to our detached garage. Sis stood alongside the Plymouth, looking scared. Mother made her wait while
she stuffed the floor well with blankets and pillows to give her
a place to sleep.

Mother, I said, where ....

She covered my mouth with her hand.

We drove three blocks in darkness 'til Daddy switched on
the headlights at Township Line, one of the main routes into
the city. A bug flashed in and out of the glare like a spark. I
peeked through the window as we drove on empty streets to the
tree-lined boulevard named after one of the Roosevelts – I was
never sure which one.

Sis was dozing in her nest of pillows when we passed the
brick lunatic asylum called Byberry. For once, Daddy didn't ask
Mother if we should drop in on her relatives.

I tried to stretch out on the back seat, but I was too excited
to sleep. What was going on? We'd taken Roosevelt Boulevard
many times, but never at four a.m. And why was everybody
so quiet? On the whole drive I'd heard Daddy make only one
comment. He said, Who'd of thought he'd sue over an awning?

I thought, Are we leaving Highland Park because of Mr.
Ehmke? That nice man?

I saw a sign on a bridge: TRENTON MAKES, THE

WORLD TAKES.

We'd crossed this bridge on U.S. 1 many times. Now I knew where we were headed.

In the far distance the sun sat atop the New York City skyline as we cruised past a pair of tri-motored Ford airliners parked alongside the highway under a sign that said Newark Airport. We passed Ruppert Stadium, the Newark Bears ball-park, a sight that usually prompted Daddy to tell us how he struck out Napoleon Lajoie on that very field with a double-breaking curve.

He steered our Plymouth onto the Pulaski Skyway, a newly constructed marvel of linked steel trusses that was regarded as one of the wonders of the world in every Jersey bar that served pierogi. The Skyway vaulted over the Hackensack and Passaic Rivers and into the mouth of the Holland Tunnel, and a driver who missed the last Jersey City exit ended up in lower Manhattan, a mistake Daddy once made to the delight of the midget navigators in the back seat.

This time Mother provided ample warning, and soon we were bumping and thumping along the pot-holed streets of her hometown. Just after sun-up we stopped in front of an un-painted four-story wooden tenement on Lembeck Avenue in Greenville, a tired neighborhood of rundown two-story homes and a few old townhouses and decaying mansions with un-kempt gardens.

My grandmother stood on the sidewalk holding Laddie on a short leash. She wasn't smiling and neither was the dog. I wondered why she was mumbling and crossing herself.

Mother got out, kissed Nanny on the cheek, then returned to the car without a word. Daddy carried my cardboard suitcase to the second landing, told me to obey my grandmother like a good boy, and jumped in the car as though someone was chasing him.

Sis was still asleep in back, and Mother was looking out the window the other way. I asked, Are you coming back for me?

Daddy said, It won't be long. Mother seemed to be trying to avoid my eyes. I wondered what I'd done wrong. Our Plymouth made a U-turn and then they were gone.

31.

In the 1930s, children were expected to ask no questions about adult matters. I always assumed that we'd fled to Jersey City to avoid paying Howard Ehmke. Years would pass before I learned the whole truth.

Daddy's company had gone under. By sad coincidence, his younger brother Edwin was enduring the same fate 800 miles away in Indianapolis. For a few months Uncle Ed kept a pile of stones just outside his front door. When his former employer's business cars came into sight, he gave chase. A few minutes later he would return to the house, huffing and puffing and spouting gibberish like, That'll bitch the sons of fixes.

Daddy's reaction to losing his job had been less vengeful but just as intense. He took every penny he could beg or borrow and put it on the nose of a longshot that had been tipped by the janitor at the Media Athletic Club. The sure thing raced to a two-length lead on the back stretch, moved out to a four-length lead on the home stretch, threw his jockey, finished first and was disqualified.

While Daddy was dumping us in Jersey City – me at my grandmother's, Sis and Mother at Aunt Ronnie's – movers had spirited our possessions to a warehouse. Eventually they were sold for failure to keep up the storage payments. My Buddy L truck, Radio Flyer wagon and Flexible Flyer sled were gone forever.

three

Lembeck Avenue: Jersey City

1.

I held back tears as I tromped up to the second floor behind Nanny and Laddie. The hollowed wooden stairs creaked with age, and the banister wobbled. I was still half-asleep and confused. What was going on? All I knew was that we'd had to sneak out of Highland Park in the dark.

I wondered what Daddy had meant by "not long." A day or two? A week? I didn't understand why we'd been dumped on our Jersey City relatives.[19] Nanny had no income except the dole. As Mother had been saying for months, the whole maternal side of our family was up against it. There was little work anywhere in the U.S. and next to none in Jersey City. Once the old manufacturing town had been the destination for trainloads of coal and oil and grain that arrived on the Lackawanna, Erie, Lehigh Valley, and Pennsy and were barged across the Hudson to New York. But now bridges and tunnels carried traffic into the big city. Freighters that once called at Hoboken and Jersey City now docked in Brooklyn or lower Manhattan. Huge warehouses that once lined the waterfront stood empty, their grimy windows providing targets for would-be Swede Olsens with rocks.

Nanny was in her fifties and suffering from rheumatism. She'd never held a job and wouldn't have known where to look. Her older son, my Uncle Bob, had given up on finding work and was now raking in $21 a month as an Army private. His younger brother, my Uncle Sonny, was newly employed as a mechanic's apprentice and on the verge of moving into a place of his own. Nanny's third daughter, my Aunt Mae, once a lovely oval-faced teenager, had borne two sons and was beginning to resemble Olive Oyl. She was just beginning a dreary career

---

19 There was an answer, but it wasn't one that a nine-year-old boy could have understood. We were entrusted to our Jersey City relatives because they knew how to be poor.

of making costume jewelry at home, bending over cheap glass beads and whistling through her missing teeth as she fashioned bracelets that her employer sold for a dollar or two at the 5&10. She retained her slender figure, permanently lacking the money to get fat.

On the first Saturday of May 1935 I was thrust into the center of this ménage. The damp spring air covered Jersey City and New York Bay like cotton batting, and the whole world seemed soggy.

In Mother's family, Nanny had always been a cardinal point of the compass. Even when she was dressed up, she was a study in restraint, usually gray and black. At home she wore shapeless print dresses and a baggy gray cardigan and the kind of men's shoes that were called carpet slippers, probably inherited from my late grandfather Robert Drecksage.

When she went on errands she put on heavily darned gray stockings and clunky black shoes of the type worn by nurses. Her glasses were steel-rimmed and usually smudged. She wore no jewelry or other personal adornments. Her engagement and wedding rings had been sold out of pawn at a shop on Ocean Avenue, as had her most prized possessions, including an ornate chest of drawers that had been hewn from walnut by her father. An oval mirror, cracked and tarnished, hung on the wall of her bedroom. The pawn shop had rejected it.

Nanny's second-floor flat wasn't electrified. On the rare occasions when the landlord sent up heat, the radiator went into convulsions, clanking and hissing in outrage at having to do its job.

Like most members of her generation, my grandmother believed that all germs traveled by air. As I soon learned, she lived in terror of drafts. Shut the door! she would yell before I even touched the doorknob. Knitting or crocheting in her wooden rocker after dinner, she would frown and glance nervously around the room. I feel a draft! she would say as she checked every door and window.

Nan was also nervous about drops in body temperature. Even on hot days, she would warn me not to take a chill. According to her, chills and drafts produced the same result: You'll catch your death, deah.

I'd thought a lot about death. Didn't death catch you?

In Nanny's flat I began to understand that there were reasons for every human being's behavior and you could learn them if you dug deep enough. Nanny's fear of drafts and chills didn't come from a whim or some quirk in her brain waves. It came from her personal history. The influenza epidemic of 1918 had broken out in a Jersey City army barracks where thousands of soldiers waited to be shipped overseas. Nanny was in her early thirties and married at the time, with five children ranging in age from the twelve-year-old Florence to the newborn William, later known as Sonny. The kids took their fears head on by joking about the epidemic:

I had a little bird and his name was Enza.

I opened up the window, and influenza.

Nan still looked stricken as she told me about the stacks of coffins that were hauled away on flatbed wagons. Crepe paper crisscrossed doorways up and down Claremont Avenue: black for adults, gray for the aged, white for children. The flu struck in the spring, was brought under control by summer, then returned in the fall, eventually taking 21 million lives, 675 thousand of them American, several from the Drecksage and Zawadzki families. No wonder my grandmother did so many decades of the rosary.

She was also sensitive about fire, and with equally good reason. As a nine-year-old in 1897, she'd watched the big new buildings on Ellis Island burn to the ground in a scary show of fireworks. Twenty years later she was asleep in her home when an explosion threw all seven members of her family to the floor.

The Lehigh Valley RR's Black Tom ammunition dock, less than a mile away, was blowing up in sequence, starting with a barge loaded with fifty tons of TNT consigned to the battlefields of France. Manhattan nightclubbers felt the hot air puff across the Hudson. All night long, Nanny and her family cowered in their rooms, not even sure what was happening.

After the final blast, the Lehigh Valley's loading docks, barges, tugboats, tracks, buildings, freight cars and locomotives were gone, pulverized. Every window in the Drecksage home was shattered. For weeks, my mother and neighborhood kids picked glass and metal from their hair.

You have to be careful around Nanny, Mother once instructed Sis and me. The flu and Black Tom made her afraid of her shadow.

2.

After a few days under my grandmother's roof, I began to realize that her life consisted of petting her dog, reciting her rosary and doing housework. She didn't read, go to the movies or take part in neighborhood activities. Every morning at seven, she swept our flat – the hall, staircase, vestibule, the skinned patch of lawn in front of the tenement and the sidewalk. I decided that she was trying to convince herself that she was living in a place worth sweeping, just as she curled the last inch of her straight hair to prove that her hair was worth curling.

The flat was chilly in the morning, and she worked in a threadbare sweater and skirt and an old scarf that she wrapped five or six times around her neck. She mopped, cleaned, dusted, filled kerosene lamps, trimmed wicks, chopped kindling, did dishes by hand, darned socks that were more darn than sock, scrubbed clothes on zinc washboards in the spooky basement, "wrenched" her dainties in the bathtub, went on rat patrol with Laddie and an old ball peen hammer, cooked on a cast-iron coal-stove, and haggled with deliverymen who were as poor as most of their customers.

On one of my first mornings with Nanny, a swarthy iceman with sloping shoulders and ropy muscles carried a block of ice up the stairs, slid it into the top of her brown wooden icebox, and said pleasantly, That'll be fifteen cents, Mrs. Drecksage.

He clicked his iron tongs as she groped in her straw purse. She mumbled and grumbled and finally said, Mrs. Shapiro pays ten.

No, she don't.

Bessie's a liar?

Fifteen cents, Mrs. Drecksage. Same price for all.

Take the ice back. I'll buy from Hogan.

Hogan died last year.

Hmmplz.

Nanny paused for a few seconds, then said, I don't mean that Hogan. I mean the other Hogan.

By this time he was starting to return the heavy block to the brown leather pad on his shoulder. Fourteen cents? he said.

Twelve.

Nobody else complains.

Nanny said, Don't start wit' me. Whattaya got? Ice made from Holy Water?

The iceman puffed up like an angry rooster. Mrs. Drecksage, he said, ice don't grow on trees.

I had the feeling I was watching a show that had been performed many times before. They finally settled on thirteen cents. Pay ya next week, Nanny said as he headed out the door.

That'll be fine, Mrs. Drecksage.

I followed him down to his truck. Look out, he warned. Don't bunk into the tailgate. Nice lady, ya grandma. You staying heah long?

I don't think so.

Lemme give ya a Joisey City popsicle.

I was excited. I hadn't had dessert in days. He chipped off a splinter of ice.

In Highland Park, Mother had enjoyed modern conveniences – gas stove, Maytag washing machine with electric wringer, Hoover vacuum cleaner, Frigidaire – but her own mother did everything by hand. She knelt on a scalloped rubber mat as she scrubbed the linoleum. Her battered carpet sweeper missed more than it collected. She washed clothes with yellow soap, then wrung them damp and leaned out the back window to hang them on a line that ran to a pulley atop a wooden pole that served three other houses. The view was of chicken coops, gnarly fruit trees, and the backsides of sagging homes with attics or garrets.

If Nan left our clothes out too long, they turned gray from the soot that sifted down from the trains that ran behind the houses on Princeton Avenue. If she hauled them in too soon, they grew mold and had to be re-washed. Even if they dried perfectly, they had to be shaken free of cinders.

Nanny would sprinkle Uncle Sonny's shirts with water from an old Feigenspan "Pride of Newark" beer bottle, remove the flatiron from the stove top, lick her finger, and touch the surface to make sure it sizzled. Then she would press out every crease and wrinkle so that her youngest child would look presentable in the saloons and pool halls where the young men of the Greenville neighborhood passed their time.

The trouble with you, I heard her tell Uncle Sonny, is you're sperled. She didn't mention that she was the one who'd spoiled him.

Nan ironed curtains, pillowcases, napkins, handkerchiefs and anything that would fit on her scorched old ironing board.

I think she would have ironed Laddie if she had a chance.

Mom, Uncle Sonny complained one morning, you don't gotta iron my socks.

You might get hit by a truck, deah. We don't want the cops to think we're Ukrainian.

All of Nanny's rules about cleanliness were based on the possibility of being run down by a vehicle and ending up naked in a doctor's office. I decided that she'd inherited that from my mother.

Breakfasts with Nanny usually consisted of leftovers from the night before or poppyseed rolls from the local Horn & Hardart ("Less Work for Mother"). The brick-hard rolls were priced at three for a dime and were usually sold out a few minutes after the counter opened. Nanny would make toast by holding a slice of bread over the hot coals, then sift on a coating of lard and cinnamon. She considered this a special treat.

When I inquired about the availability of the Breakfast of Champions, Nanny said that Wheaties weren't sold in Jersey City and even if they were, they would be too dear. I asked around and learned that there was no such thing as day-old Wheaties. You paid eleven cents a box or you did without.

At lunchtime on one of my first days with Nan, she served me a cup of re-heated lentil soup and a side dish of sliced tomatoes sprinkled with sugar. I was so hungry that I enjoyed it. I gulped down a treat that she called coffee 'n' milk – a glass of milk with a teaspoon of coffee and a little sugar. I'd never tasted coffee before. I asked for seconds and, to my surprise, she poured me another glass. I think she felt guilty about the Wheaties.

On a walk along Princeton Avenue with Nanny and her dog, we passed a couple of young women who wore bright-clothes and swiveled their hips and seemed to be taking a special interest in passing cars. Nanny told me not to look. A skywriter had written COCA COLA over New York Bay, and the message trailed away in long gray-white ribbons.

After a while I said, Nan, I got a tummy egg. That was the family phrase for stomachache, based on my sister's baby talk. In our family, childhood mispronunciations were memorialized as though they were quotations from Shakespeare. Carolyn could say stomachache as well as the next seven-year-old, but the rest of us continued to say tummy egg in her honor.

Nan, I said, it hurts.

She jerked Laddie to a stop and said, Maybe you need an enema, deah?

When I declined her offer, she said, How about a bottle of citrate? She pronounced it baw-ul.[20]

I'd already learned that citrate of magnesia was my grandmother's second choice for any ailment short of death. After swallowing a baw-ul of the lemony fizzwater, the patient spent the rest of the day sitting on the toilet.

I shuddered. No thanks, Nan, I said. I feel a little better.

It was another of Nanny's miracle cures.

I found it hard to get accustomed to the toilet down the dark hallway. The trip was always an adventure. The light bulbs had been stolen from the two fixtures and the small window at the far end was covered in grime. Even under my seventy pounds, the floors squeaked and creaked. I never made the trip barefooted.

The bathroom was barely big enough for a child. The water closet was way up on the wall and equipped with a pull-chain, an innovation that I hadn't seen before. I had to stand on the seat to reach it. A cardboard sign advised, Our aim is to keep this place clean. Your aim will help. An empty book of matches rested on a ledge, and the air smelled of sulphur, urine, and mil-

---

20   When I was in my teens, my grandmother's brightest daughter, my Aunt Ron-nie, explained that this was called a glottal stop. She pronounced it glaw-ul.

dew. Strange-looking people walked in and out.

Is this the smoking room? I asked a passing neighbor on my first visit.

Uh, no, the woman said.

What's the matches for?

For cooking! she said in a snotty tone. What're you, nosy or sumpin?

I'm not from here.

Gee, I never would of knew. You from Bayonne, or Union City?

I didn't answer. I'd never done well on multiple choice.

3.

After a week with Nanny, I began to yearn for home. I knew I should be out on the street making friends, but tomorrow would be time enough – or maybe I would put it off 'til next week, or next month. I didn't like the prospect of meeting strange kids, playing on city streets, ducking in and out of traffic, maybe getting lost. I was plain scared.

As it turned out, Jersey City was no place for a skinny little shrimp with a foreign accent. Of course I wasn't yet aware that I talked funny. I thought the whole world said *wooder* for water, *iggle* for eagle, *murry* for merry, and expressed *grateetude* for *beauteeful* things. It didn't take long for problems to develop.

One day Nanny served tea to a middle-aged visitor and said, Jackie, this is my friend Gloria.

I already knew her last name. I'd seen her collect her mail, and her name was inscribed on the box: O'Boyle.

Hoi there, Mastuh Jack, the stranger said, patting my head. I'm Mrs. O'Burl.

I hated to be patted or called Master Jack. How long would

that go on? 'til I was thirty-six?

I thought it was odd that she didn't know how to pronounce her own name. Please to meetcha, Mrs. O'Boyle, I said, displaying my suburban good breeding.

It's O'Burl, the woman said.

Oh, okay, I said. O'Boyle.

Nanny said, He's from Philadelphia, hon.

Mrs. O'Boyle said, I soitinly hope he gits over it.

She stepped back and looked me over. How old? she asked.

I'll be ten next month.

You're kinda small. D'ya smoke?

I told her that kids my age didn't smoke. She burst out laughing.

A half-hour after Mrs. O'Boyle left, a deputation of three boys banged on our door. When Nanny opened up, the tallest kid said, Where's he at?

As I came out from behind her skirt, she said, This is my grandson Jackie.

The blond boy looked about fourteen or fifteen. He said, Dis guy's been making fun of our name.

He sounded like a Dead End Kid. It was annoying to be discussed as though I were invisible. What'd I do? I said. Ain't your name O'Boyle?

Nanny jerked my arm and said, *Ain't* ain't in the dictionary.

It's O'Burl, the tall boy said, moving a step closer. O'Burl. What're ya, deef?

Nanny ushered the boys out, crossed herself, and shut the door. Later I took another look at the mailbox. Their name was O'Boyle.

I spent hours trying to solve the mystery. For my age, I was usually quick with words, but it took a long time for me to catch on that the letter *R* was pronounced one way in Highland Park and another in Jersey City.

My first breakthrough came on the word *sugar*. Out in front of our tenement, I asked the second oldest O'Boyle brother to say it slowly and distinctly.

I'll bite, said eleven-year-old Harry. Su-gah.

See? I said. You're not saying the R!

Yes I am. Sugah. Shu-gah.

It's shugarrrr.

What're you, a expoit?

No, but I speak Amurrican.

Don't start wit' me, ya little bastid. Mind ya own beeswax.

I thought, I'm gonna be plenty mad when I find out what *bastid* means. I said, You oughta be able to speak your own language. Say it again: shugarrrrr.

Harry grabbed me by the front of my shirt and said, It's shugah, joik. Shugahhhhhhhh, willya? Whattaya, deef in one ear and can't heah out da udda? What was you, behind the door when the brains was passed out?

I still didn't realize that when he said *sugar* I heard *shu-guhhh*, and when I said *sugar* he heard *shu-garr*.[21] In my own ignorance, I was accusing him of being ignorant. I said, Jeez, don't you go to school?

He slapped me hard across my right eye. I saw Arcturus, the Bear Stars, and Halley's Comet. I'd never been hit. Highland Park boys didn't fight; we ran home and told our mothers.

Out of concern for my concert piano career, I didn't strike back. Harry grabbed me by the collar and said, Quitcha bawlin'.

---

21   Years would pass before I learned that I came from the only part of the east coast where the terminal R was sounded. Everybody was out of step except those of us in the Philadelphia-Baltimore corridor. Long after that spring of 1935, I also learned why Nanny, the O'Boyles, and other North Jerseyites said *terlet* and *erl* for *toilet* and *oil*. They were parroting the speech patterns of Dutch West India Company members who crossed the Hudson from a little town called New Amsterdam and settled the Jersey City region in the 1600s. Jerseyites and New Yorkers who spoke of *Toity-toid Street* and *Toid Avenue* were influenced by the same archaic Dutch tongue. Nanny and the O'Boyles weren't ignorant; they were historic.

Say my name!

I said, O'Burl O'Burl O'Burl through gulps and tears. I would be at the mercy of these bullies 'til I got back to Pennsylvania, and I didn't want to be found dead on the sidewalk in my first month.

I offered my hand like Tom Mix in the movies. That's what good guys did, even after a bloody gunfight. Okay, Harry? I said. Friends?

His spit just missed my sneaker. Ya sistuh's! he said. Go home and tell ya mudda to call ya.

I wondered: Doesn't he know I'm living with my Nanny? That my mother's on the other side of town at Aunt Ronnie's? I turned and walked away. I'd always prided myself on knowing when I wasn't wanted. Nuts to you, Harry, I said under my breath.

My mother, a chameleon who mimicked the locals wherever Daddy dragged her, told me that when she was a girl, she could tell if a speaker was from Jersey City, Hoboken, Bayonne, or Union City. She passed her linguistic acuity down to me. Even today, I can recognize Union City residents by their accent. They speak Spanish.

Nan cut a potato in half, pressed it against my eye and told me it would drawr out the swelling.

Joe Palooka uses beefsteak, I said.

Who's Joe Palooka?

He's a prizefighter. In the comic strips.

I'll buy you some tendalern tomorrow, deah.

She pressed a little harder. We shared the potato for supper.

4.

The abused martyr whimpered and simpered through the night. Every hour or so I would hear a car and pray for it to slow down, park, and disgorge Daddy. Whenever I started to fall asleep, unfamiliar noises reminded me that I wasn't home. In the tree canyons of Highland Park, silence fell over the neighborhood at dusk and lasted 'til dawn. In Jersey City a low hum was constant. Kids ran the streets 'til late. Trains rattled our walls. Switch engines huffed and clanked in the nearby Lehigh Valley yards. Tugboats crisscrossed New York Bay like the coffee bugs on Naylor's Run. Sometimes an ocean liner would cut loose its basso-profundo foghorn and rattle my grandmother's iron bed.

After I finished my breakfast poppyseed roll, Nanny told me to go outside. She said I looked a little weak in the knees and needed some fresh air. I was standing on the sidewalk when two slightly older kids emerged from our tenement. The boy frowned and the girl began scrooching up her nose like a lost bear cub. I must have passed the sniff test because they introduced themselves as the Dallesandro twins from 3-C.

I'm Petey and dis's my sistuh Rose, said the one with the darker moustache. You from dis neighborhood?

No, I said. I'm from Philadelphia. I'd already learned not to mention Highland Park or Upper Darby. Nanny said it would sound like bragging.

The girl asked, Who you stayin' wit'?

My Nanny. In 2-A.

The Polock lady, the boy whispered.

Petey! Mrs. Drecksage is Polish.

Yeah, sure, and we're Eye-talians, hunh?

He had a heavy way of saying *huh*, as though there were an "n" tucked in there just before that final *h*?

I tried to remember what Daddy had taught me about Eyetalians, and I recalled that they were excitable and ate spaghetti. So far, he was half right.

I said, Nanny's Polish, but I'm ... I'm not sure what I am. Amurrican, I guess.

Petey said, Nobody's poifect. You look like a Polock to me.

His sister said, Well, Petey, somebody's gotta be Polish.

I began to feel besieged. I was nine years old and sooner or later I would have to stand up to people like the Dallesandro twins, or every kid in Greenville would be after me with brass knuckles and stilettos.

J'ever hear of Kosciusko? I said, my voice skittering up toward lyric soprano. I'd seen the Polish general on a U. S. stamp. I said, J'ever hear of Paderewski? I remembered him from conversations with my Aunt Ronnie.

I'd run out of famous countrymen, but then I came up with another. I said, Who d'ya think built the Pulaski Skyway? Some Eye-talian? It was Samuel Pulaski! From, from ... Warsaw!

Petey said, No skin off my ass.

I gave him a final shot: J'ever hear of Alfred Einstein?

He stepped up 'til our noses almost touched. He said, J'evuh heah of Primo Carnera?

His twin hustled him away just in time.

I went inside and sat in the vestibule. I felt alone in the world. I decided that I had to stick close to Nanny. It was life or death. It was true that I'd never lost a fight. On the other hand, I'd never been in one.

5.

To my surprise, my stolid Polish grandmother seemed to sense that I was having a hard time and began to warm up a little. As a pre-schooler, I'd had pleasant moments with Nanny, but since the death of my grandfather Robert Drecksage, she'd changed. Mother told me that after the funeral, Nanny said, Well, that's life. Then she stopped smiling for good.

So I was pleased to find that she could be a pleasant companion for a boy from another planet. Behind her glum exterior, a sense of humor began to peek out. For no reason at all she would burst into poetry:

>Fire, fire, false alarm
>Baby peed on Papa's arm....
>Chinky chinky Chinaman
>Sittin' on a fence
>Tryin' to make a dollar
>Out of fifteen cents ....
>Holy Moses, King of the Jews
>Sold his wife for a pair of shoes.

I didn't understand every reference, but I appreciated her effort. Maybe we could cheer each other up a little.

I'm beginning to like it here, I said, lying a little.

Nanny said, I see, said the blind man.

One of her favorite expressions was Only for beer we wouldn't be here, which reached my Philadelphia ears as Only fuh bee-ah we wouldn't be hee-ah. I missed the joke, but I laughed so I wouldn't seem stupid.[22]

Nanny had always used antique expressions like I dasn't, I swan, dear me, I daresay, do tell. She didn't merely tell the truth, she told the God's honest truth. Unlike my parents and teachers, she was willing to discuss earthy subjects as long as they didn't involve the church. She referred to farts as whistleberries and even joked about them. The Secaucus hog farms[23] were

---

22   A half-century later, *Esquire* magazine ran a clever piece about the lovemaking cycles of ethnic groups. Under Poles, it listed no sexual activity from Sunday through Friday, then "twice on Saturday night." I laughed out loud in Nanny's honor.

23   Now the site of the Meadowlands Stadium, home of the New York Football Giants.

eight or ten miles to our west, and if the wind was just right (or wrong), we could smell every pig and piglet. If someone passed gas, Uncle Sonny would scrooch up his long thin nose and ask, Who farted? But Nanny would call out like a bus driver: Secaucus next stop!

She asked me if I'd heard about the little skunk that went to church and sat in his own pew. That was as much blasphemy as her devout Roman Catholicism would tolerate.

When I asked a question about Jesus, she said, Don't talk about Jesus. It's sacrilegious.

Eventually I came to realize that Nan had her own strong set of values, but they weren't easy for a kid to figure out. She was death on pomposity and fakery. When a woman put on airs, Nan would lift her chin and say, Oh, how bad she feels. Overdressed or overpainted females were hotsy-totsy girls. If Nanny felt that something was beneath her notice, she would say, I couldn't be bothered, which I heard as couldn't be boddid. If you talked too much, she would say, Siddown! which meant shut up. Guh 'head meant Go ahead. If something amazed her, she reacted in the plural: Boys oh boys! When she said, Get outa heah!, it didn't mean get out of here. It meant, How surprising! For a long time I thought Nan might be hard of hearing. I would tell her something and she would respond, Tell me about it.

But Nan, I would say, I just told you about it.

Since her husband's death, my grandmother had spent most of her time alone, but she still had conversations. When Uncle Sonny stomped out the door after an argument, she turned to a kitchen chair and said, See what I get from my family? When he returned without apology and disappeared into the bedroom, Nanny addressed the floor lamp: Din't I tell you?

She wasn't concerned that her electricity had been turned off, since she preferred cooking on a coal stove and reading by the light of coal oil lamps. I asked her where coal oil came from, and she said, I thought you was suppose to be bright. Big machines squeeze the coal.

She also said, You can't see electric or hear it, deah, but you dasn't get too close. It's bad for the gonads.

I asked her what gonads were and she told me she was just quoting a doctor on WOR who said that males should be careful of electrical currents. At least you won't go bald, she added. The reference was to a Polish cousin in Paramus, a locksmith by trade, who'd stuck a table fork in a 220-volt receptacle. As the family story went, his hair turned as crisp as won-ton noodles and fell to the floor. When my grandmother first told us the story, Daddy said he was from Missouri, but Mother said she wouldn't be surprised.

It took me awhile to learn the ins and outs of Nan's most important possession: her cast iron stove. Four iron discs were inlaid flush with the hot surface, and she lifted them with a metal tool that fitted into a slot on top of each disc. You had to bear in mind that those iron plates were just a few degrees short of red-hot, something I learned when I burned up a potholder. A strict protocol was observed in the unfortunate event that you accidentally touched the hot discs, and I learned it when Uncle Bob came home on a three-day pass from Fort Dix. If you dropped one, you said Damn! If the disc hit your foot, you said Goddamn! If you grabbed it barehanded, you said, Goddamn son of a bitch! It was a lot of memory work for a nine-year-old.

6.

In certain ways the hard times of the 1930s might have been easier on my grandmother than on the rest of our family. Nanny and poverty were old acquaintances. I heard her say, Great Depression? What's so great about it?

Nan had lived a hard life, making do for five children on a printer's income, then raising two bumptious sons after her husband died without insurance. Every Monday she handed a dime to a collection agent for her burial plot. We had to cremate your grandpop, she explained to me. I'd rather die.

At the time of my summer visit in 1935, Nanny was in her second year on welfare, known at the time as "relief." She would trudge to a collection center and pick through wilted greens, soggy fruit, bins of moldy beans and dented cans, then fire up the coal stove with wood scraps that she'd collected in back alleys.

Sometimes supplementals became available to those who were willing to swallow their pride and wait "on line," as Nan called it. On a cold wet afternoon we waited for supplementals outside a grim bastille of a church on Ocean Avenue. Waves of drizzle rolled up from New York Bay to mix with rotten-egg and chemical smells from factories and refineries. The sound of sneezing and coughing rippled up and down the line. Greenville had turned into a pulmonary ward.

Nan's forehead furrowed as we waited in the rain. Like everyone else in line, we were afraid that the food would run out. Still there was no nudging or shoving, no cutting in or outbursts of temper. We supplicants acted as though we didn't need this handout; we were just killing time on a soggy afternoon.

The church building was crusted with soot, and grayish rainwater dripped off the stone wall and down our backs. By the time we reached the entrance, Nanny's white cloche hat had lost its shape. Laddie shuddered and trembled like a pup.

In the vestibule an overweight relief worker smiled and offered us a can marked MUTTON. Nanny smiled back and asked, How about my grandson heah?

The woman's face went blank. Same family, ain't? she said.

My grandmother slowly shook her head. One can per household, the relief worker said. You know the rules, missus. You want pickled pig's feet instead?

Nanny held the canned mutton at arm's length as though it might explode. No, thanks, she said. I'll keep the feet Our Lord gave me.

She took my hand and led me away. On the sidewalk she commented how bad she feels. She let me carry the can.

Nan seemed able to survive on a chipmunk's diet, but my stomach started growling on the day I arrived and didn't stop 'til I left. Delicacies like chocolate mint ice cream, tapioca pudding and Tastykakes were unknown at Nanny's. Most of the time we lived on soup: lentil, barley, pea, turnip, chicken, tomato, noodle and beet. (Nanny never called her beet soup borscht, out of respect for the ghost of her father.) On a feast night we would split a frank with a side dish of dandelion greens she'd picked in the backyard. We shared boiled vegetable dishes evenly; I ate the vegetables and Nan drank the water.

A friendly butcher on Ocean Avenue saved bones for Laddie. Nanny would crack them open with a hammer, make a tasty dish she called marrow soup, then smash the boiled bones into bits and mix them with leftovers for the dog. Neither Nan nor Laddie would have understood commercial pet food. She probably would have eaten it herself. (I already had.)

Sometimes she sent me to an Italian restaurant on Ocean Avenue to harvest food that remained in the kitchen pots at closing time. One of my grandfathers had befriended Mr. Scalise, the owner. Thus I learned about *polenta* fifty years before it would cost me fifty cents a serving in Bologna and sixteen dollars in San Francisco. I learned that *tripe* was tasty if you were hungry and the cook used plenty of tomato sauce. I began to consider *tartuffi* shavings a mere flavoring, *porcini* a condiment, and sun-dried Siciliano tomatoes a nice topping for a *radicchio* salad. *Mortadella* was still mortadella and not yet bologna, and it seemed to consist mostly of fat and garlic garnished with a few dots of almond and olive. If you slapped it between two slices of day-old bread, it was as tasty as the best veal loaf.

My grandmother said that her father Francis always joked that when he walked into the roundhouse with mortadella on his breath, the other machinists would call him Giusepp'. She said that hadn't kept him from eating it just about every day, so that the smell of garlic became for her the smell of her father ... and Poland.

One night as the dinner hour approached, Nan said, Never went hungry a day in your life, didja?

The pantry and ice-box were empty and her relief check wasn't due for two days. She said, An empty gut's a good physick, deah. Clears the bowels.

A fly went zzzp-zzzp against the mustard-colored flypaper that hung in a lazy spiral from the ceiling. Laddie stood up as though to point, but apparently realized that the fly was neither a small bird nor a Norwegian.

Eat a piece a ice, Nan told me. Your belly'll think you're at Schrafft's.

An hour later I was seeing visions of Mother's rice pudding and butterscotch pie and the Highland Park School cafeteria's yellow cake with chocolate icing. Out of heartfelt sorrow for my plight, I couldn't help but sniffle.

Siddown! Nanny yelled from the other room. She was in the habit of sitting on the side of her bed, fingering her beads, mumbling to herself, and slowly rocking under the pictures of the Immaculate Heart of Mary and the Sacred Heart of Jesus with its dripping gobs of blood. Her plaster statuette of Christ on the Cross always made me ask myself, Was that my fault? When her rosary string broke, Nan fell to her hands and knees and scrabbled around on the floor 'til she recovered every last bead. You'd have thought they were the crown jewels of Silesia.

Around bedtime I was reading a comic book in the kitchen when she said, I daresay Mrs. O'Burl could spare us a dime for some poppyseed rolls.

My heart leaped, but then I realized that Horn & Hardart was closed. It's too late, I whined.

I meant in the morning.

After another long pause, she said, C'mere, Jackala.

I didn't know where she came up with the nickname, but it sounded friendly. She scribbled something on a piece of paper. Heah, she said. Take this to the Boylans.

Mr. and Mrs. John Boylan, locally pronounced "BER-lin," were Nanny's lifelong friends and the parents of her son Bob's fiancee Helen. They lived a few blocks away in a Princeton Avenue rowhouse backed up against the Jersey Central's mainline. Mr. Boylan had infinite patience with inquisitive boys. I'd met him when I was five and thought of him as a favorite uncle. When Mr. Boylan was laid off after twenty years of clerking in Manhattan, he kept the news to himself. Every morning he took the ferry to Lower Manhattan and strolled around town for six or seven hours. After he collapsed from what the Irish call "the hunger," Mrs. Boylan discovered that her husband hadn't worked in five months.

Now he was standing on his tiny porch reading Nan's note: I GOT NO FOOD FOR THE BOY. He went inside and came back with a half-loaf of bread.

I pressed the package against my side and ran for Lembeck Avenue. All the way home I tasted toast covered with lard and cinnamon. I hoped Nanny gave me seconds. The rain fell in fat cold drops, more persistent than before.

Here! I told Nan. I was completely out of breath.

She opened the wrapping on the kitchen table while I dried

out by the oven. Mother of God, she said.

Two slices lay on the oilcloth. The others must have slipped out as I ran.

There was no point in re-tracing my steps. By now the bread would be beyond eating, even by a hungry kid who'd once dined on dog food. My grandmother spread lard on one slice, handed it to me and said, We'll save the heel for breakfast.

7.

The next morning I decided to make amends and be a hero at the same time, thus combining two lifelong faults: grandiosity and impulsiveness. I headed for Hudson Boulevard and the Big Bear, New Jersey's first supermarket. I was skipping along, as usual, 'til a cop stopped me and said, You're not from heah, huh, kid? Look, don't skip in Joisey City. Take my woid ....

Two teenagers were standing next to the front door when I arrived at the market. I breezed past as though I were a paying customer and not some punk trying to muscle in on their jobs, and they graciously spared my life. I spent fifteen or twenty minutes studying the delicacies on the shelves, and by the time I went back outside the killers were gone. I took up a post next to a stall that was heaped high with potatoes – three cents a pound. Potato pancakes were a Drecksage family specialty. A dime would buy us a couple of delicious meals.

A man emerged with bags in both hands. I started to ask if I could help, but he just said, "Ya mudda's" and kept walking.

A middle-aged woman carried a sack of something that looked like charcoal. Help ya? I asked.

Go 'way. Ya bodda me.

My third prospect chucked me under the chin and said, Does mommy know you're here? When I reached for her grocery bag, it ripped open and three packs of Red Indian chewing tobacco fell out. She picked them up and scurried off without looking back. Nuns were never good tippers.

I pictured Nanny back in her dreary flat, nibbling at a heel of bread, trying to make it last. No, half a heel. The other half was for me.

A few potatoes had fallen from the bin. One was dented, but to my eyes the others looked as fresh as the day they were picked. I grabbed two and started walking.

A male voice shouted, Hey!

It didn't occur to me to run. Everything in Jersey City seemed so threatening. If I ran, I would be brought down by an artillery shell or a machine-gun bullet.

A hand grabbed my shoulder and spun me around. The man was about thirty years old and wore a smudged white apron and a pencil moustache. Whatcha got, joik-off? he asked. I'd heard that word once or twice before, but I had a vague impression that it was something you did, not something you were.

Uh ... nothing, I said. Uh, just these, uh, smooshed potatoes.

He grabbed the back of my shirt and duckwalked me through the store. Customers fell back at the sight of Jack the Ripper. He pointed to a wooden box in a rear office and said, Siddown and shut up! Guh 'head! Then he left.

I pictured myself inside the New Jersey State Prison at Rahway, a forbidding pile of bricks that Daddy never failed to point out on our drives from Philadelphia. I was hemmed in by boxes that almost touched the ceiling. The room smelled like Quaker oats.

A few minutes later he returned with an older man who wore a black leather bowtie, rimless glasses and a name-plate that read "Haggar." He asked me what was going on here.

I tried to answer but dissolved into whimpering, then sniveling, and finally to hysterical bawling.

Hey, little fella, Mr. Haggar said, nothing's that bad. He turned to the man with the moustache and said, What should we do with this dangerous criminal, Sam?

Call duh Mickey Mouse, Sam said. I can't keep nuttin' in those stalls no more. Yesterday dey got a watermelon.

Mr. Haggar said, I'll take it from here.

With Sam gone, Mr. Haggar told me to settle down and tell my story like a big boy. I was wracked by gulps, quivers and tremors as I confessed in fits and starts that I picked up the potatoes because I lost a loaf of bread in the rain and Harry O'Boyle was mean to me and the kids made fun of the way I talk and I want to go home to Highland Park and please don't send me to Rahway.

The man seemed to listen closely. He said, You're not from here, are you?

No, I said. I'm from ....

I got a vurry good idea where you're from, he said. He handed me a paper cup and said, Have some wooder.

With my vocal chords lubricated, I continued the story of how I was spending the summer with Nanny, and my mother and sister were staying way across town with my Aunt Ronnie and I didn't know where my Daddy was and Nan's relief check was late and our pantry was empty and I needed to make some money, and anyway everybody in Upper Darby knew I wasn't a stealer and I only picked up the potatoes because they fell on the ground and they were wormy anyway. I wasn't taking potatoes. I was taking worms.

Mr. Haggar shook his head as though a close friend had let him down. C'mere, son, he said. He took my hand and led me through stacks of canned goods, past pallets heaped high with Rinso and Ivory and out a back door to a loading area where two clerks were bagging vegetables. He handed me a sack of potatoes and said, Take these home. We were giving them to the fathers.

He led me back through the busy store, past the glowering Sam and out the entrance. When he let go of my hand, I made a beeline for Lembeck Avenue.

Wait up! Mr. Haggar called out. I'll walk you across the boulevard.

I was relieved. In Highland Park we had no four-lane thoroughfares with blaring horns and ten-wheel trucks and heavy buses and traffic darting in and out and changing lanes. As Mr. Haggar helped me across, I kept hearing his words in my head: Wait up. I'll walk you....

Back home we used those phrases all the time: I'll walk you to the store .... Wait up, I'll walk you home .... I said, Mister, are you from Philly?

He said, I'm from Camden. Right across the Del-wer.

Philadelphians called the Delaware and the Schuylkill "Del-wer" and "Skoo-kill." I was relieved. It was turning into a beauteeful day ....

As the mother-in-law of a man from Missouri, Nanny was dubious. Boys oh boys, she said. That's five pounds of spuds. The guy give 'em to ya?

Yep.

Get outa heah!

After I told the whole story again, she said, Jackie, that was stealing.

No, it wasn't, Nan, I said, adding a little simper for dramatic effect. The potatoes were laying on the ground. I was – sniff-sniff – hungry.

I should have known not to overact in front of my grandmother. Listen heah, Sarah Boinhawt, she said, it's stealing even if you're starving. Stealing's against the lawr. Do you wanna grow up to be like .... She stopped abruptly. I knew where she was headed. Like your father .... I'd always sensed the bad feeling between them. When was he coming to take me home?

8.

Early the next morning Nan dropped a few potatoes into a paper bag. Heah, she said, run these ovuh to the Boylans. Put on my sweatuh, deah. I don't want you taking a chill.

On the way back, I detoured along the Lehigh Valley freight siding to explore for a mineral called Iceland spar. I'd read in *Boys Life* that it bent light two ways and made your words double. There was no earthly reason why a rare mineral should be lying along the railroad track, but I still had the childlike attitude that if you looked for something hard enough, it would turn up. If Buck Rogers and Wilma Deering could fly through the air, why couldn't I find Iceland spar in a railroad yard?

My attention was diverted to pieces of black coal scattered in the ballast. Wouldn't she be proud of a good little boy who brought her potatoes and coal on the same day? I filled my pockets, then used her threadbare sweater as a coal-carrier. When it was stretched to twice its size, I slung it over my shoulder and headed home.

Nan was darning socks when I dumped the coal on the kitchen table. You know what this is? she said.

Coal, I said. For my Nanny.

Do tell. This is soft coal. I use anthracite, deah. This stuff don't drawr.

She explained that smoke from the bituminous coal would leak out the openings in the stove and drive the tenants into the streets, if not to the Jersey City Medical Center, if not to the morgue. A family on the third floor had been overcome by coal smoke a year or two earlier. The family survived, but the parrot didn't.

I headed for our community bathroom. Judging by the

smell in the hall, one of the families was preparing a delicious rope lunch. I reviewed my situation in private. In one month in Jersey City I hadn't done a single thing right. Maybe it was a matter of geography. Highland Park boys belonged in Highland Park. If a Jersey City boy visited Highland Park, he would make mistakes, too. What would happen if he went to our A&P and asked for sugahhhh?

Seated on the throne of knowledge, I concluded that I had to find a summer job. It would help Nanny and make the time go faster. There hadn't been much work for boys in Highland Park, but Jersey City was a big town. I was trying to decide whether to go into the delivery business, landscaping, floral sales, or banking when a gravelly voice asked, Didja fall in?

Before I made my exit, I pulled the chain to prove that I'd had a genuine need.

Nanny boosted my spirits by serving potato pancakes for lunch and again for supper. I declined her offer of coffee 'n' milk, and for once I didn't go to bed with a tummy egg. In the morning I saw her dusting with her old sweater. I'd turned it into a dust-rag.

After Nan cashed her relief check, she marched me straight up to the Big Bear and handed a dime, a nickel, and five pennies to the cashier. What's this fuh? the woman asked.

Potatoes, Nanny said.

What potatoes?

Don't ask.

It was another Joisey City expression I would hear again.

9.

The Dallessandros in 3-C kept homing pigeons cooing and fluttering in rooftop coops, and their prize roller Giorgio flew straight through our window during an electrical storm and knocked himself out against Nanny's plaster-of-Paris statue of Our Lady of Lourdes, which Uncle Sonny had won at a St. Anthony's bazaar by throwing softballs at priests who wore padded leggings and kept moving.

I was trying to revive the prize Lithuanian red rock with an eyedropper of kerosene when my grandmother came into the kitchen and crossed herself. A squab, she said. It's a miracle.

No, Nan, I said as I flapped a rag in front of the pigeon's face, he ain't a squab. He's Giorgio.

He flies through my window, he's a squab.

Nanny, he's the Dallessandros'! He's a roller pigeon!

That was yesterday.

She picked up the unconscious bird and dangled him upside down. There was a hard gleam in her eyes. Poor Giorgio, I said to myself. Your first enema ....

In one snap she broke his neck. It sounded like a mousetrap going off. She dipped a finger into her can of used lard and shook a lump into her iron frying pan. While the grease was melting, she made the feathers fly. As she plucked, she mumbled to herself. I think we got a coupla leftover peas.... I wonder does Agnes have oregano....

Laddie was whimpering and clawing the linoleum and going on point. Sit, Nan said softly. The dog settled down after the bird began to pop and sputter in a bubbling mix of flour and pigeon juice. Laddie pointed the quick but not the dead.

How's the squab? Nanny asked as we nibbled the meat off translucent bones not much thicker than toothpicks.

Good, I said.

You like the peas?

Peas is peas.

As I ate, I remembered how Petey Dallesandro had bragged that Giorgio was his best boid and won a blue ribbon at a show in Patterson. Whenever I saw Petey after that, I had to suppress an urge to tell him he'd been dead right. I've had squab four or five times since my dinner with Nan. It doesn't come any better than Giorgio.

10.

At the end of a month with Nanny, I began to realize that there was one thing worse than being bullied by kids and that was being holed up with the same human being day after day. My grandmother certainly wasn't an unpleasant woman and I was a well-behaved boy, but we'd begun to grate on each other. Nan spent three or four hours a day saying her rosary.[24] Then she would play a few games of solitaire with cards so old you could read the *Jersey Journal* through them. While she played she listened to an Emerson radio that Uncle Bob had left behind when he joined the Army. It had no chassis, just a metal base and a few tubes and controls. Every song seemed to be about money ... "We're in the money" ... "Brother, can you spare a dime?" ... "I found a million-dollar baby" ... "With plenty of money and you" ... "Tomatoes are cheaper" .... The few songs that weren't about money were about girls. I found girls pleasant and interesting, but I would feel foolish singing about them.

Once in a while Nan launched into reminiscences about her father Francis Zawadzki, her sainted mother Balbina, life in an immigrant family, how the Greenville section had gone to pot, the flu epidemic, Black Tom, the greatness of FDR, the corruption under Mayor Frank "I am the Law" Hague, and other subjects of towering disinterest to a kid from Highland

---

24 Decades later, on assignment in France for the Chicago *Sun-Times*, I bought Nanny a rosary and had it blessed by the Bishop of Lourdes. When she died in 1960, the undertaker found it in her bedding.

Park P-A. I couldn't decide whether she was trying to educate me or bore me to death.

One morning I left in the middle of a John Philip Souza concert over WOR and decided to do a solo reconnaissance of the neighborhood before the O'Burls and Dallesandros and other kids had a chance to man their sentry posts and obey their standing orders to shoot any foreigners who said *vurry* for very or *iggle* for eagle. Yesterday's coffee grounds had dried overnight on a sheet of newspaper and Nanny was pouring them back and forth as she listened to a man with a hog-caller's voice sing about his mammy. I didn't need to be reminded that I missed mine, and my daddy and sister, too, and the man's voice hurt my ears. I said, I think I'll go for a walk, Nan.

Don't go near the white road, deah.

White road? What the heck's the white road?

Nanny didn't answer.

I was tiptoeing across the n- man's-land in front of our tenement when Harry O'Boyle squirted out of the alley on an old bike with balloon tires and a deep basket over the front wheel. It was too late to flee. Hey, Philly, he called out, where ya been at?

I said, I, uh – I been doing things, uh – with my Nanny. We, uh – we went over to New York.

New Yawk, huh? he said. What'd you and grandmommy see in New Yawk?

I tried to think of a fib that would work. The, uh – the Umpire State Building, said. The, uh – the park.

Central Pawk?

Yeah.

Big pawk, huh?

Must be a city block, I said.

Harry laid his bike down and walked over. Before I had time to defend myself, he threw an arm around my shoulder and said confidentially, Hey, you wanna go on my paper route? It's collection day. I'll loin you duh neighborhood.

What a joke. Did he think I had a choice?

We went up Lembeck and turned right on Garfield, Harry slowly riding his bike and me jogging behind. He collected from two or three houses, meanwhile keeping up a friendly conversation. When we sat on the curb for a break, he said, Hey, wanna hear a song?

How could I turn him down?

> My gal's a corkuh
> She's a New Yorkuh
> She lets me fawkuh
> Whenevuh I please.

I said, You got a nice voice. He smiled and sang another one:

> Sally is a frienda mine
> I can fawkuh anytime
> For a nickel or a dime
> Sally is a friend of mine.

I didn't want to admit that I didn't know the word *fawkuh*. Something told me not to ask Nanny.

Harry and I spent another hour collecting along Pearsall and Winfield before we reached the stores and rooming houses on Ocean Avenue. Jersey City was the service entrance to New York City and Greenville was the service entrance to Jersey City, so there were no luxury restaurants or fancy hotels in sight. Harry said he liked this part of his route the best. Woikin' people, he said. Good wit' kids.

After he'd collected at a saloon that advertised a free lunch, he told me his family planned a seashore vacation and he hadn't been able to find a replacement for his route.

Would I think about it?

I was thunderstruck. Yesterday I was the dumbest joik on

Lembeck Avenue, and today .... Harry O'Boyle would trust me with his paper route? At nine, the human organism is a bundle of naivete, so I said, Sure, Harry, sure!

We returned to his collections. It was a cool misty morning, but Jersey City began to look like Atlantic City to me. At the head of a cobblestone alley, Harry instructed me to walk to one of the back doors with him and observe his technique. I stood quietly as he knocked and called out, *Joisey Joinal.* Collect!

An old man with a beard and a funny hat opened the door, plopped a dime in Harry's hand and uttered a few words. I asked Harry what *Geh gesunt* meant, and he said it meant see ya around.

What language? I asked.

Jewish.

What's Jewish?

Harry said, What was you, raised in a dump?

I dropped the subject.

A bakery's back door was opened by a red-faced round woman who paid Harry his dime and asked us to wait. She returned with two warm sugar doughnuts.

At the rear of Morphy's Tonsorial Parlor, a burly man in an apron looked up and down the alley before opening the door. Ah, Harry me b'y, he said, ye'll bankrupt me yet!

He threw in a nickel tip.

See? Harry said as we walked away. Nice people. Woikin' people.

After a few more stops, he said it was my turn to make a collection. I followed his bike to a tenement building with greenish sheets of copper flapping loose on the roof and a rusty fire escape dangling in front like a claw. He told me to walk to the far end of the second-floor hall, knock hard on 2-G, call out *Joisey Joinal.* Collect! and accept some money from a customer named Lemon Lee.

Lemon? –

– Lee. Takes in laundry. Nice guy. Woikin' people.

Why do I have to knock hard?

He's a chink. The pigtails cuts off their hearing.

I climbed sagging wooden stairs and started down the long hall shaking with excitement. Would I be as successful with the *Jersey Journal* as I'd been with radishes? Would the Lembeck Avenue boys accept me now? I had to make good. My whole summer might be at stake.

A grimy lightbulb in a wire cage seemed to make the hallway darker. I guided myself by dragging my fingertips along the wall. The place smelled like coal smoke, dog poop, stew, urine, and cigars. Someone was practicing trombone and someone else was vacuuming. One sounded like the other.

I banged hard on 2-G. Nothing stirred. I decided that I would wait here the rest of the morning, if necessary. I did not intend to fail on my first Jersey City business opportunity.

After three or four minutes I slammed the wooden panel with the flat of my hand. The door jerked open, a bright patch of light made me blink, and a shadow took form. I made out a flushed face, a little black hat shaped like the top of the Flower Observatory, a black shirt with cloth buttons, and a pigtail. Who could this be but Lemon Lee? Persistence and patience had paid off.

Joisey Joinal, I said. Uh, om, uh – collect!

The man turned away from the doorway as though reaching for the money, then whirled around. Clackuh? he yelled in my face. Clackuh? What? Did you say *clackuh*?

He grabbed a broom and shoved it in my chest.

A piercing scream almost made me faint 'til I realized it was me. I sprinted the length of the hall, bouncing off the dark wall. I took the stairs four steps at a time and didn't slow down 'til I reached Lembeck Avenue.

Nanny and Laddie were standing in the patch of grit and dirt that we called a front yard. I ran upstairs and flopped on our ratty couch. After Nan served me an order of coffee and milk, I said, I saw ... this ... Chinaman. I was ... helping ... Harry ....

Oh, my grandmother said. You tried to collect from Lemon Lee.

11.

Everyone in the neighborhood except Laddie enjoyed a big laugh at the new kid's expense. Lemon Lee ran the Chinese Lottery in Greenville and he'd been jerking Harry around for six or eight months. At first Harry hadn't worried; plenty of his customers were on the arm. But after six months Lemon Lee's account stood at three dollars and he was still chasing Harry away with cries of Clackuh? Clackuh?

The O'Boyles sent littlest brother Matthew to our door to ask if I wanted to join the Jersey Bumps. When I paused to consider, he said, Skeeter says don't worry about Lemon Lee. That was your initiation. You're in the club now.

I dragged myself downstairs and met a delegation of club members including Skeeter and Harry O'Boyle and the Dallesandro twins. Skeeter asked the others, Whattaya say we cut him open and see what he eats?

Petey snapped, On your back, punk.

Before I could argue, Skeeter took my ankles and Harry grabbed me under the armpits and they began swinging me like a sack of onions. They chanted:

> A rump dee dump
> A rump dee dump
> I t'ink I'll give you da Joisey Bumps ....

With each swing my rear end came an inch or two closer

to the sidewalk. I flinched when I nearly hit, gave a mighty jerk and ran to our vestibule. Just before I slammed the door, I heard Skeeter yell, You gotta be initiated. Like it or lump it!

Halfway up the stairs I decided to lump it.

After my experience with the Jersey Bumps, I swore an oath on my Buck Rogers ring to have nothing to do with the Lembeck Avenue kids whether I stayed with Nanny for six more days or six more years. They didn't know how to treat a nice suburban kid. I cried rivers of self-righteous tears and pounded my lumpy pillow and wrote a lament to Mother at the address on seedy Boyd Avenue where she and Sis were living with my Aunt Ronnie. I missed them both, missed the Tanners and the Saroyans and Billy Glossop, missed my teachers and my Valentine Lulu Abernethy, missed every maple tree and squirrel and Baltimore oriole in Highland Park. I also missed regular meals, not including liver and asparagus. I was so forlorn that I didn't care what happened to me, my family, or President Franklin Rose Velvet or the whole state of New Jersey.

Nan tried to cheer me up, but it wasn't in her job description to be pals with a whiny kid. God intended her to be a mother and grandmother. I told her that Jersey City needed a cow like Mrs. O'Leary's to kick over a lamp and burn the darn place down. Nanny crossed herself and told me I should be ashamed. She said that Greenville had come close to burning down after the Black Tom explosion, and it was nothing to joke about. She told me that you could still see the burn marks from the white road.

I could tell she was in one of her storytelling moods, but I was feeling restless.

Laddie needs a walk, I said.

As I was leaving the tenement with my protective escort, Harry O'Boyle rode by on his bike. Hey, Philly! he yelled. Didja rat on me to ya granmudda?

He disappeared up the alley before I could settle with him.

12.

One cool May morning Nanny cashed her relief check and gave her mopey houseguest a penny. Here, she said. I'll blow you to a Hooton's. Take Laddie.

The candy store was a block away at the corner of Linden and Princeton, which also marked the farthest point that I now considered safe for boys with Philadelphia accents. Right behind the rowhouses on Princeton Avenue ran the main line of the Jersey Central Railroad, whose locomotives my Polish great-grandfather had helped to repair at the Communipaw Avenue roundhouse.

I sat on the bench outside the little store for a few minutes of bliss. Hooton's milk chocolates were about an inch square and a half-inch deep, but in my Memory Hall of Fame there was more old-fashioned chocolate flavor in a penny bar of 1935 Hooton's than there is in a whole box of Hershey bars. I never understood why Hooton went out of business and Hershey became a town.

Something in the sheer chocolateness of the moment muted my fears about the neighborhood. I walked back inside the store and asked, Is there a white road around here? My nanny keeps talking about it.

The man jerked his thumb over his shoulder and said, Across the bridge. He didn't even look up from a tray of fudge he was cutting into squares. The white road was behind his store? He'd pointed in the direction of New York Bay.

Laddie and I walked east on Linden Avenue 'til we reached a rickety wooden viaduct that crossed two sets of rails about twenty feet below. The overpass seemed barely substantial enough for a boy and a dog. As we picked our way around cracks in the asphalt, I felt cinders through the soles of my Keds. A steep flight of wooden stairs led to the tracks and a waiting area in front of a stationhouse bearing a weather-stained sign: "Greenville." The windows were broken and the door hung by a hinge. I guessed that locals had found a better way to get to Journal Square and the Hudson River ferry.[25]

I stood in the middle of the viaduct and looked north. About a hundred yards away a curtain of knotted ropes hung over the tracks to remind roof-riders to duck. Next to it was a semaphore tower. As I watched, the pointed arm jerked upward from a nine o'clock position and the light changed from red to yellow.

I felt the old urge to walk the tracks to their end, but I also felt apprehensive. The bridge railing was shaky and some of the crosspieces had rusted out. Laddie whimpered as though to warn me.

I looked east toward the bay and saw a ribbon of concrete sloping away 'til it disappeared from sight in the marshland behind the Statue of Liberty. In my closed suburban mentality it had never occurred to me that solid land existed east of the Jersey Central tracks, let alone that it was serviced by a road. The white road!

I felt like exploring, but I'd been gone for almost an hour and Nanny would be worried. I gave a light tug on Laddie's leash just as the semaphore arm clicked into an upright position. The light turned green, and far down the tracks I saw something

---

25 My friend Mr. Boylan informed me that most of the Greenville residents who worked in New York City had moved out to suburbs like Rutherford and Hasbrouck Heights and commuted to New York by bus. A few years later my Uncle Bob Drecksage and the Boylans' daughter Helen married and rented a house near a young couple named Nancy and Frank Sinatra. Uncle Bob told me that Frank was a pretty good singer for a fleaweight, but he wasn't well-liked in Hasbrouck Heights because he had a chip on his shoulder. Thirty years later I learned this the hard way when he tried to get me fired from *Time*.

that resembled a whirling ball of smoke. As I watched, the ball got bigger and darker and the viaduct started to hum. I wondered why the engine seemed to be struggling. There was still no sound as I gripped the iron railing and stared.

The locomotive approached a little unsteadily, swaying a few inches from side to side, smoke pouring from its stack and steam blowing from its sides, a dim ugly yellow light and a clanging bell clearing the way. It wasn't low and sleek like the stainless steel Burlington Zephyr or other streamliners you saw in newsreels. It put me in mind of a steel ingot on wheels.

Laddie yanked at his leash as the planks began to tremble under our feet. The engine was a hundred yards away and closing fast. At fifty yards it gave off a bluish-purplish cast through the smoke. The dog reared up on his hind paws and bared his teeth. I could tell he was barking, but all I heard was an overpowering *whoosh*.

A shock wave jolted my body and I was enveloped in a black cloud. I shut my eyes and tried not to breathe. Even with my ears covered, the noise was deafening. Hot air puffed through cracks in the bridge deck and up my short pants. I sneezed and gasped and coughed. I thought, Why isn't there a warning sign? Stay off bridge when train approaching ....

The noise lessened and I wiped my eyes on my shirtsleeve. I heard the cars rattling and squealing. I looked south and saw the purple train riding on its own smoke. On an observation platform two men in Panama hats were sitting side by side as though they were enjoying a rock 'n' rye in their favorite club. I thought, If I could change places with them, I would give up Hooton's for life. I watched with my mouth open 'til Laddie whined and rubbed his nose against my knee. He looked as though he wanted another crack at the big purple dog. So did I.

On the way home, I thought, I could walk the Pennsy tracks for ten years and never encounter a sight like this. This is better than Arcturus, better than Donkey baseball or cantaloupe ice cream from Hap's. This is better than looking at every bare heinie in Highland Park School.

Lembeck Avenue, Greenville, Jersey City. What a neat place.

After a dinner of barley soup with a cube of salt pork, Nanny asked me to deliver a recipe to her friend Mrs. Boylan, and while I was there I recounted my adventure to my pal and mentor. Mr. Boylan explained that I'd seen The Blue Comet, the Jersey Central's crack excursion train. By the time the Blue Comet passed behind the Boylans' flat, six blocks south of the Linden Avenue viaduct, its smoke trail had thinned and they were treated to a fine view of the stained-glass and polished brass. Mr. Boylan told me that a round-trip ticket from the CNJ Terminal in Jersey City to Atlantic City went for $5. A two-night excursion was $12.50 and included a Boardwalk hotel. Mr. Boylan wanted to take his wife, but in thirty years of marriage they hadn't been able to afford the fare.

I asked him why the engine looked purplish and he said it must have been an optical illusion caused by the hot smoke. The Blue Comet was painted in the colors of the sea, sky, and sand of New Jersey. Every car was named after a comet, and Mr. Boylan rattled off the names: Tuttle, Holmes, Westphal, D'Arrest, Faye, Spitaler, Winnecke, Brosen, Halley, Encke, Giacobini, Tempel, DeVico, Biela.[26] The personnel wore fancy blue uniforms, and the napkins in the dining car were embossed with short-tailed comets that were right out of the Buck Rogers comic strips.

Years would pass before it entered my mind that there might have been a visceral, spiritual, or even genetic connection between my first exposure to the Blue Comet and my family history. On the May morning in 1935 when the great old train scorched my underpants, it had started its journey in the same rail center where my immigrant grandfather had worked. May-

26 He recited them from memory. I had to look them up.

be the ghost of Francis Zawadzki arranged the timing. Why else would a skinny kid stand on a rackety old bridge and allow himself to be terrorized by a hellish wall of sound, his body enveloped in a stinking cloud – and enjoy it! Maybe if I'd kept my eyes open, I would have seen Great-grandpa's face in the soot and the ash and the smoke.[27]

13.

After lunch the next day I retraced my steps to the viaduct and down the white road. I passed a turnout where kids must have had a party. Three or four deflated grayish-white[28] balloons were scattered on the sandy hardpan. I didn't stop to investigate. I was overwhelmed by the scene that opened in front of me as the sun burned off a few patches of fog. An ocean liner moved through the Narrows, flanked by a fireboat squirting plumes of water. A tugboat with a tall smokestack nudged a bargeload of boxcars toward Hoboken.

Another tug pulled a scow heaped high with what looked like a year's leftovers from Mr. Scalise's restaurant.

As I approached the shoreline, I saw broken docks and wharves and railroad tracks, piles of scrap, wrecked outbuildings, a donkey engine half-buried in the sand, wooden pallets with cracked slats, a railroad sidecar with morning glories sprouting from its bed. A rusting crane lay on its side like a giant mantis. Miss Liberty's backside presided over the ruins. My eyes bugged out. I was always drawn to wreckage.

---

27 I tried to visit the Blue Comet at the CNJ Terminal a few months after my sixteenth birthday, but it had been decommissioned. One of the luxury cars ended up as a diner in Pennsylvania and the others were scrapped. Mr. Boylan provided the epitaph: They don't make 'em like that any more. R.I.P. Blue Comet, February, 1929-September, 1941.

I walked faster 'til I reached a wooden wharf where three barges were snubbed to iron bits by rotting hawsers. A sign hung from a collapsed shed:

LEHGH VALEY

The barges rode high in the water. Black scars made me guess that they'd once hauled coal. Squeaks and creaks came from the covered decks. I imagined armies of rats but soon realized that the sound was being made by the timbers as they twisted and strained in the breeze. The ropes had aged a light green; a broken rat-guard dangled from one. The air smelled of salt, creosote, and tar.

A squiggly railroad track ran parallel to the wharf, but no locomotives or freight cars were in sight. A coating of powdery rust showed how long the tracks had been out of use. Farther down the wharf I came to two men, one sitting on the cap log, his legs dangling above the oily water, the other sitting on a canvas chair. Both wore overalls, high-top army shoes, and fedora hats with the rims cut off and holes punched for ventilation: the basic uniform of the unemployed workman. In Highland Park I'd seen hoboes in the same outfit.

Three small fish lay on the concrete apron. The biggest was about the size of my palm. I asked if they were sunnies. I remembered the sunfish in Naylor's Run, small and round and reflecting blue and pink and orange in the sunlight.

Nope, Tomcod, the man in the chair said. See the whiskers? Ever tasted tomcod, little man?

I was too excited to reply and just shook my head. The fisherman said, Cat got his tongue, professor.

A fire of sticks and trash was sputtering. Hey, kid, the fisherman said, we're outa wood. He pointed to a pile of trash on the far side of the tracks and said, Make yourself useless!

I dragged over the remains of a packing box, and the bossy fisherman stoked up the fire. A few minutes after he resumed his seat on the caplog, he let out a whoop and jerked on his handline. A fish flew through the air and fell at my feet with a splat. This one was whiter and brighter than the tomcod, and it had no whiskers. That's a sunny, I said.

Kid got sunfish on duh brain, the fisherman said. Where ya from?

Highland Park, I said. Just outside Philadelphia.

That's the way they talk, the older man said. You wouldn't know that language, Davey. They call it English.

The professor wore Ben Franklin glasses over pale blue eyes and had a fringe of milkweed hair. He looked twice as old as his friend. He lifted the fish as though it were a fine piece of China. Nice specimen, he said.

I watched as the fish opened and shut its mouth like a guppy. Right before my eyes its silvery-white sides began to fade.

Is that a tommycod, too? I asked.

Tomcod, the professor said. No, this is another species.

He reeled off something in a foreign language. I must have looked puzzled, because he pulled out a pencil stub and wrote two long words on the inside of a matchbook. That's the species, he said. He printed the words as easily as if he'd been writing See Spot Run.

How do you say that? I asked.

Davey giggled and said, Cunner.

After I'd spent a few sociable hours with the fisherman and the professor, two black men arrived. One had graying hair like Brillo and at first I thought it was a cap. It turned out that they were also unemployed, laid off from a highway gang. Davey was a longshoreman who'd stopped attending morning shape-ups because the bosses demanded bribes. The professor was on involuntary leave from a South Jersey junior high.

I asked where they lived, and Davey gestured in a vague southerly direction. All I could see was a sea of reeds.

After a while the fishermen set me to collecting grass shrimp for bait. They showed me how to shinny down to the water, reach under the surface and feel around the pilings 'til I got pinched. It was scary at first since I didn't know whether I would encounter a shrimp, a crab or a sea serpent. My blind trust seemed to impress my friends.

Can you swim? the professor asked.

No, I said.

Don't worry, Davey said. We'll pull ya out. We ain't lost a kid in two, t'ree weeks.

The translucent shrimp attracted snapper blues that flashed under the surface, the most exciting fish I'd seen. Ya gotta be quick, Davey explained as he retrieved an empty hook. Snappuhs is lightnin'.

The professor explained that snappers were the baby version of bluefish, a prized saltwater species. Bigger than sunnies? I asked.

He laughed, but since we were friends by now, I didn't feel foolish. The professor invited me to return the next day for angling lessons. Davey said, We'll loin ya how to catch smoked sturgeons.

The professor said, They're bigger than sunnies.

One of the black men said he wanted to catch an eel or two now that the sun was going down and they would start to bite. How's dem snakes taste? Davey asked.

The black man said they were delicious if you skinned them first and roasted them over an open fire.

You people eat anything, don'tcha? Davey said. I bet you eat rats, too.

You tell 'em, brother, the black man said. I stutter.

Everybody laughed. The fishing friends were still needling one another as I headed back up the white road. The last rays of the afternoon sun caught the tip of the Statue of Liberty's torch. A gull pecked the water and flew off with a minnow. I took a deep breath of salty air and felt like the legal owner of New York Bay.

14.

It was almost dark when I reached Lembeck Avenue. The smell of beet soup filled my grandmother's flat. Nan! I said. You ever eat tomcod? Cunner? Snapper?

She said, You missed dinnuh, deah. I was gonna send fuh the Mickey Mouse.

Mickey Mouse was Jersey City-talk for the police. When a Lembeck Avenue kid spotted a cop, he would shout, Cheese it, the Mickey Mouse! and the boys would disappear into the air like steam from a kettle.

Nan said, Suppose your fawthuh came to getcha and I didn't know where you was at? Huh?

In the delirium of my adventure, I hadn't considered this possibility. If Daddy drove back to Highland Park without me, I would drown myself in Nanny's washbasin. He could bury my body by the Flower Observatory.

It's bedtime, deah, she ordered.

What about dinner?

She pointed toward Laddie, curled around his feet in his corner. He opened one eye and burped.

The night noises from the railroad yard didn't sound as interesting with my navel pressed against my backbone. Around nine, my grandmother's usual bedtime, I thought I smelled soup. I walked out in my junior BVDs and heard the lid rattling on an iron pot. A kerosene lamp cast a yellowish glow on the ceiling.

This is the last time, she said as she ladled out a bowl of

barley soup. This ain't Schrafft's. Mark my words.

After I'd put away two helpings, Nanny said, What'd you do all day?

I related my adventures on the white road. She asked how many fish my friends had caught, and I told her five or six, the biggest about eight inches. Let's see, she said, frowning and pretending to count on her fingers. That makes, uh, two bites each. That's probably all they had to eat.

Those guys don't fish for food, I explained. They fish for fun.

Nan's gray boyish bob whisked around her neck as she shook her head. Take my woid, she said. They fish fuh food.

15.

I got up at dawn for my first full day of fishing. I had no idea that this warm summer morning in 1935 would mark the start of a lifelong obsession. To my young mind the art of catching snappers from a wharf seemed simple. If somebody like Davey could do it, so could a kid who'd skipped the third grade.

Nanny was already up, frying a leftover potato pancake for us to split. She lent me a ball of string on threat of death if I didn't return every inch. I borrowed a couple of thin nails from Uncle Sonny's supply and tied the head of one to the end of the string. Whattaya gonna do with that? Nan asked.

You'll see, I said.

Bring me back a nice filet.

I had snappers in mind for the same reason that I later became fascinated by the lunges and dashes and swirls of trout. Snappers and trout were alive; they were quick and cunning; they were a mystery, a force of nature, a challenge. Cunners and tomcod just nibbled at the bait, and I suspected that eels did the same. Anyway, who wanted to catch snakes? To fool snappers, you had to be smarter than the fish.

Which I wasn't.

I spent the first daylight hour alone. A mile or so to the southwest, across acres of reeds, tidal creeks, mud flats and sloughs, the Lehigh Valley railroaders were making up trains. The couplings clanked as the boxcars rolled down the incline to hook up with other cars. A tugboat chugged past Caven Point. I watched a white ribbon of steam spurt from a pipe above the cabin, followed in a split second by a low moan that could have come from a locomotive, the kind of sound that always made me lonesome for places I'd never been.

But the fishing – well, there wasn't any. I would thread a wriggling grass shrimp on the tip of Uncle Sonny's nail, lower the string into the milky-gray water, and wait for the snappers to bite down hard and impale themselves. I waited and waited. And waited. Every few minutes I would retrieve an empty hook. It didn't occur to me that something must be wrong with my technique. The water made a *slpp-slpp* sound as it washed against the wharf.

I was groping under the pilings for a fresh supply of grass shrimp when the professor arrived with his fold-up chair and a paper bag. Well, well, he said. If it isn't Jackie from Philly. Landed any smoked sturgeon?

It was seven a.m. on a weekday in the first week of June. I'm sure of the date, because my tenth birthday was coming up on Sunday and Nanny had mentioned the possibility of a jelly doughnut from Horn & Hardart. But this waterfront event was more important than a birthday treat. Here, in the oily backwaters of New York Bay, I told the first fishing lie of my life.

Nope, I told my new friend. But ... I had one on.

Davey showed up an hour or so later with two seedy characters who looked like hoboes from Highland Park. The professor said, Jackie lost a smoked sturgeon.

Davey said, No shit?

I said, It was a tough fight.

I didn't know what they were laughing about. They began passing a cigarette back and forth, arguing about who was "lipping" it. They sounded like me and Sis fighting over a piece of coconut cream pie. Butt me, one of the men kept saying. Butt me! I was glad when they settled down to fish.

The professor cleared up the mystery of the disappearing bait and why I hadn't been catching any tomcod, cunners, or snappers, let alone smoked sturgeon. Fish are sneaky, he explained patiently. They don't impale themselves on every sharp point that comes down the pike. They have to be teased, fooled, then hooked.

No one had mentioned these niceties the day before. My friends had also neglected to tell the green kid from Philly that the bay was home to a scavenger so clever that he could steal your bait and your wallet and run off with your wife without arousing the slightest suspicion. I'd wasted the first hour of my day providing breakfast for crabs.

My bayside companions had no extra fishhooks, but they told me they were available at ten cents a dozen in the little shop that sold Hooton's chocolates on Princeton Avenue. The same store would sell me a handline-and-spool combination for a quarter.

Thus equipped, I could tackle anything that New York Bay had to offer, from cunners on up. I imagined the grateful look on Nanny's face the first time I brought home a smoked sturgeon. It would probably feed us both with some left over for Laddie.

I was starting to head home when I saw Davey bringing in his line inch by inch.

Whatcha got? someone asked.

A Brooklyn trout, he explained.

I said, Is that a filet? My nanny asked me to bring home a

filet.

Davey said, Tell your nanny the filets weren't biting today.

He held up his catch, a gray-white balloon like the ones I'd seen on the side of the road. He twitched it off his hook as though it might bite. One of the new arrivals said, Ya look at dis bay, ya'd t'ink all we do is fuck and eat oranges.

16.

As I hurried back up the white road to be on time for lunch, I thought, That must have been a pretty good joke, the way everybody laughed. I'd hardly ever heard that bad word. It wasn't in popular use in Highland Park P-A – but I knew that it was in the same family as heinie, pee-pee, and bagina, only with more bite.

I ran into the D'Alessandro twins in my vestibule. Hey, Petey, I said, grabbing him by the arm. I got a good joke.

Me too, he said as Rose backed off. What's the difference between Eleanor Rooz-velt and the Panama Canal? The Panama Canal's a busy ditch!

I'd heard that one when I was five. It would have been hard to come up with an Eleanor joke that I hadn't heard in our Republican neighborhood. I took a few seconds to get my waterfront joke straight in my mind. Then I said, If you take a look at the bay, all we do around here is eat and fuck oranges.

Petey jerked away so fast that a couple of pigeon feathers dislodged from his jacket and floated to the sidewalk. Rose put on a sour face and said, Watch ya mouth, joik. We're Cat'lic. The two of them hurried off, looking over their shoulders.

For the next week I began every day at the Lehigh Valley wharves. When Nanny found out where I was going, she said, Don't talk to strangers. When I asked why, she said, Nevuh mind, deah. Mark my words.

Even though I'd invested in a dime's worth of barbed hooks, I caught nothing but "killies," minnows the size of my fingers. Either the tide was wrong or the fish weren't feeding or I didn't set the hook fast enough or I was just plain unlucky – my fishing companions always came up with an excuse for me. They used my killies for snapper bait and told me I would catch on with a little practice. A decade or two....

17.

By July my grandmother was getting tired of answering questions about when my parents would pick me up and take me back home. They'll be heah when they get heah, she said, over and over.

Yeah, I would whine, but when's that?

She would say, Siddown and let your feet hang.

Lying in bed at night I tried not to cry, and my throat felt as though a scorpion had me by the tonsils. Nothing in my childhood ever hurt as much as holding back tears. When I was little, one of Mother's purple-dyed ice cubes had stuck in my throat and I thought I would die before it melted. Trying not to cry hurt worse.

Late one night I was thinking about Mother's beaver coat and how it changed color. I pulled the pillow over my head and was trembling with self-pity when Nanny came into the room carrying a kerosene lamp. She put it on the side table, tuned the wick into a slit of yellow light, and perched on the side of my cot. I wanted to tell her not to worry about me, but no words came out. The only sound was her beads.

It was a long time before I began to feel sleepy. Just before I dropped off, I felt her hand lightly pat my back. All she said was *Jackala*.

18.

After two months in Greenville, I still had no friends. The D'Allesandros had given up on me even though they didn't know about Giorgio. I decided that they just didn't like me. What was there to like? I tried to convince myself that friends didn't matter. Tarzan had Jane and a monkey. I had Nan and Laddie. Who was better off?

I kept waiting to hear Daddy drive up and beep his horn. If I heard him, I would take the staircase four steps at a time. I would fly to our car.

To take my mind off my problems, I began to explore the sandy trails that led off the white road. The reeds were taller than my Uncle Sonny's six-foot-four and grew in thickets, walling off the paths on both sides.[29] A few steps into the wetlands put me out of touch with Greenville and Jersey City and the rest of the world. I was alone with the birds, padding along mystery paths with no idea where I would end up. The sounds of Upper New York Bay mixed with the screeches of gulls and the chirps of English sparrows. Red-winged blackbirds sounded like ringing doorbells. I heard a thin shriek and spotted a hawk with something in its claws. The biggest rat I ever saw turned out to be a muskrat. Sunflowers and cattails and a few stunted pin oaks and red maples grew on hummocks and provided cover for small birds that I'd never seen in Highland Park. The professor called them dickie birds.

I expected to find something new and different around ev-

---

29   Years later I learned their scientific name: *phragmites australis*. They were common in most parts of the country and the dominant reed of the Jersey Meadowlands.

ery corner, and I was seldom disappointed. Most of the narrow trails led to the shoreline, where I picked through saltgrass to find stranded jellyfish, skate carcasses, crab shells, broken buoys, driftwood, bottles, floats, mollusk shells, shattered cargo pallets, a half-box faintly marked FL KE, a khaki life jacket, an oarlock, the transom of a dinghy with the name worn off except for an L. Almost every object hosted barnacles and tube worms and smelled of salt and iodine. The wreck was colored a pale green from sea slime, and some of the sea grass was so long and fine that it could have been parted and combed.

For a week I turned these Jersey tidelands into my private dig. The area, just across New York Bay from Brooklyn and an inlet or two south of Ellis Island, was drenched in history and folklore, and yet I never saw another boy or another adult in the marsh. The kids were too busy playing stickball on Lembeck Avenue and racing pigeons and delivering papers and swimming at the municipal pool and showing off for girls in the hot weather.

Who would want to play on crowded city streets when he had New York Bay to himself?

Jack Olsen was who.

It wasn't just that I craved companionship. I'd always been easily bored, and it wasn't long before I began to grow tired of the marshlands and the bay. I would pull out one of the phragmites and launch it through the air root-ball first, something I couldn't have done in Highland Park. But after several hundred throws the thrill was gone, especially if there was no one around to impress or hit.

On the wharf, my fishing pals began to run out of patience with the dumb kid who never caught anything longer than his index finger. I began to wonder if I would see my old schoolmates again. I even missed Miss Eggie-heinie! Would I be stuck in Jersey City the rest of my life? When was Daddy coming to pick me up?

I thought about making friends with the O'Boyles, but I had no idea how to start. Matt and Harry hardly acknowledged me, and Skeeter, the fifteen-year-old leader, had whacked me with a stickball bat when I interrupted his game one day. I tried impressing the brothers with a story about walking the Jersey Central tracks to New York City and peeking out of the underground to watch the crowds strolling on Broadway. Gimme a break, Harry said. I bet you took the Hoboken Ferry to Chinar, too, din'tcha?

I followed the tracks, I said. I seen a couple guys wearing top hats. I think one was the mayor.

Ten years old, Harry said, and already fulla shit. Go peddle ya papers.

The D'Alessandros were always busy with their pigeons. When Petey caught me on the roof conversing with one of his rollers, he threatened to kick me in the slats if I wasn't out of his sight by the count of ten. I was gone by two. When I asked Nanny what part of the body the slats were, she said, What am I, deah? A doctuh? It was the language problem again.

With nothing else to do, I trudged back down the white road and found a side trail that I hadn't explored. Out on the bay, fog covered the water like the meringue on Mother's pies.

The temperature was in the nineties. I was soaked in sweat by the time I decided that this path probably went all the way to Florida and I'd better turn back. I heard a faint splashy sound, as though someone was swimming a slow crawl. I rounded a bend and blinked at the sight. An old wrecked ferryboat was heeled on its side at the end of a narrow inlet. The shattered prow was half-buried in the sand and the stern bobbed lightly in the water. The carcass of a rowboat lay alongside. A seagull buzzed my head.

As I approached I saw that the planking of the ferryboat

was holed. I thought of crawling inside, but the memory of the Mudmen and Zarkov and the Frankenstein monster steered me away from the cracked ribs and purple shadows. Instead I hauled myself toward the deck hand over hand. Nothing bad ever happened in sunshine.

I was halfway to the rail when I heard a scraping sound. A hairy face peered over the side. It had dark skin, a big nose, snaggleteeth and a red bandana.

Blackbeard!

I hit the sand with my legs churning like an eggbeater and didn't slow down 'til I reached the white road. Crossing the viaduct I stumbled and fell, unable to take another step, probably forever. In case a train came along I covered my face with my hands and took in great gulps of air. I saw my tombstone: Jack Olsen, 1925-1935. He should of stayed home.

After a few minutes I opened my eyes. No one was in sight. I brushed myself off and decided not to tell Nanny. She had enough on her mind. Blackbeard would be one worry too many.

That wasn't no pirate, ya dumb sap, Rose D'Alessandro explained. She was the first person I encountered on the way home. She said, You seen Mac.

It seemed that every kid on Lembeck Avenue knew about the beached ferryboat and its squatter, just as every kid knew about Lemon Lee. Mac didn't shave, bathe, or socialize.

A few years back, a Lehigh Valley railroad bull had broken his arm with a nightstick. Mac had fled to the bayshore, splinted the fracture with driftwood, and resigned from the world. Nobody knew what he lived on, but it was probably seafood and seaweed. He was harmless.

Oh, good, I told Rose. I'll go back and make friends.

Mac don't talk, she said. He wouldn't unnastan' you anyway.

That night Nanny told me about other human derelicts who'd haunted the backwaters of New York Bay since her childhood days. Black Tom Island had been named after a dark-skinned fisherman who lived on the tiny island before the ammunition dock was extended out from the Jersey shore. Nan said there'd been rich shellfish beds in the Arthur Kill and Kill van Kull and plenty of oystermen and clammers.

Didn't I eat plenty ersters when I was a goil? she said in her Jersey City Dutch accent. They musta been safe. I'm heah, right?

I told her I would try to dig some in the morning.

Do tell, she said. Listen, I can't spare no more sweaters.

19.

Just when I was beginning to doubt that I would ever make a friend on Lembeck Avenue, Skeeter O'Boyle walked up to me with a smile and said, Hey, Shorty, how's your hammer hangin'?

I knew enough to smile back at the muscular blond kid even when he didn't make sense. It turned out that they needed one more player for a game of stickball. You wanna try? he asked.

Sure, I said.

You only had to watch one game to understand stickball, Greenville style. It wasn't that different from stoopball, punch ball, boxball, and curb-ball, the local variants of baseball. Greenville stickball required three players on a side: a catcher, a pitcher, and a fielder. The pitcher bounced the rubber spaldeen to the batter who swung at it with a cutoff broom handle and ran to a base in the middle of the street. The game was simple enough for a kid who'd played baseball.

When it was my turn to hit, I swung so hard at Skeeter's first pitch that I turned into a human corkscrew. I swung even harder the second time and ended up on the seat of my pants.

I stepped away from the plate and told myself to ignore

the laughter. I just needed to swing nice and easy. I took a deep breath and hit the next pitch across Princeton Avenue for a home run. Before Skeeter finally got me out, I'd scored four runs and put Petey and Rose D'Alessandro and me into a lead that we never lost. Good going, Limey, Rose said after the game. You're not such a joik as you look.

Skeeter asked where I'd learned stickball. I told him we played every day in Highland Park – one of the silly lies that I repeatedly told the Lembeck boys out of nervousness. I said I'd been taught by family friends like Howard Ehmke, George Earnshaw, and Herb Pennock. At the mention of Pennock's name, Skeeter made a face.

Just when we were starting to get along, I'd said something wrong again.

Herb Pennock, huh? he said. Tell me about it.

I made the mistake of thinking that he really wanted me to tell him about it, the same mistake I often made with Nanny. Well, I said, my dad used to pitch for the Detroit Tigers....

My fawda was Woodrow Wilson, Skeeter said. He changed his name from O'Burl when he was elected president.

I realized that neither the O'Boyle brothers nor the D'Alessandros wanted to hear the truth, so I changed the subject. Hey, I asked, why'd you call me Limey?

'Cause you talk funny, Skeeter said. It turned out that the brothers had seen *David Copperfield* at a moviehouse in Journal Square and agreed that Freddie Bartholomew had the same weird pronunciation as the kid from Philly. So now I was Limey. I wasn't sure if this was meant as a compliment. But I knew what Skeeter meant when he told me I was as fulla shit as a Christmas goose.

I told him it was nice of him to say so.

The next afternoon Mrs. O'Boyle dropped in and said I had a big imagination for a little twoip, telling stories about my father pitching in the major leagues.

Nan said, His father's Swede Olsen.

Swede ... Olsen?

I said, Right! That's my daddy.

Mrs. O'Burl said, Nevuh hoida no Swede Olsen. Who'd he play fuh?

Nanny said she hadn't followed his career.

The Detroit Tigers, I said.

Yeah, sure, Mrs. O'Burl said.

When Nan and I were alone, she reminded me to stop trying to impress people. Why didn't I try to be a modest little boy like the others?

We were grating on each other. A tension came from living within the same four walls, going nowhere, skimping on meals, having little in common except blood, both of us beginning to lose hope that anything would change. Nan had spent thirty years raising her own flock. For the first time in her life she could look forward to peace and quiet. Except for me.

I didn't help matters by turning up my nose at dinner. Gee whiz, Nan, I said. Again?

She took a little taste and explained that her recipe for beet soup came from Poland and called for a touch of apple vinegar. Every autumn she collected fallen apples around the neighborhood, but this year the neighbors had beaten her to the drops. I've only got two hands, deah, she reminded me.

I waited for her to add, Mark my words, but instead she said, Boys oh boys, and slowly shook her head.

I felt an inch tall. I felt like taking the advice that Billy Glossop had given me in Highland Park: Whyn't you stick your head in the toilet three times and take it out twice?

My grandmother was struggling to provide what my parents couldn't. She could barely feed herself and her dog – and now a spoiled brat was griping about her soup. But instead of apologizing and giving her a little squeeze, I turned away. I was an Olsen.

20.

By late July, nearly three months after my arrival in Jersey City, I'd become a member of the Lembeck Avenue gang. I discovered that I could get into trouble with the best of them. I helped them hook grapes from backyard vines and apples from backyard trees that had been bearing fruit since Greenville was open farmland. I stood watch on the night Petey D'Alessandro and the O'Boyles stripped the raspberry vines of the two old sisters who lived in a spooky old mansion two blocks away on Garfield Avenue. I began hooking Hooton's chocolate bars from the little store at Linden and Princeton.

The Lembeck boys yanked trolley cables from overhead tracks, creating showers of sparks and sputtering motormen. We threw mudballs at passing cars and the Mickey Mouse. We intercepted girls who sauntered along Ocean Avenue and subjected them to sophisticated comments like *Whoo hoo!* and *How's every little thing, toots?* We chased intruders from our turf and administered the Jersey bumps. The only thing we didn't steal was cash. Hooking money is wrong, Petey D'Alessandro announced. We're not crinimals.

I began to suspect that lawlessness might be part of my nature. I'd learned rote morality from my parents and teachers, but I'd also learned that it was okay to cheat Howard Ehmke. The subject of right and wrong was confusing, and I was too busy to puzzle it out.

By mid-summer I'd become a real problem for Nanny. She was nearly fifty, couldn't chase a healthy ten-year-old kid, and had no male muscle to back her up. If your grandfather was alive, she told me, he'd be toining in his grave. I hadn't seen my parents in weeks. Daddy was in Philadelphia, or maybe he was just ... gone. Mother and Sis were with Aunt Ronnie on the other side of town. I was free to steal and carouse and run wild.

At my urging, Petey D'Alessandro and I graduated to two-man jobs. I would engage a store clerk in conversation while Pete stuffed fig bars or a brick of halvah down his shirt. We became so proficient that one day we hit the same store twice because I had a craving for Hooton bars with almonds.

After a string of easy scores we developed an approach based on every kid's favorite: exotic cheese. Velveeta display-boxes were the perfect size and shape to hold baseball cards, and they were at a premium among boys. I would put on a beatific look and ask the grocer if he could spare an empty box or two, which usually sent him shuffling to the rear of the store. He was repaid for his kindness by a shortfall in his inventory.

I was having such a good time that I developed an unchar-acteristic bravado. Security guards were unknown in those days, and the Mickey Mouse were busy with other matters. Petey D's father told me that the local cops had been on the take since Peter Stuyvesant. He said, They're so crooked they gotta screw 'em in the ground when they die.

It was an easy excuse for being crooked ourselves.

21.

In the mystery memories of childhood, there are always a few incidents that can't be explained logically no matter how often they're recalled and dissected. It makes no sense that I would fling a stickball bat into the front-wheel spokes of a bicycle that a boy was riding along Lembeck Avenue. It makes no sense that this Nelson kid from Bayside Park was riding in the gutter instead of on the sidewalk. It makes no sense that my bat would find its way between his spokes, bend the bike's front fork and pitch the poor kid over the handlebars.

But it happened. And the oddest thing was that I did it on purpose. With split-second reflexes. With malice aforethought. With deliberate cruelty. On that, my memory is clear, if not my conscience.

The boy jumped up with clenched fists. His nose gushed blood. He was twelve or thirteen and wore short pants and a tattle-tale gray undershirt. He was crying and snuffling and looking wide-eyed at the blood on his hands. He jerked around with a crazy look and cocked his fists. Before he could take a swing, Skeeter and Petey pinned his arms.

Limey didn't mean it! Harry O'Boyle yelled. He didn't mean it!

I was bawling right along with my victim. How could I explain that I did mean it, that I'd seen his bike out of the corner of my eye, that some evil impulse made me sling my bat at his wheels?

After threats and counter threats, the Nelson boy offered to settle for a new bike. When Skeeter laughed in his face, he said he would settle for a new front fork. When we didn't bite, he offered to settle for twenty-five cents for repairs. During the Great Depression, there were few childhood beefs that couldn't be settled for a quarter. I ran upstairs and told my grandmother I had to have the money or I'd be in trouble.

Do tell, she said. I just gave my last dime to the insurance man.

I wiped my drippy nose on my shirtsleeve and stumbled down the stairs. My Nanny's broke, I told the Nelson boy through gulps and tears, and my mother and father are, uh – they're gone.

I hoped to convey the impression that I was an orphan.

He began to edge away, pushing his stricken bike. I'll get my bruddas, he said over his shoulder. We'll fix youse doity bastids.

We'll be waiting, Skeet said.

I thought, Speak for yourself, pal. I'm leaving town.

After Nelson disappeared around the corner, Skeeter slapped my cheek hard and said, Why'd you do a cockamamie thing like dat, Limey? Now the whole gang'll be on our ass.

What'll they do? I asked.

Oh, nuttin' much. Prolly just kill you. When he saw my stricken look, he said, Don't worry about it.

Huh?

You're wit' us now, shrimp. One for all and all for one. He paused, and added, Well, wit' you, we might make an exception....

Just before dark a glowering teenager skatemobiled onto Lembeck Avenue to deliver the official challenge. He was the oldest Nelson brother, head of the Bayside Park gang, and he warned that if I didn't pay up, his gang would settle the matter at noon. I said I couldn't raise a nickel, let alone five of them.

See you tomorrow, he said. Then he disappeared around the corner.

I asked Harry O'Boyle, What's gonna happen?

War, he told me. Gang fight. We'll beat their ass. Then we'll beat your ass.

I barely slept. I'd seen street fights in movies and some nice kid always ended up hurt or dead. I didn't see myself as a movie hero, and I didn't want my first fight to be a gang fight. I wanted it to be with a midget or a girl or an old guy in a wheelchair. I wanted my first fight to be on the familiar turf of Highland Park – radishes at ten paces.

I thought about hitchhiking home and placing myself under the protection of old friends like the Tanners and Saroyans.

But then I remembered our 3:00 a.m. getaway. The Upper Darby cops were probably still on the lookout. I imagined Daddy's face on a wanted poster. Maybe Mother's face, too, and mine. If we returned, we could all end up in prison.

I had visions of bloody fists, knives and pistols flashing in the sunlight, razors, machetes, tommyguns. I dreamed of ambulances lining both sides of Lembeck Avenue with their motors running, a hearse with an open back door, doctors and nurses huddling together at a Red Cross first-aid station and nervously puffing on cigarettes.

For the first time since my arrival in Greenville, I was up before Nan. You sick, deah? she asked as she entered the kitchen in her robe and carpet slippers. Took a chill?

Nah, I said. I just got up to, uh ... think.

Do tell, she said. Yeah, I thought I smelt somethin' burnin'.

22.

Skeeter knocked around eleven and announced that my stupid ass was required outside. Our gang was assembled on his porch, and every member was holding a rolled-up magazine.

Where's yours? he asked.

My ... what?

Go back up and ask your grandma for a magazine.

What for?

What fuh? Fuh fightin', stoopid!

I returned with a tattered copy of the *Readers Digest* that I found in our bathroom. Skeet was saying that we would be battling for the honor of Lembeck Avenue. We'd beaten the joiks from Bayside Park before and we would beat 'em today. We would hoit 'em so bad they'd never come near here again. I thought, With ... magazines?

Skeeter dismissed the troops and turned to me. You got ... *Readers Digest?* he said. How you gonna fight wit' *Readers Digest?*

He went inside and returned with a thick *Saturday Evening Post.* Then he gave me a little history lesson. Greenville boys had been squaring their beefs with magazines for years. There was a set ritual, aimed at providing satisfaction but not over-burdening the Medical Center or the Bayshore Cemetery. The O'Boyle, Drecksage, and Zawadzki families were already well represented in the shabby old graveyard.

Skeet and I stood on his front porch while he outlined the rules of engagement. Each side was limited to the same number of fighters. The battleground extended from our tenement to Princeton Avenue and from curb to curb. The idea was to force the opponents out of bounds by whacking them with rolled-up magazines. Anyone who stepped outside the lines was dead. The last gang standing was the winner. After the fight, the beef would be considered settled. No one had been seriously hurt in a Greenville fight since Buggsy Endresen lost an ear.

The Bayside Park kids arrived early and fell to their knees along the curb while we Lembeck kids huddled in front of the O'Boyles'. I remarked to Skeet that they were praying. He told me to take another look. They weren't praying; they were rolling their magazines as hard as crowbars.

A fan club of four or five backers, including two teenage girls, accompanied the visiting gladiators. We had fans of our own, including Ethel Pearson, who resembled Barbara Stanwyck, and Virginia States, who put me in mind of Dick Tracy's girlfriend Tess Trueheart, plus a half-dozen other local girls and a few grown-ups.

The age-spread of the Bayside boys appeared to be the same as ours, from a redheaded kid of about ten to a wiry black-mus-tached teenager who wore a beanie hat and looked like a match for Skeeter. I turned my back when I caught sight of the Nelson boy. Now that his nose wasn't bleeding, I saw that he was about the right size for Harry O'Boyle but several sizes too large for me. He kept slamming his magazine into his palm as though he couldn't wait to crack a head. It sounded like a billy-club thwacking a cantaloupe. I knew whose head he had in mind.

It turned out to be the hottest day of the summer. The asphalt squooshed under my sneaks as I nervously flattened tar-blisters. Only one car was in sight, parked up by Garfield Avenue. It seemed to float a few inches in the air.

The O'Boyles tightened my *Saturday Evening Post* 'til it was hard. Skeeter and the big kid from Bayside Park lined up their gladiators in the middle of the street, then crossed their rolled-up magazines like fencers. I hung back, hoping to be overlooked or excused for illness – a sudden attack of gout, the return of the 1918 flu. What're the chances of another Black Tom explosion?

Suddenly everyone was whacking away. I hadn't even heard a signal! The scene put me in mind of those cockfights where the birds squirt upward in a shower of claws and feathers and one comes down dead. All I saw were floppy shirts and raggedy pants, dirty overalls, white arms and legs, shredded magazines, torn hats and reddened foreheads.

I kept doing the old soft shoe around the edges, trying to avoid the Nelson kid. Little guys smacked big guys in the knees and big guys bopped each other over the head. Petey D turned into a whirligig, holding his magazine straight out and spinning hard 'til he made contact with flesh and bone. Unfortunately one of his first victims was little Matt O'Boyle, who twisted off-balance, stepped across the curb and was dead. Our teammate Armand Cataneo ran to the sidewalk shrieking, He hit me in the jools. He hoited my jools!

Skeeter was fighting the big kid in the beanie who kept missing with wild swings 'til Skeet sent him sprawling with a wallop across the eyes. The Bayside fighter jumped to his feet, and the two gang leaders clinched and yanked each other across the curb. The fight wasn't two minutes old and they were both dead.

I was marveling at how few fighters were left when something came down hard on the back of my neck. I turned and saw the Nelson kid cranking up for another swat. I evaded two or three blows, then decided that I wanted to see Highland Park again. I'd almost reached the safety of the curb when I saw Nanny hustling out our front door. She'd heard the racket while hanging out clothes.

As I turned to locate Nelson, his magazine caught me in the Adam's apple. It felt like a lead pipe. We whacked at each other for a minute or two, but most of our blows missed, perhaps because I adopted the clever strategy of fighting at a range of five or six feet. At last he backed me into a corner, and we parried with our magazines like Douglas Fairbanks. Then he sprang forward, hit me hard across the back and knocked me down.

Get up, Limey! someone shouted. Get up!

Someone else yelled, Hit him in the nuts! It sounded like Nan.

I staggered to my feet and reeled backward as Nelson pummeled my head and shoulders. He didn't intend to allow me a second wind. Out of the corner of my eye, I saw that we were the last boys on our feet. It was me against Nelson for the honor of Lembeck Avenue! It was Hairbreadth Harry versus Rudolph Rassendale, Ming the Merciless against Flash Gordon, Popeye vs. Bluto. It was Dr. Zarko against –

He kicked me in the shin and gave me a shove. The lights went out.

A formation of Douglas Airliners, zeppelins, and Baltimore orioles soared high above.

Giorgio the roller pigeon broke into a double whistle, and the Mobilgas flying red horse flew past with Lulu Abernethy in the saddle, her bloomers showing.

When I finally opened my eyes, our two Lembeck beauties were kneeling over me, acknowledging my existence for the first time. Ethel Pearson gently fanned me with a silky handkerchief that smelled of rosewater. Virginia States gripped my wrist and appeared to be counting. I felt my heartbeat in the back of my head.

What happened? I asked weakly.

The joik tripped ya, a male voice said. Ya bunked ya head.

As I lay in the gutter, two more faces swam into focus, one covered with fur. After Laddie licked me, Nanny said, Get up! Her face was white.

The crowd parted and the sniveling victim was escorted across a battlefield littered with scraps of paper. Nan grabbed me by the upper arms and half-shoved me up the stairs to our flat, safely away from drafts, chills, and Bayside Park wolfpacks.

I was still a little groggy and couldn't figure out why she kept telling me that I needed some mice on my bump. She iced me down and gave me a glass of coffee 'n' milk.

Jackala, she said, what's next on the program? Swim to Canarsie? Jump off the Chrysler Building? Guh 'head, tell Nan.

I'll be a good boy, I said.

I realized it was a tough assignment. I was still trying to figure out why I'd thrown my stickball bat into the kid's wheel.

I heard footsteps on the stairs and a knock. Skeeter's voice called out, Limey? Y'okay, Lime?

Jackie's okay, Nanny said as she opened the door.

I waited to be condemned by the gang I'd failed. How would they punish me? The Jersey bumps? 'til every bone was broken?

Ya done good, Skeet was saying. I heard laughing in the background and wondered what was so funny.

Ya din't back down, Harry put in.

A high-pitched voice said, Prouda ya, Limey. It was Rose D.

I mumbled, I lost the fight and that's not right.

Skeet giggled and said, You're a poet and don't know it!

But your feet show it, Harry added.

After the merrymaking, Skeet explained that I hadn't lost the fight and neither had Lembeck Avenue. I'd fallen, yes, but on the curb, not across it. By the rules of the battlefield, that didn't render me dead. When a spectator ran to the police call box, the Bayside Gang disappeared like flour through a sieve. Skeeter sent word that my body was at the morgue, so they weren't expected to return for a year or two. The way Skeet saw it, Lembeck Avenue won, thanks to good old Limey. Who was I to argue?

Late into the night I thought about my victory. From now on, "Limey" wouldn't mean a skinny little dope who couldn't speak his own language. Limey was a neat guy who didn't back down. No one seemed to realize that I'd spent most of the fight in search of a separate peace. They were too busy with their own opponents. I decided not to disillusion them with the truth.

23.

The sky, the street, the air, smells, sounds – everything seemed better the next day. Skeeter took the gang up to the sweets shop on Ocean Avenue and ordered egg creams. He raised his glass and led the gang in a toast:

Hooray for Limey

Hooray for Limey

Hooray for Limey

He's a horse's ass.

I said, Aw, Skeet.

He said, Back in ya hole, rat!

In the Lembeck gang there was no greater praise. The proprietor shooed us out, but we didn't argue since we hadn't paid. We jacked around all the way back home, and I felt so proud to belong.

A car was parked in front of our tenement. I was a little surprised. Our street was almost always empty. Once or twice a day the Mickey Mouse drove through, but otherwise there was hardly any traffic.

As we drew closer, I saw that the car was a Ford Model- T sedan with a man at the wheel. I wondered if Uncle Sonny had traded in his motorcycle. A puff of smoke curled out of the driver's window. I caught a whiff of Bayuk Phillies. The man stepped out and said, Hello, there, Sonny boy. How ya was?

My heart thumped. I was so happy to see him. I'd been with my grandmother for three months and it was time to go home. But ... what about the Lembeck Avenue Gang? My new friends? And what was Daddy doing in a Tin Lizzie?

He shook my hand as though we were business partners. Then he pointed to the passenger's seat and said, Time to go. Shake a leg!

My friends drifted away. I saw my duffel bag on the back seat. I asked where we were going, and Daddy said, Aunt Ronnie's.

I gulped and said, Aunt Ronnie's?

Yep.

On Boyd Avenue?

Yep.

My heart sank. I hated everything about Boyd Avenue. There wasn't a bird or tree in sight.

Daddy knelt over the front of the car and inserted the crank. He held his body at an odd angle as though his insides hurt. I was glad that my pals had disappeared. I would die of embarrassment if they saw Swede Olsen, former Detroit Tiger ace, cranking a Tin Lizzie.

After a few turns the engine caught and he jumped inside.

Wait! I said. Can't I say bye to Nanny?

Not, uh ... now. She's a little upset.

Upset? Nanny?

She says you're turning into a ragamuffin. Almost got yourself killed yesterday. Says she can't handle you no more.

How could I argue? What could I say? That I'd become the best stealer in the gang and helped to win a street fight? Through the tears, I saw Nanny's point. She was getting old and she'd raised her share of kids. She didn't need a Jackala around her neck.

four

Boyd Avenue: Jersey City

1.

The family reunion was low-key. Mother gave me a light hug and Carolyn shook hands. I was informed that I would share a bedroom with Sis and our pretty little cousins Barbara and Bernice. Uncle Bill Johnson had erected a Japanese screen between the beds to separate the sexes. The closet was filled with little girl clothes, so I slid my bag under my cot.

Don't worry, Daddy said. I ain't leaving you here long.

He'd used almost the same words when he dumped me at Nanny's a hundred years earlier. But I believed him. He was my Daddy.

After he left for Philadelphia, Mother told me what had happened to our Plymouth PV.

Easy come and go, she said in a flat voice. She'd finally learned the meaning of the word *repossess*.

The Tin Lizzie was borrowed from a friend.

She told Sis and me that Daddy had made friends with a race track steward and was on the inside about a boat race and some jockey benefits.[30] He planned to win a few big races, pay off his arrears with the bookie, start a business of his own, retrieve us from Jersey City, and give up gambling forever.

She told us that if Daddy didn't make good with the bookie, someone might perform surgery on his kneecaps. She didn't go into further details. Later that night she came out of the bathroom shaking her head. I asked, What's wrong, Mother?

My first gray hair, she said.

She was twenty-nine.

---

30   A *boat race* was a fixed horse race. *Jockey benefits* were races in which groups of riders held back their horses to enable a selected jock to win. Jockey benefits were often given in lieu of wedding presents or baby showers.

2.

In August Boyd Avenue was a steam bath. No one played stickball on the narrow street. There were no railroad tracks to walk,
no fruit trees to strip, no barges, no beached ferryboats, no via-
ducts or Blue Comets or marshlands – just block after block
of two-story rowhouses with backyards the size of my radish
garden and a bunch of tough kids with names like Carracci,
Loretto, Ramelli, Sanzio, and others I found hard to pronounce.
On my first day, one of the locals asked my name.

Olsen? he repeated. Is that Sicilian?

Most of the locals spoke Italian, and they spoke it long into
the night. On steamy summer evenings Boyd Avenue turned
into an asphalt town meeting. Grandmothers fanned themselves on the front steps and missed Palermo. Mothers sewed
and knitted on their second-floor fire escapes and exchanged
mementos in wicker baskets that they lowered from a string.
The men of Boyd Avenue, mostly unemployed bricklayers,
painters, masons, stevedores, carpenters and laborers, filled clay
demi-glasses with "Dago red" made from Concord grapes that
dangled from back fences in weeping clumps that attracted
yellowjackets. Fathers and grandfathers lobbed bocce balls or
played a card game called *tresette* or a finger-counting game
called *mora* that Aunt Ronnie's husband Bill Johnson told me
had been banned in Italy because it caused so many murders.
He did his own impression of the game: *Cinque! Due!! Otto!!!*
BANG!

Uncle Bill competed with our neighbors for day-laboring
jobs, and he had a long list of hateful names, including *guinea,
wop, dago,* and *greaseball* (pronounced greezeball). He referred
to the single Jewish resident as a *sheeny.* In a domestic argument
he called Aunt Ronnie a *dumb Polock.* When she called him a
squarehead, he bloodied her lip.

Prizefighting flourished on Boyd Avenue, usually around

dinner time. Sis and I were tense and unhappy and fell into our old ways. We were on the undercard.

For most of that summer of 1935, we residents of Boyd Avenue went around in our underwear. It was like living in warm syrup. Mother and Aunt Ronnie spent most of their time chatting in the kitchen, sometimes joined by the third sister, Aunt Mae. Their slogan seemed to be: If you can't say something bad about our relatives, try harder. Our women were reluctant to light up the gas stove. It seemed as though every meal consisted of Shredded Wheat, a half-biscuit per kid, sometimes pre-softened with sugar water, or a piece of bread with a dab of lard in the middle. Our mealtimes were as jolly as Sunday School.

When Mother made a chocolate cake, Sis and I fought to lick the batter.

Sis got more!

Jackie's tongue's too big! That's unfair.

She always gets more!

He's the same old crybaby! ...

When we weren't fighting, we listened to the radio or played checkers, Parcheesi, Fish, and Spit in the Ocean with our cousins. There was no reading matter, not even a comic book. Uncle Bill subscribed to a labor newspaper, but we never saw him open it.

When he wasn't at work or pulling out his pretty wife's blonde hair, he was drinking beer and eating onion sandwiches.

The days passed as heavy and dull as stone.

3.

Toward the end of August the heat wave relaxed its grip and the temperature dropped into the eighties. Uncle Bill insisted that I go outside and meet some of the neighborhood boys.

Despite his low standing with Nanny, we'd become friends, maybe because we were the only males in the household.

Get outa heah, he said. These ain't bad boys. They can kill you but they can't eat you.

But I couldn't bear the thought of more arguments about sugarrr and sugahhh or proving myself in another street fight, this time with knives and grenades.

Uncle Bill was a wiry little man who worked part-time at Dixon Pencils and Congoleum Flooring and other Jersey City factories and brought home souvenirs like a box of gold-plated pen nibs and a dozen rolls of adding machine paper. His best score was a government-issue diving suit that he claimed fell off the back of a truck. He cut off his T-shirts at the shoulder to display Popeye arms, plastered his slick brown hair to his scalp, and trimmed his moustache to the width of a knife edge. He played endless games of solitaire and taught me the correct odds in craps and how to deal seconds in poker. Like Mr. Boylan, he never seemed annoyed by my questions. But he liked to tease and joke. One day he pointed at my fly and said, Hey, Jack, ya hobby's open.

When I looked down, he cracked, Is that ya hobby?

After Aunt Ronnie left the room shaking her head, he said, Hey, Jackie, what's them little things that screw on the wall? Flies!

When cousin Bernice brought over a friend's pet rat, Mother jumped on a chair and yelled that a rat in the house was bad luck.

No it ain't, said Uncle Bill. You're thinking of anudda animal.

What's that? I asked.

A giraffe.

One day I asked Uncle Bill where a kid could go fishing without having to walk all the way to New York Bay. 'Dja try the aquarium? he asked.

He directed me to a city pond a few blocks away and told me he'd seen big goldfish breaking the surface. That turned out to be the problem. Goldfish are weed-eaters and next to impossible to catch on hook and line. I returned the old fishing gear he'd lent me and asked what else a kid could do to pass the time. He told me that he'd seen a carnival setting up at Yale Avenue and advanced me three nickels. Try the concessions, he told me. If you win more than a grand, we'll dump these Polock broads and go to Florida.

I was excited at the prospect of winning money. Imagine a place where you could run fifteen cents up to a thousand dollars! Maybe I wouldn't be that lucky, but forty or fifty bucks would make a nice bankroll for a kid. I imagined the look on Nanny's face when I brought her a bag of fresh poppyseed rolls and some potatoes.

At the fair I heard a Victrola playing a tinny version of "Take Me Out to the Ballgame" at a concession stand featuring six metal bottles set in a pyramid. At Woodside Park in Philadelphia, Daddy used to play that game and fill our arms with prizes.

The barker held out three balls and said, C'mon, kid! Knock 'em down and win a prize! He had a coal-black moustache like Smilin' Jack's and wore a battered Yankees' cap. On the wooden shelves behind him were dolls and gewgaws that looked expensive. My gambler's heart beat faster.

How much? I asked.

Ten cents, podna. The tenth part of a dollah.

If I ever saw a sure thing, this was it. I handed over two nickels and the man in the straw hat gave me three mushy baseballs. I wound up and fired and hit the bottles square in the middle of the second row. The topmost bottle wobbled and fell on its side.

I decided to throw hard at the bottom row to wipe out the pyramid's support. This time I left one bottle standing. Then I dumped that one – a direct hit. Simple enough for a pitcher's kid.

I'll take that one up there, I said, pointing to a sequined doll with carrot-red hair. Sis and my little cousins would love it.

Try again? the man said, pushing three more balls at me.

No, thanks, I said. I'll just take that doll up there.

He told me I was a cinch to win on my next try. I pointed out that I'd knocked all the bottles down, and he said they had to be knocked completely off the stand. I fussed and argued 'til I noticed a cop heading toward the booth.

I gave up and walked past a red and black printed sign:

> When you're weary in the noodle
> Just drink an RC doodle
> And you'll feel like Yankee Doodle
> Come ... to ... town!

I blew my last nickel on a 12-ounce RC. It was bubbly, cold, and delicious, but it didn't make me feel like Yankee Doodle. Another unfair claim.

When I got back to Boyd Avenue, I complained to Mother that I had nothing to do. She told me to sit down and let my feet hang.

4.

Trying to sleep in the steambath bedroom, I came to the conclusion that if I had to spend much more time on Boyd Avenue I would spontaneously combust and my ashes would join my maternal relatives in Bayside Cemetery. Lately I'd been thinking a lot about death. What would the world be like without Mother and Daddy? Sis? Uncle Bill and Aunt Ronnie? What would the world be like without Nanny? I couldn't imagine. And yet she paid her burial insurance every week, so she must be planning to die. Even I had to die. It wasn't fair. What would the world be like without ... me? It was after midnight when I made my decision: I was going home. I didn't intend to suffocate in a bedroom furnace in Jersey City.

I got up before anyone else and crammed some dry Shredded Wheat in my mouth. I hooked eleven cents off the mantle and walked out the front door. It was already hot, but I wore my heavy sweater in case I had to sleep outside for a night or two. Highland Park was ninety miles away.

A block and a half to the east, Boyd Avenue turned into a marsh. I felt a glow of recognition when I spotted phragmite reeds with their feathery cottony bolls, but I didn't relish the thought of picking my way along more blind trails. I'd walked for a few minutes when I smelled smoke and heard voices. In a clearing alongside a river, two skinny men stood next to a shack made of wooden boards, tarpaper, and flattened tin cans. The roof was covered with reeds. A scrapwood fire guttered under a pot that rested on an off-kilter tripod. Off to one side was a stack of baldy tires.

I'd already turned to leave when one of the men called out, Step right in, young man. Don't be bashful. The mulligan's on.

I'd seen Hoovervilles on the outskirts of Philadelphia and along U.S. 1 and realized that I'd bumbled into one. I wondered if it was safe. An assortment of faces peeked from the shacks, and several men stepped out for a look. One man's German haircut seemed to be rusting.[31] Another had bare feet like Alley Oop's and skin like sliced bread. The soles of a younger man's motorcycle boots flapped when he walked.

They seemed fascinated by the fact that I was from Philadelphia. One told me he was from Bristol P-A and another

---

31   A sign of protein deficiency, as I learned later.

said he was from Scranton. I held back the news that I was running away but hinted that Boyd Avenue wasn't my idea of vacationland.

Neither's this dump, one of them said. But the rent's fair.

More hoboes joined the circle. It didn't seem to bother them that I talked funny or that I was small for my age. I happened to mention that my father had pitched in the majors. One of the men brightened and said, Ole Olsen! I seen him pitch in D.C. It was three, four years after the war.

That's my dad, I said. He could break off a curve in two directions.

Left-handed, huh? A reliever? Come from Maine, Rhode Island, somewhere up there. Ain't that right?

He was a rightie, I said. He came from Indiana.

I tried not to show my disappointment at hearing that Daddy had been a relief pitcher. I'd always thought he was a starter. Relief pitchers just helped out and didn't make much money. I couldn't think of a single famous relief pitcher.

What brought you to Joisey? an older man asked. Patches of white hair looked as though they'd been glued to his skull, and his tattered shirt drooped across bony shoulders. He seemed to have trouble breathing.

Howard Ehmke, I said.

Da pitchuh?

Yeah. We didn't pay for the awnings.

The old guy seemed more impressed with my mention of Howard Ehmke than anything I'd said about my father.

One of my new friends walked me around as if he were showing off fancy homes on the Main Line. He chewed on a lumpy pipe and emitted smoke that didn't smell like tobacco. I saw hand-scrawled signs on the walls: All equal here. No straw bosses. Work or walk....

The one I liked best read, Thanks Mr. Hoover & kiss my

cock.

A three-legged dog nibbled at a bone outside an empty shack. I figured that the owner was picking trash or looking for work. Each place had a tin smokestack held up by guy wires; most of them leaned a little off center. My guide told me the residents kept warm in winter by burning tires in steel drums.

After a while I began to notice an odor. The men told me it was from the Hackensack River. They pointed to where the brackish water spilled into Newark Bay, just to the south. The surface was the color of stained silverware. We were standing almost directly below the Pulaski Skyway, and from underneath it looked like something made from a giant Erector Set.

I asked if sunfish lived in the river. One of the hoboes said, There's some kinda fish in there, but we don't get that hungry.

I'd heard that story before. I saw a chance to resume my angling career. A nice catch of sunnies or snappers might change my view of life on Boyd Avenue.

I would worry about the smell after I'd caught a few.

5.

I started fishing at daybreak and didn't get a bite even though I used real hooks and a revolutionary bait that should have made the fish line up: blood-red grapes from Mr. Giamfacaro's Concord grape vine. When I came back home, Uncle Bill told me that he'd never fished the Hackensack, but as a young man he'd caught a few blue crabs before the river became so fouled with sewage and garbage that you could almost walk across to Kearny. He took me into the basement and pulled a rusty wire crab-trap from a pile of junk. He told me to use fish heads and guts for bait. Crabs're like the goddamn Swedes, he said. They don't eat fish 'til it smells like shit.

He was the only member of our family who used cuss words around me. It made me feel an inch or two taller.

A Bergen Avenue fishmonger wrapped some old parts in newspaper and warned me that they weren't for the table. I was followed to the river by a bobtailed tomcat the size of a bulldog.

Who died? one of my hobo friends said. He interrupted his whittling to peek into my sack. He asked, D'ya know what the blind man said when he walked past the fish market?

No, I said.

Hello, girls.

I laughed but didn't get the joke.[32]

Down near the bank I picked up a rat by the tail. The skin came off and the carcass slipped to the ground. I bent over for a closer look. Maggots crawled on maggots. I walked away fast.

I baited my trap and pitched the apparatus five or six feet out from shore. While it was soaking, I set out to explore the bank below the Pulaski Skyway. I was looking for piers or pilings and dying of curiosity about what I would find around the next bend. A drowned cat bobbed in the current, its white body bloated to the shape of a circus balloon. Coots paddled through the debris. They didn't seem concerned about sanitation.

I came to a tidal creek about a foot too wide to be jumped. A mossy crossing plank was just awash. I stepped onto the slimy surface and teetered to the other side. A couple of bends farther, a low-lying bird's nest confirmed that few humans used this path. I flushed a flicker that got up with a chirr like a rubber-band model Helldiver. Birds chattered in the weeds; I figured they didn't care much about sanitation either.

The air stank. It was as though B.O. Plenty had jumped out of a Dick Tracy comic strip and was walking a bend or two ahead.[33] A Brooklyn trout floated by, but there were no signs of

---

32 Mother and Aunt Ronnie didn't get it either.

33 In 1950, a reform politician and pig farmer named Henry Krajewski demanded

oranges.

On my way back I couldn't find the little plank-bridge. I wondered who on earth had filled it up, but then I saw its sheen just below the surface of the tidal creek. I took a step, slipped and skidded feet-first into the water. Flailing and gasping, I imagined my sad little body being swept into Newark Bay to be nipped by snappers and cunners, and on into the Atlantic to be finished off by sharks and smoked sturgeons. I came up covered with mud and wearing the rotting roots of reeds and cattails. The creek was a foot deep. Luckily it was a hot day, so I was almost dry by the time I reached my crab trap.

It was gone.

At first I thought it had been swept downriver, but the current didn't seem strong enough. Someone must have stolen it. I'd been crazy to leave my uncle's property behind while I meandered all over the map. I glanced toward the hobo jungle. What made me think I could trust men who lived in tin sheds and smoked funny tobacco?

No, I ain't seen no crab trap, one of them told me.

How would I explain to Uncle Bill? He'd lent me the trap as a favor.

Then I heard the giggles. Two men emerged from a tarpaper shack, one holding my trap, the other a burlap bag. Lookee, said the one with the bag. He pulled the top open to show a rattling mass of claws, feelers and shells. You hit Keno, son, the other hobo said. He had little side whiskers like Felix the Kat. He said, Too bad they're fulla poison.

A dozen blue crabs wriggled in the sack. I thought, I may not eat them, but I'd sure like to take them home. Then maybe I won't be treated like an outcast in a leopard colony.

One of the men warned me not to touch my catch. As he

---

the clean-up of the area. He said that it smelled like embalming fluid. That was where I was walking.

spoke, he picked at his ripped shoe. He said, Din't you see the shit in the river?

Wasn't that plants and stuff?

That was shit and stuff.

6.

When I reached Boyd Avenue I remembered a night a few years back when Mr. Boylan brought home some crabs from the Fulton Fish Market and my share was half a claw. I could still taste the sweetness. I was ready to devour my crabs, shells and all. Health was no longer the issue. Hunger was the issue.

As I emptied the sack into the laundry sink, I heard a familiar voice. Boys oh boys! Jackie brought home a shore dinner.

I wanted to hug Nanny, but I knew she only hugged Laddie. I started to thank her for coming to visit me, but it turned out that she'd come to see her daughters. She gave me a friendly pat on the shoulder, but she didn't call me Jackala.

In the bottom of the soapstone sink, the crabs clicked and clacked like one of Mother's mah-jongg games. Nan rooted around in the cupboard and came up with an iron pot. Ye Gods and little fishes! Aunt Ronnie exclaimed, her favorite expression these days.

Mom, you're not gonna cook those filthy things? Did you ever hear of amoebas! Blood flukes?

Aunt Ronnie had been the family's health advisor ever since winning a biology prize in high school. We kids knew she was smart because she read books and wore glasses. Several other Drecksages and Olsens wore glasses and a few members of our family read books, but Aunt Ronnie was the only one who did both.

Nanny said, Get me some salt, deah. She began to fill the

pot with water.

Uncle Bill acknowledged that it was a nice mess of crab but said nobody on the docks would touch Jersey blue crabs with a stevedoring hook. When he lifted little Barbara over the sink by her ten-inch waist, Sis and our other little cousin Bernice ducked behind their mothers. Barbara reached down, jerked her hand back and said, Oooh! It bited me!

As soon as the water reached a boil, Nanny threw in an onion and some mystery spices, probably from an old Polish recipe. I looked away as she grabbed a live crab by one of its feelers and dangled it above the bubbling water. Up to then I'd been uncertain of the process, but of course it wouldn't include boiling the crabs alive. Would it?

I fell back against the table and cried out, That's torture!

Uncle Bill draped an arm across my shoulders. They don't feel nothing, he said. Crabs is crabs.

I tried to toughen up. It seemed as though I'd been bawling ever since I got to Jersey City – or trying not to. Most of the time my throat felt as though a surgeon had ripped out my tonsils.

In a few minutes the blue crabs turned into red crabs, and Nanny pronounced them done. Not for me, Aunt Ronnie said. She and Mother took Bernice, Barbara, and Sis for a walk to shield them from the horror.

Nan laid several sections of the *Jersey Journal* across the kitchen table and asked Uncle Bill for a hammer and screwdriver. She banged and ripped and picked 'til she'd removed every shred of meat. I stared as she filled a cereal bowl. This is what grandmas are for, she confided to me.

Up to then I'd thought they were for making soup and petting dogs and putting up with grandsons.

Nanny and I agreed that it was the best meal we'd had in months. Around six the angelus rang from a church up near

Bergen Avenue. I said, Hey, Nan, remember the day we stood in line for mutton?

Stood on line, she corrected.

Remember the night I dropped the bread?

She said, You're forgiven.

Uncle Bill opened a bottle of bock beer and said, I hope da two of youse is still wit' us in the morning.

That was the last big haul I ever made in the Hackensack. One of my hobo friends offered an explanation after another wasted day at the river. You dropped that trap on a crab hotel, he said. You caught the guests. The rest checked out.

I promised Aunt Ronnie that I wouldn't bring home any more crabs. Thank you, she said. We'll sleep better now.

7.

By September I'd been in Jersey City for five months, and for the first time in my life I missed school – not just any school, but Highland Park Elementary, home of Miss Eppeheimer and my Valentine Lulu Abernethy and pals like Billy Glossop and Warren Wigo. Mother assured me that I was registered for the sixth grade and we would be home in plenty of time.

Now there was even less reason to make friends on Boyd Avenue, and I continued to steer clear of the neighborhood kids. I watched their performances from our front window. If they weren't beating up outsiders, they were pounding on one another. One day I spotted them playing dodgeball with a rock the size of a hand grenade. Apparently you won the game if you drew blood – double points for fractures. They squared their beefs with fistfights, pummeled each other senseless, then shook hands and wandered off arm in arm. I knew where they came from. They came from the planet Arcturus.

With my dad in the very early days.

At 15 months in Gainesville, FL, at the
Whitehouse Hotel. I was holding a Gideon's
Bible, already devout.

Age 3. Might have been wearing Daddy's cap

May 13, 1928. Only 3 and already resembling
Babe Ruth.

Great-grandpa Zawadzki in his Imperial Polish Army uniform - or was it a Jersey City fraternal order outfit?.

"If my grandmother was in a hugging mood, she reached for Laddie."

At six, ready to play ball like my dad.

In my pirate stage, ready for the 4th of July parade, 1931.

Fishing on the Jersey Shore – 1937.

Ready for Upper Darby Junior High School

Either George Washington or Little Lord Fauntleroy – May Day, 1936, at Henry C. Lea School.

Doc Raymond of Raymond's Pharmacy. He "seemed to know what made boys laugh."

Fishing, 1942, this time in Oxford, PA.

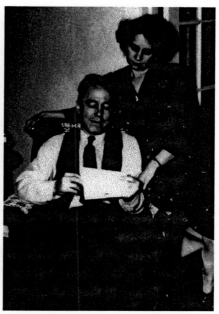

Mother and Father in the early '40s.

In cap and gown and saddle shoes. A high school graduate.

High school graduation photo.

The star-dwellers' footwear tended toward flap-tongued sneakers with openings for ventilation, usually in the soles. A few kids went barefoot on the hot asphalt. When a car appeared, one or two boys would try to hook onto the bumper for a free skate ride. That was how the twelve-year-old Van Dusen kid from across the street shattered his wrist in four places. A few days later I saw him grabbing at a Ford pickup truck with his good arm.

Uncle Bill said that no Boyd Avenue kid wanted to admit he'd come in second to a car, even if he had steel pins in his wrist bones.

Some of the kids were working on beer bellies like their fathers'. I said to Aunt Ronnie, They're sure getting plenty to eat.

They call that malnutrition, she explained. Those are banana bellies. Aunt Ronnie didn't always make sense.

One day I watched several boys chase a street-repair truck, swipe gobs of pitch, and stuff them in their mouths! When I told Uncle Bill, he said, They're not eating, they're chewing. It's cheaper than Wrigley's.

But ... it's black!

Yeah, he said. Pitch is black. You got some eyesight, kid.

He explained that fresh-fired tar made teeth whiter, cleaner and stronger. Also, it was free. I decided to take his word.

I watched through the front window as street kids built scrapwood fires against the curb and baked the big lumpy potatoes they called *mickies*. Outdoor cooking was against the law, and the boys fled at the first sign of the Mickey Mouse. The last boy to leave would perform a juggling act with the hot potato as he ran down the alley.

One morning a red-faced cop knocked at our door on the trail of a well-known curbside chef. Missus, he told Aunt Ronnie, in case youse engaging in said misdemeanor, I'll pinch every perpetrator in dis jernt and let the judge decide what to do wit' youse.

To my Philadelphia ears, the long word came across as *pipe-a-tratuhs*, and I wondered if Aunt Ronnie was one. After he left, I said, Are you a pipe-a-tratuh?

No, she said. She told me that residents of Jersey City knew it was wiser to agree with the Mickey Mouse than to argue with them or even try to make sense of their police doggerel. If you squawk, she said, he might pull out his ticket book, and if he pulls out his ticket book, you better have a dollar bill ready.

8.

One day Uncle Bill intercepted me as I returned from an expedition to the Hackensack marsh to hunt rats with a tack hammer. Your old man's in town, he said. He got ridda dat Tin Lizzie. He just drove Flo downtown in a new Auburn.

He pronounced it *Au-boin*. Auburns and Cords were the hottest cars on the road and cost more than a house. The boat-tail Auburn Speedster was the fastest car going.

What model? I asked.

I t'ink it's a V-twelve. Supercharged. The one wit' the exhaust pipes on da hood.

Boys o boys! I said. What color?

Uncle Bill said it was pooce. It didn't matter to me if our new car was striped, speckled or polka-dotted. Auburns could go a hundred miles an hour without breaking a sweat. Billy Glossop, the Tanner boys, and the Saroyans would be wild with envy when we arrived in Highland Park in our Auburn.

I got out my spaldeen and played stoopball against the front steps to work off some of my excitement while I waited for Mother and Daddy to return from the market. One of the local boys walked up and said, Hey, punk, I ain't seen you 'round.

Where you from?

I said, Joisey City. I gotta go in now.

Soon a black car chugged down the street from the direction of Mallory Avenue and pulled up to the curb. Mother and Daddy climbed out. He was wearing a new pair of wire-rim glasses that he must've picked from the bin at McCrory's five-and-dime. It entered my mind that he'd bought the car in the same place.

Uncle Bill had been playing the wiseguy again. I hoped the Boyd Avenue kids didn't spot the blue-and-yellow Pennsylvania license plate on the black Ford Model-A. Not that it mattered much whether we drove home in a Ford, an Auburn, or another Tin Lizzie, as long as we got to Highland Park.

I jumped from the top step to the sidewalk. Hello there, Sonny, Daddy said. How ya was?

Before Mother turned away, I noticed that her eyes were red. I guessed she was overcome about going home after all these months.

Daddy gave me his major leaguer's handshake and said, Let's go inside. I got something to tell you.

He handed me a paper bag with ears of corn sticking out the top and said he'd stopped at a roadside stand in South Jersey. I looked inside and saw that the radishes weren't top grade. I wondered if we would take this stuff back to Highland Park or leave it with Aunt Ronnie and the others. They were always so hungry.

Then we went inside for the news.

I bawled all night. Sis cried too. I covered my face with a pillow, but I'm sure that cousins Barbara and Bernice had a hard time sleeping for all the sniveling and gulping and shuddering that went on next to them.

Daddy must have been back in Philadelphia by the time we got up in the morning.

It's not so bad, Aunt Ronnie said as she handed me a burnt piece of toast. Your mother and I went to Jersey City schools. Didn't we turn out okay?

Jersey City Schools. The words hit me like bricks. Jersey City schools were penal institutions, and the students came from Murder Inc. Jersey City schools had no trees or yards or playgrounds. I didn't know the system and didn't speak the language. I would rather enroll in the pen at Rahway.

Mother came into the kitchen in her robe and advised Sis and me to possess our souls in patience. Your father'll be back in a month, she said. Two at the most.

I asked if I could lay out of school 'til we left Jersey City. I'll read *Huckleberry Finn*, I promised. I'll learn my multiplication tables. Please, Mother?

She said it was out of the question, and if she remembered her own days in the Jersey City school system, I'd better start practicing my penmanship.

9.

Mother and Aunt Ronnie took Sis and me to Journal Square for clothes and supplies. I'd brought only summer wear for my stay with my grandmother, so I tried on a pair of heavy corduroy knickers and almost collapsed when the saleslady brayed, How are they in the crotch?

Mother bought me a matching corduroy lumber jacket and a hat unlike any ever seen on Boyd Avenue. The last time I'd worn a peak cap I was three years old. It made me look like a coal miner then; it made me look like Little Lord Fauntleroy now. Mother said, Jackie, that hat's perfect! Aunt Ronnie said I looked cute.

That was just the problem. I told Mother that I would be

stabbed and shot and mutilated if I tried to wear that hat to school. I didn't want to look cute. I wanted to look tough. I wanted to look like Pretty Boy Floyd or Alvin Karpis. I wanted to look so mean that Jersey City school kids would flee at my approach.

Mother didn't understand and refused to discuss the matter. I asked if we could wait and leave the decision to Daddy. Great idea, Mother said. You'll end up in a derby.

Every social problem I'd had on Lembeck Avenue was worse at my new school on Virginia Avenue. Too many teachers had been hurt while trying to break up fights, and a nonintervention policy was in effect. Hardened P.S. 24 boys fought to the end. They made the O'Boyles and Petey D and the rest of our Lembeck Avenue gang look like candidates for a nunnery.

As usual, my Philadelphia accent made my own problems worse. Even though I'd begun to sound a little like a Jersey City kid, I still rounded my D's like Freddie Bartholomew and bit hard on my R's. I was coming across as a snotty little jerk who considered himself a higher order of life, or as one of my new classmates put it, You t'ink ya shit don't stink.

I said, Well, in all sincerity, it certainly does!

He acted as though he didn't believe me. Nanny had always reminded me that Jersey City kids didn't like braggarts.

P.S. 24's faculty turned out to be more demanding than any teachers I'd encountered in Highland Park. My arithmetic teacher was cruelly unwilling to accept answers like "74, more or less." My history teacher refused to believe that General John "Black Jack" Pershing had lived in Highland Park. The cook told me where I could stick my shepherd's pie. The hall monitors threatened to kick my ass. In front of the whole 6-A class the gym teacher told me that if I kept on smoking, "you'll be a runt the rest of your life." When I said I'd never smoked, she laughed. Then she insisted that a boy of ten should be able to chin himself and do two or three push-ups. I proved her wrong.

Late each morning my sixth-grade class spent a fifteen-minute recess milling around a concrete playground that was a few gun turrets short of a prison yard. I found a hiding place, but the janitor told me his supply room was off-limits. He said, You're new heah, aincha?

Yes, I said.

Stay outa fights. If you fight, make sure you win.

Why?

'Cause we don't break 'em up. School policy. Let the little bastards fight it out.

You never stop a fight?

Well, sometimes we got no choice. Like, I mean, if a kid's unconscious or something. Dead, maybe.

Has that ever happened?

Not in a long time.

My fellow students didn't challenge me to fights, but they thought it was fun to put me in an arm lock and push my arm upward 'til the tibia started to crack. They sneaked up behind me and collapsed me by ramming a knee into the back of my leg. They Dutch-rubbed my head 'til my hair came out in clumps. Tripping and goosing seemed not only acceptable at P.S. 24 but compulsory. I was insulted, ridiculed, shoved, and subjected to Jersey bumps and half-nelsons.

My second day was worse. A sixth-grader cocked a fist and said, Two for flinching! I felt the bruises on my upper arm for a week. From then on I gave her a wide berth.

An eighth-grade boy no bigger than Oliver Hardy asked me, What's a ship do when it reaches da dock? Before I could answer, he said, Ties up! and flipped mine into my face.

A skinny kid asked if I wanted to play a game. Without waiting, he said, Look at your thumb. Gee, you're dumb! Then he said, Knock, knock. I was alert enough to ask, Who's there?

but not alert enough to notice that another boy was crouching behind me on his hands and knees.

Ovuh, the first boy said.

Over who?

Ovuh yago!

I scrambled to my feet and wiped my eyes on the sleeve of my new lumberjacket. Pay attention, bawl-baby, the boy said. Knock knock.

I wondered what was coming next. Decapitation?

Who's there? I said in a trembling voice.

Ben.

Ben who?

Ben down and kiss my ass.

I turned away, but he wasn't finished. Knock knock, he said.

Who's there?

Bob.

Bob who?

Bob up and kiss it again!

I was working on a firm reaction when he was saved by the bell.

10.

On most mornings of my indeterminate sentence, Mother packed a sack lunch consisting of a sandwich wrapped in wax paper, a hard-boiled egg, an apple, and one of the little hard candies, chicce, that she bought for a nickel a bag at the Italian grocery. By local standards, I was overfed.

A gang of older kids began scavenging my lunch and soon were eating every bite. Now and then they rejected a sandwich that failed to meet their standards, but they seemed to approve of most selections. The exception was a boy who had a reddish moustache and was already muscle bound. He grabbed me by the collar and said, Tell ya mudda no more of dis peanut buttuh shit. Stick wit' da lunchmeat. He stuck his face in mine and added, We know where youse live.

He had my chicce on his breath.

After two weeks of going hungry, I cowered behind my forearm and asked my tormentors, Can I taste my sandwich today?

The words were hardly out before two boys, both wearing scallop-edged hats that looked as though they belonged on a grease monkey named Spud, flanked me front and back, joined hands under my crotch and lifted. After they bounced me a few times, I gasped, Is there – any special kind of, uh – food you'd like?

Nah, said the bigger of the two. Just tell ya mudda – put mayo in da tunafish. And more onion.

I promised to pass along his request.

11.

It snowed heavily that winter of 1935 and Santa brought me a black pocket comb and a red diary with a gold clasp. My first entry was a description of Christmas day on Boyd Avenue:

WEATHER IS C-O-L-D.

Daddy didn't show up for the holidays. He's busy, Mother explained. Don't worry. It's always brightest before the dawn.

I learned later that he was working a temporary job at the Post Office and selling encyclopedias door-to-door. He'd bought another car but Mother hadn't bothered to find out what kind. She never seemed to realize the importance of models and styles and whether a car had free-wheeling or balloon tires.

The day after Christmas I grew tired of letting my feet hang and decided to visit my friends at the hobo jungle. It was too cold to crab or fish, but I enjoyed their company. There was something about their free-booting nature that appealed to me.

Panes of ice crunched under my feet as I picked my way among the frozen puddles on Boyd Avenue. I thought, Isn't this just like this darn town? In Highland Park I could be sledding and snowballing and having a good time. But here the cold weather only made things worse.

As I threaded my way through the reeds, I missed the pungent smell of burning tires and millican soup or whatever it was called. The only sound was the chatter of birds in the reeds and the whir of the cars on the Pulaski Skyway. I looked up at the bridge to see if just by chance Daddy was slowing down for the Jersey City exit. Then I realized that I didn't know what kind of car to look for.

The hobo jungle was gone. The only trace of my friends was a few scraps of scorched paper that the wind had blown into the reeds. The earth was dark where the tires had been stacked. A hand-printed sign read, No trespassing. This means YOU. Someone had scribbled, We got rights. NRA WPA Fuck you 2.

Returning on the trail, I ran into the man who'd been so impressed by Howard Ehmke. He said he was taking a look around before heading south. He'd lived in the Hooverville for two years and needed a warmer climate for his asthma.

I asked him what happened to the place. At first he told me I didn't want to hear about it. Then he said, Some palooka got stabbed is all.

Is he ... dead? I asked.

He nodded. I tried to get more details, but he seemed vague. Maybe he didn't think that murder was a fit subject for a kid. As near as I could determine from a few hints, the victim was the prankster who'd temporarily stolen my crab trap, the one with side whiskers like Felix the cat. I ran all the way home. It was my first brush with the crime of homicide, and I hoped it would be my last.

12.

P.S. 24 issued report cards three times a year, and after two months of dealing with new books, new subjects, new teachers, and new classmates, I was apprehensive about my marks. The arithmetic teacher, who might have been cartoonist Chester Gould's model for Gravel Gertie, still seemed disturbed by my difficulties with the multiplication table and could not accept the fact that I was stuck on 8 x 8.[34]

One of the kids told me that our English teacher had started teaching during the French and Indian Wars and had taught Pocahontas to ask permission to go to the terlet. This teacher asked where I'd studied grammar, and when I told her, she said, Hmphhh, as though to express her contempt for Philadelphia snobs.

A few days later she gave our class a lecture about dangling participles and split infinitives and ended by asking if there were any questions.

Yes, I said. I have a question.

Guh 'head.

I don't understand split infinitives and dangling participles.

She yelled, That's not a question! And she made me stay an hour after school.

My grades for the semester ending January 31, 1936, averaged 75 and ranged from excellent in spelling to very poor in arithmetic. A printed note on the back of the card stressed that a grade of VP "should be a matter of immediate inquiry."

---

34   By now I was well aware that the correct answer was 62.

It was. Everybody in the family started drilling me. My little cousin Barbara was chanting Twee times twee nine! in her thin high voice when there was a knock on the front door.

It was Daddy. He'd arrived in a 1931 Ford Model-B Roadster. Four horses, he told Uncle Bill Johnson proudly. Look at them cowl headlamps.

Sis and I were ordered to pack. Before we left, Daddy borrowed two dollars from Uncle Bill for gas.

I didn't know what excited me more – that we were finally going home, or that we would be traveling in a Model-B with canary-yellow wheels, a maroon finish, and chrome bumpers. But Mother threw a fit. In a loud voice, she asked, How much?

Four-seventy-five, Daddy answered.

Payable when?

Nothing for three months. Flo, we stole this car! Look at the canvas cover on the spare! Check them side windows! How about them spoke wheels?

Mother yelled, How about that rumble seat?

Daddy looked flustered. Uncle Bill looked amused. Aunt Ronnie frowned. Nothing in her knowledge of biology had prepared my intelligent aunt for a specimen of mankind who would consider stuffing two children into a rumble seat and driving three hours in the dead of winter at night.

13.

The first few miles over the Pulaski Skyway and through the Jersey Meadowlands were exciting. The suitcases and boxes that were piled around us cut some of the wind. But by the time we passed Newark Airport my teeth were clacking and Sis was turning blue.

I tapped on the isinglass window and Daddy pulled over.

We squeezed into the front for the rest of the drive, me in the middle and Sis on my lap. I don't know whether I fell asleep or lost consciousness, but I missed my favorite sign – Trenton Makes, The World Takes.

I woke up just as we began to thread our way through the narrow Philadelphia streets and under the elevated tracks on Market Street. I wondered why we made a left turn at 48th Street. We should be going straight to 69th and then up the hill on West Chester Pike.

Where're we going, Daddy? I asked.

A tense silence made me drop the subject. I spotted a parked police car on Walnut.

Cheese it! I said. The Mickey Mouse. It was just a little joke.

Daddy's voice was sharp. This ain't Jersey City, he snapped. Don't act dumb.

I heard Mother whisper, He's only a boy.

Daddy said, He's too damn fresh.

Something about the conversation convinced me that Daddy wished Sis and I had stayed in Jersey City. Maybe he wished Mother had stayed, too. But he'd been working hard and driving hard, so I dismissed the idea. I knew that Daddy loved us even though he never said so. Mother loved us, too. It was their secret.

West Philly was covered with a dirty crust of snow. We parked in front of a three-story rowhouse on a tree-lined block of Cedar Avenue. Daddy said, This is it. Everybody out!

We followed him up a narrow flight of stairs to a third-floor apartment. Mother took one look inside and said in a choked voice, Ole, you know I'm afraid of fire!

Daddy said, There's a fire escape in the back.

He led us to a rear window and yanked open a metal canister attached to the wall. Out fell a long section of rough hemp, knotted every few feet. Mother said, That's ... a fire escape?

Daddy looked sheepish. I couldn't imagine Mother sliding down three stories.

Carolyn was strong for a girl and might have a chance. I knew I could do it, and Daddy still had his muscles from baseball. So in a fire we would only lose Mother. It was a scary thought, so I decided not to think about it.

Otherwise, I felt fine about the new apartment. Sis was smiling. We'd both taken note of its most desirable feature: It wasn't on Boyd Avenue.

five

West Philly

1.

In that Arctic cold January of 1936, mounds of snow and ice turned Philadelphia streets into frigid wind tunnels. Boys climbed atop the snow and played King of the Mountain, which involved punching and kicking and pulling at body parts numbed by the cold. I watched but decided not to participate 'til I recovered from Jersey City.

Day after day the last entry in my diary would be WEATH-ER IS C-O-L-D or BRRRrrrrr. It was a winter of yo-yo exhibitions by little tan men, jai-alai contests with paddles and rubber balls, dish nights and bank nights at the movies. Every day I shoe-skated to Henry C. Lea School, a half-mile away, and every day I thanked God that I was ninety miles from P.S. 24, never mind the ice and snow. And glad to be in a place where I spoke the language. If a friend showed grateetude for the clean wooder in our beauteeful city, we both knew what he was talking about. The Philadelphia Iggles was the best team in the National Football Lig and the *Inquire* noospaper was so good it was read as far away as Balmer, Merlin. If a boy had one blonde hair, he was Whitey. When Jersey City kids wanted to claim something as their own, they said dibs on it; we said yax. We said sugarrrr and riverrrr. And we never said hello or hi; we said yo. If you didn't say yo, you were dog poop.

The possibilities for exploring in West Philadelphia weren't as promising as they'd been on the salty shores of New York Bay and the sooty mainline of the Jersey Central, but there were interesting people to gawk at and plenty of other diversions. Black Oak Park, a square block of old established trees, swings, fat squirrels, fatter infants, twittering birds, and hidden acorns, was a ten-minute walk from home. One day I saw Daddy sitting on a bench on the far side of the park. He was with a woman in a green hat. By the time I reached the bench, they were gone. I figured he was trying to sell her some encyclopedias. At the dinner table, I said, I seen you in Black Oak Park today.

No, you didn't, he said.

Mother told me to pass the peas.

I still missed my waterfront friends from Jersey City, especially when I spotted bindlestiffs picking through trash and knocking on doors. City tramps seemed different from the Hooverville residents – they didn't have much to say, and if you tried to strike up a conversation, they looked around nervously and hurried off. Seven years had passed since the crash of 1929. I concluded that they must be getting weak from hunger.

2.

In my second month at H. C. Lea School, I met a friendly boy named Isaac Schindler who lived two blocks east on Cedar. He was eleven and I was ten and a half.

Schindler, huh? Daddy said when I mentioned my new friend's name. I think that's Jewish.

I said, What's Jewish? I'd heard the word, but it hadn't registered.

Daddy said, Jewish is just ... Jewish. Everybody in this neighborhood's Jewish. Don't worry none. I'm looking at a house in Highland Park.

I started to ask why I should worry about Jewish, but the look on Mother's face told me to drop the subject. I wondered how many Jewish people I'd met without realizing they were Jewish. Who was Jewish anyway? Was Earnshaw a Jewish name? Pennock? Connie Mack? No, Mr. Mack had changed his name from McGillicuddy because nobody could spell Mc-Gillicuddy when he started playing ball. And McGillicuddy certainly wasn't a Jewish name. Was it?

I did a little research and asked a few questions at school

and finally decided it was silly to try to identify Jewish people by name. They weren't all Goldbergs and Horowitzes and Finkelsteins. Some had Italian names, like Shapiro. Some had German names like Gottlieb. Some had English names like Cohen. Were the SPHAS Jewish? I knew better. They were the South Philadelphia Hebrew Association.

For a while I wondered about "Olsen." Could we be part Jewish? We were part Polish, weren't we? Didn't we live in a neighborhood where Daddy said everybody was Jewish? If everybody was Jewish, and we lived here, then so were we. Logic was logic.

I asked Isaac if Schindler was a Jewish name. He gave me a funny look. Who wants to know? he asked.

Me, I said. My, er – my father and mother, I guess.

What're you?

Whattaya mean, what am I?

What nationality? German? Methodist?

I dunno, I said. Part Jewish, I guess. How can you tell?

Isaac said you couldn't tell unless you were a doctor.

As I was walking home from his house, I realized that he hadn't answered my question.

After several weeks of field study, I reached some conclusions of my own. You could spot Jewish women by their chest expansion. My 6-A teacher Miss Horowitz was raising a pair of seal pups under her peach-colored V-neck knitted dress. Her colleague Miss Templestein appeared to be concealing honeydew melons. If you got too close to Mrs. Rappaport, the student teacher, you risked being impaled. I tried to look away when these teachers bent forward. I thought it was only fair.

Mother explained that we were all Americans under the skin, but that under our particular skins Sis and I were half German with some Danish and Polish, not that it was necessary to mention the Polish in public.[35] No, we most definitely were not Jewish. Moving into a Jewish neighborhood didn't make you Jewish.

When I reported back to Ize, he said, You're prolly a Polock, you know that? You even look Polish.

What's Polish look like?

Uh, I dunno. Just .... Polish, I guess.

Well, I'm not Polish, Ize. Not Jewish, either. I guess I'm Amurrican. What're you?

That's for me to know and you to find out.

C'mon, Ize. Are you ... Jewish?

I yam what I yam and that's what I yam.

I recognized Popeye the Sailor Man, so I just dropped the subject. I didn't mention that I'd heard enough on the subject. Friends were friends. Isaac owned a whole set of Horatio Alger books, a toboggan, a taped-up hockey stick from the Philadelphia Arrows, and a puck. Cedar Avenue was covered in ice and snow.

Who the heck cared if we were Jewish?

Daddy cared. At dinner he asked, Who's that kid I seen you with?

That's the friend I told you about. Isaac Schindler.

Isaac, huh?

I could tell by his face that it mattered.

---

35   With the coming of another millenium such distinctions became less important. My daughter Sara once computed that she and her brother Harper were three-eighths Swedish, three-eighths German, one-eighth Danish, and one-eighth Polish, but we were 100 percent Northern European. On just about any map, a dime covered our ancestral places of origin. By that time most members of our family had lost interest in the subject. At last we were one with Great-grandpa Zawadzki: No Pole. No Polack. Greasy.

3.

Sis and I both were beginning to wonder what happened to the Daddy we'd known in Highland Park. This one seldom smiled or made funny remarks or cracked jokes. If we ate at a lunch stand, he didn't tell the waitress that one must be good, girlie, or ask what was on the desert, or demand to know the total incurred indemnity. If a driver offended him, he made no comments about Sunday drivers or how to make angels or "blow your nose; you'll get more out of it."

He left our apartment every morning and returned late at night, too tired or bored to bother with us kids. Whenever I asked if we could play a little catch, he was busy. He didn't reminisce about his days on the All-Phillies or All-Nations or talk about friends like Eddie Gottlieb and Herb Pennock, and he stopped listening to Bill Dyer and Byrum Saam broadcast the A's and Phillies games on the radio.

His strangest reaction was to his old major league team. I'd kept up on the Tigers ever since I was old enough to spread the sports pages on our living room floor and flop on my belly to check the box scores. Of course I read the results of the Phillies and A's games, but only after checking the Detroit box. I was so close to the Tigers that I referred to the players by their nicknames. Schoolboy pitched a shutout today.... Hank hit another one.... Jo-Jo took a homer away from Gehrig.... I could recite the official statistics on Chief, General, Goose, Mike, Gee, Flea, Firpo, and Heinie. My heroes were Hank Greenberg, the American League's Most Valuable Player in 1935,[36] and Charlie Gehringer, known as the mechanical man because you could wind him up every spring and he would hit .300 and drive in 100 runs. My pals Hank and Charlie were the stars on a team

---

36 Thirty years later I interviewed him in depth at his Manhattan brownstone, preparing a series for *Sports Illustrated*. After each session, I had to restrain myself from asking for his autograph.

that went from fifth place when I was nine to World Series champs a season later.

Daddy didn't seem to care. One day he said, Don't tell me no more about the Tigers, okay, son? I went to my room so he wouldn't see my look. I was proud that he'd worn the Gothic D on his cap, but I wondered if his old club had done something to hurt him, to make him feel resentful. He didn't seem to understand that I was a Tiger fan because of him, and I would never change.

I looked for my heroes on Movietone News or Pathe. I was impressed by big Hank as he circled the bases after a home run, and the way Charlie handled the pivot, and how far Billy Rogell could range to his left, and the break on Tommy Bridges' roundhouse that you could see from the center field bleachers.

Daddy didn't want to talk about it.

We began to see less and less of him; sometimes he would disappear for a week. Mother would say he was out of town, earning our living. Don't worry. He'll be back.

Each time he seemed to be gone a little longer.

Late one night I awoke to sounds from my parents' bedroom. Mother was crying. I heard her say, You did. You did! You called me Lily!

I did not, Daddy said. I called you ... my lily. The lily of my life.

You called me Lily! Don't deny it, Ole.

I stuck my head under the pillow.

Daddy drove away in the morning and was gone for two weeks. When he came back, he acted as though he had a permanent toothache. Where had he gone? What happened? Daddy wasn't Daddy anymore.

In the daytime I would slip into the bedroom to sniff the bay rum on his pillow. I got out his cracked old pitcher's mitt and pounded it 'til the pocket was perfect. It just got crinklier and crinklier on its shelf. When I asked him to bring home some neat's-foot oil, he said, We don't need that stuff no more. Then he pulled the *Daily News* over his face and kept on reading.

He certainly hadn't been a perfect father, but I missed laughing at his funny remarks and watching him yell at his players from the coaching box and ordering bowls of floating butter at Henri's on 69th Street and threatening to turn the car around when Sis and I went at it. Mother didn't complain, but I was sure there were moments when she missed being told that she was a good jane. He used to laugh and say, You're the only girl I ever loved – one at a time. We didn't hear that anymore.

4.

I buried my frustrations in exploring, roaming the city on roller skates after the snow melted, sometimes finding myself two or three miles from home at sundown and hitching to the back of a bus or trolley to get back in time for dinner. After Mother washed the dishes and Sissy and I dried, we would sit in the living room and listen to Fibber McGee & Molly, Fred Allen, Ed Wynn, Joe Penner. We laughed when Charlie McCarthy told W. C. Fields, So help me ... I'll mow ya down, and the ex-Philadelphian replied, Go 'way – or I'll sic a woodpecker on ya.

Most of the radio shows seemed to originate in Chicago or New York, and when the signal faded we would grab a wire in the back of the radio and hold hands to form a human aerial. Sis was sure we would be electrocuted. I would go *sssst*! in her ear 'til Mother made me stop.

After several months on Cedar Avenue, Daddy started tuning in to talks by a Catholic priest named Father Coughlin. I noticed that he kept the volume down. One night after we'd heard Eddie Cantor sing in his high tenor voice that he loved to spend each Sunday with us, Daddy pointed out that Cantor's real name was Isidore Iskowitz. When Jack Benny came on (Well!), Daddy informed us that he'd been born Benny Kubelsky. Al Jolson was the son of a rabbi named Yoelson. Sophie Tucker was Jewish; and Sarah Bernhardt, and Eleanor Roosevelt probably had a little Jewish blood. Daddy relayed this information in a confidential tone, as though revealing something evil.

At dinner one night, he told Mother, You know, Flo, I'm a little suspicious of Morgenthau. And that other guy, uh – Harry Hopkins. What's he up to, sneaking around the White House all the time?

Mother asked, What're you suspicious about, Ole?

He lowered his voice. The only word I heard was "Jews."

Mother said, Please, Ole, it's … Jewish people.

They dropped the subject, leaving me more puzzled than ever. Why should Jews be called Jewish people? Were Christians Christian people? Were Methodist-Episcopalians Methodist-Episcopalian people? Where did Lithuanians fit in? I decided to keep on being Amurrican people. It was simpler.

Of all the comedy shows, Daddy seemed to prefer Amos 'n' Andy. The sillier the two black men acted, the louder he laughed. One night he said, We use to listen to them shines when they was Sam 'n' Henry. In twenty-eight, wasn't it, Flo?

Mother nodded toward Sis and me and said, Hush!

I wondered why she was so emphatic. I also wondered when colored people had become shines. What did it mean? Our cleaning lady Amanda had referred to herself as Negro. I wished I knew more about Negroes, but not a single one had attended Highland Park Elementary School and there were only a few in H. C. Lea. All I knew was that most of them were skinny and poor and talked funny. But … shines? What the heck was shiny about Amanda?

I started to ask Mother, but she backed away from the subject. Just remember, she told me, you can't tell a book by its color.

5.

One evening Daddy struggled up our stairs with an upright L. C. Smith typewriter that he'd bought from funny Mr. Geldberg on the first floor. Mr. Geldberg was a hen-shaped little man whose apartment was crammed with sale items, some of them in factory boxes. The first time we met him, he told Daddy that the cold weather reminded him of a Japanese gymnastic meet.

How's that? Daddy asked.

There's a little Nip in the air.

No one knew Mr. Geldberg's occupation, but the pry bar that he carried in his waistband might have been a clue. I'm a flautist by trade, he told me when I asked what he did.

What's a flautist?

A Jew that plays the flaut. I used to play flageolet, but I quit because I always lost.

What's a flageolet?

What're ya, writin' a book?

Daddy told us that Mr. Geldberg had asked six bucks for the typewriter, half the regular price in stores. I jewed him down to four, Daddy said.

I thought, How do you jew down somebody who's Jewish? If Mr. Geldberg bargained with Daddy, did he Christian him down? I decided that such matters were too confusing for someone who was still having trouble with multiplication. Maybe I would figure it out after I turned eleven.

Although I'd spent many hours trying to impress my parents by pretending to listen to the Metropolitan Opera, I had no real interest in music or drama, but after I was cast as George Washington in the sixth-grade play I began to consider an acting career. Acting, huh? Daddy said when I told him. Ain't no money in that.

Mother said, Jackie's always been an actor.

I finally began to develop an ear for music; all kinds of tunes seemed to burst into my head and repeat over and over. Isaac Schindler became musical at the same time and announced that he intended to search for the lost chord, with my assistance, of course. We planned to start in the sheet music stores on 52nd Street. Somewhere in those stacks of music we were bound to find a clue, if not the chord itself.

In those first icy months of 1936, I began to have peculiar reactions to songs. The first time I heard "Beautiful Dreamer," I felt like bawling. I reacted the same to "Danny Boy" and "All Through the Night." "Juanita" made me want to hug the nearest female, even my blimpish civics teacher. After hearing "Marching Along Together," I thought about going to the recruiting office and signing up as a drummer boy. "Little Old Lady" made me miss Nanny. "I Dreamt I Dwelt in Marble Halls" made me yearn for a fine ancestral home.

When I heard "Indian Love Call," I was ready to join the Mounties.

The tone-deaf brat who'd once abhorred piano recitals was suddenly open to all types of music, even jazz.[37] Mother took Sis and me to a matinee on Market Street, and before the feature film we watched a short subject featuring a song called "Hot Lips." It was played by an orchestra that once would have made me cover my ears and run. The cornetist was Henry Busse, described by the narrator as the man who invented shuffle rhythm. I had no idea what shuffle rhythm was, but I couldn't sit still.

---

37   Just as I would become open to girls when I was 13, to pinball when I was 16, and to asparagus when I was 43.

On the radio at home I caught the last strains of a performance by a trumpeter named Clyde McCoy. He made his instrument growl, sing, purr, and wail. Before the last note of "Sugar Blues" faded away, I knew that I had to hear more of his music. I also had to take music lessons, play a trumpet with a mute, and own a Victrola.

What I got was a ukulele. Mother bought it at a rummage sale for 40 cents and reminded me that music hath charms to clothe the savage beast. My Bakelite uke came with a coffee-stained instruction book that showed how to tune the four strings to A, D, F#, and B, or the old familiar "My dog has fleas." Daddy brought home a mandolin that he'd accepted as part payment for a set of encyclopedias. I tuned the four double-strings to "my my dog dog has has fleas fleas" and strummed it like a ukulele. Now I could brag that I played three instruments, counting the piano.

A harmonica became my fourth, purchased with money that I earned sniping deposit bottles from trashcans. Then I replaced the harmonica with a $5 Hohner Chromonica that played sharps and flats. Now I could breeze through "Santa Lucia" and "Captain Jinks of the Horse Marines." To add to the joyous musicality in our furnished apartment, I finally caught on to double-whistling, blowing two tones in such quick succession that they sounded like a chord. Such talents cannot be taught, and there weren't many sixth-graders at the H. C. Lea School who could whistle the duets from "Naughty Marietta." Mother had always known the technique, and so had her grandfather, Francis Zawadzki. I figured it had something to do with the Polish blood that we never mentioned.

6.

I finished the sixth grade with a B average and only one negative comment on my report card: "Dental needs." In the 1930s, struggling parents saved money on their children's mouths. Neither my sister nor I had ever seen a dentist, which was fine with us. With my "needs" now a matter of record, Mother dragged me to a store-front dentist who agreed to fill five teeth for ten dollars and throw in a cleaning, a bottle of mouthwash, and a tube of Colgate's latest formula toothpaste that would clean my breath while it cleaned my teeth.

I showed up alone a week later with the first installment of two dollars and endured thirty minutes of medieval torture. Novocain was in wide use but apparently hadn't reached this part of West Philadelphia. For my remaining four appointments, I waltzed past his office to a nearby Baltimore Market, one of a chain that advertised Teach Your Dollars More Cents. The store featured Milky Ways at a nickel each and chocolate-covered graham crackers at a quarter the sack. For a few weeks, I believed there was hope for the dental profession.

Mother decided that such a self-reliant young man deserved a happy birthday and informed me that Daddy was working on a surprise. They knew about my obsession with fishing and that I'd sent away to the L. L. Bean Company in Freeport, Maine, for a catalog.

On my eleventh birthday, June 7, 1936, I became the recipient of a five-foot boat rod for ocean fishing, a four-ounce dipsy for surfcasting, an L. L. Bean flyreel for trout, and a red-and-white Bass-O-Reno plug with three treble hooks for bass, pike, muskellunge, and Mako sharks. I carried my gear fifteen blocks west to a polluted little brook called Cobb's Creek, found a pool that was eight feet wide and six or eight inches deep, made a mighty cast and waited for action. The leaden dipsy dragged the plug to the bottom, where it wobbled tantalizingly in the current. I held my index finger against the line to feel the slightest nibble. A shadow sniffed at one of the nine hooks but didn't bite. It was about half the size of the Bass-O-Reno.

After a few frustrating hours I trudged toward home. I arrived just in time to see Daddy pull up in a gray 1936 Dodge. We were moving back to Upper Darby. I was eleven years old, and we were going home.

six

Taylor Avenue: Drexel Hill

1.

The green community of Drexel Hill adjoined Highland Park and resembled the rest of Upper Darby Township except for the absence of the Tanners, the Saroyans, and other friends of my grammar school years. On the first night in our furnished rental on Taylor Avenue, our duplex neighbors introduced themselves: Joe Reminger, a pleasant ex-Milwaukeean who sold Buicks; his wife Rhoda, a dignified homemaker from the Pennsylvania Dutch country; their daughter Mary, tall and dark and destined to break my heart two or three times a week; and her younger brother Johnny, a bright and talented boy of my own age.

Early the next morning Sis came running into the kitchen yelling, Mother, Mother, look out the window. The lady's driving her car backwards!

It was Mrs. Reminger, backing out of her driveway in a boxy old Chevy sedan.

Mother said, Well, I never. It was the first time we'd seen a female driver. Daddy said the roads wouldn't be safe anymore.

For the first few months the Olsens and Remingers stayed at arm's length even though we shared a front porch and lawn. The common wall was thin, and every day we heard our neighbors go up and down their stairs, flush their toilets, sing, train their dog, and listen to the radio. We heard Mary and Johnny recite their lessons while Rhoda and Joe corrected them. We didn't hear the Remingers argue because the Remingers never seemed to argue. But we heard Johnny practice his clarinet, usually at dawn or around bedtime. He had an uncanny ability to hit E-flat, but only when he was reaching for D-sharp or even A. Daddy considered buying him a new reed, but Mother said that the Remingers might take it as a complaint.

Johnny and I soon developed a mutual interest in baseball cards. A nickel bought a player's picture, statistics, life story, and five pieces of bubble gum, a tasty product that we were proud to learn had been invented in Philadelphia. We collected cards and gum from Goudey, Delong, Diamond Stars, and American Caramel, but our favorite was Fleer's, a local company that had outlasted its competitors.

Johnny and I played odds-and-evens and variations. He was skillful and patient and usually cleaned me out. Still, I managed to avoid the disaster that befell our mutual friend Chris Jacobsen, who lived a block away on Huey Avenue. His grandfather had given him a Cy Young card, showing the legendary Cleveland pitcher wearing a tiny glove, a narrow-billed cap over his eyes, glossy high-topped shoes and black socks. The card had been issued in 1911 and was reputed to be worth hundreds of dollars.[38] Chris lost it in an odds-or-evens game with a stranger he met in the 69th Street Terminal. He told his father, I didn't think it was worth anything. It was so old.

My talented nine-year-old sister landed a role in "H. M. S. Pinafore" at Garrettford Elementary School and came home to tell us that her music teacher thought Gilbert and Sullivan were the equal of Walter Damrosch.

Are they having another sale? Daddy asked, looking up from his *Evening Public Ledger*. Mother said he was probably thinking of Frank & Seder.

For a week Carolyn went about our frame house singing "Poor little Buttercup, dear little Buttercup." At first we enjoyed the free preview. Toward the end we wanted to put a sack over her head. Meanwhile I blew, banged, and strummed nine different instruments: ukulele, mandolin, fife, Chromonica, penny whistle, Jew's harp, snare drum, piano, and straight harmonica. Daddy threatened to confine me and Sis to the coal bin.

Mother enrolled her eleven-year-old prodigy in Upper Darby Junior High School, a fifteen-minute ride from Taylor

38 Now thousands.

Avenue on dyspeptic school buses that reeked of incomplete combustion. I had boisterous reunions with old pals from Highland Park, especially Billy Glossop, who said he was goddamn glad to see me and I could come over to his goddamn house anytime even though I'd begun to talk a little funny. I told Billy to siddown and mind his own beeswax. We boys were thrilled that Jesse Owens won four events at the Berlin Olympics, and marched up and down the halls chanting, Jes-see! Jes-see! [39]

By now I was experimenting with five or six cuss words, but I was still too priggish to use the worst of them. My friend Tom Still's mouth had been rinsed out with Lux for saying "damn" to his aunt, a Seventh Day Adventist missionary to Mexico. I hadn't known that the Adventists sent out missionaries. I wasn't even sure what Seventh Day Adventists were, but if they believed in seven-day weeks, I was on their side. I was pretty sure they weren't Jewish because none of our friends looked nervous when you said "Seventh Day Adventist."

I ran into my astronomer pal Thomas North Jackson in study hall and was glad to see that he wasn't much taller. He had a new set of friends but seemed pleased to see me. Lulu Abernethy welcomed me with a loud Arf-Arf-Sandy and kissed me on the cheek despite our shared indiscretion, or maybe because of it. Lulu had never been as upset as her mother by the incident. You'd have thought it was Mrs. Abernethy who'd pulled down her bloomers, not her daughter.

I kept looking for the Tanners 'til Billy explained that Catholics had their own schools so they wouldn't be exposed to hot dogs on Fridays and end up frying in hell along with the hot dogs.

---

39 Three decades later he would go on record that I should be hanged. I'd written a series of articles suggesting that over-emphasis on sport was damaging the futures of athletic young African Americans. Owens angrily disagreed. I saw it as proof that experience is the worst teacher.

2.

Almost a thousand students attended UDJHS. The building was a handsome rectangle in colonial Georgian style, with six pillars in front, a bell tower suitable for Paul Revere, and an enclosed inner court with shrubs, grass, and flowers. Daydreamers like me could stare out the classroom windows and see green in any direction.

In my first week of school, mechanical drawing joined math as my main problems. Not one of my introductory sketches was recognizable as a cube, a trapezoid, or a cylinder. I thought I'd drawn a neat rectangle, but the teacher said I'd forgotten the moustache. Nor did I understand the basic geometry that went with the course. I grasped the idea of isosceles triangles – they looked flatter – but what was so cute about the other triangles? And why was the sum of the angles always 180 degrees? I drew several triangles and measured them with my protractor. One came to 176 degrees and another 188. So much for the teacher's arrogance. I had enough trouble with know-it-alls at home.

I'd put on weight and gained a little muscle over the summer, but Phys. Ed. remained a stumbling block. I'd hardly set foot in my seventh grade home room before Chick Bramble took me aside and said, Did you hear we gotta strip?

Strip? I said. For roll call?

For gym.

Not me, buddy.

Not me neither.

I'd never seen my mother naked. I'd never seen my father naked. I hadn't seen my sister naked since she was a baby, and even then I'd turned away. I didn't like to see myself naked. After fifteen minutes in the bathtub my fingertips wrinkled and my wee-wee almost disappeared. Why did I have to show such personal items to people I didn't even know?

Chick's warning proved all too true. In our first week, we

male seventh-graders spilled into the boys' locker room and were outfitted with gym suits in the school colors, buff and blue, plus sanitary sweat socks and a cardboard box containing a protective male undergarment. We were assigned combination locks and our own lockers. The problem was that somebody else's locker was right alongside, and there we were: thirty kids in a row, all looking sideways. We were ordered to get into our gym suits right now. Of course that would involve taking off our clothes. There appeared to be no appeal from this sentence, although some of us kept hoping for a phone call from the governor.

Nicholas Sanson requested permission to go to the office and phone his mother.

That was the last we saw of Nick. He transferred to a private school where we were sure that every kid had a private dressing room and a valet.

The rest of us hemmed and hawed and finally followed the example set by Billy Glossop and three or four other boys who regularly met at a summertime swimming hole called Brass Beach where they smoked cattails and gloried in the human form divine. In the locker room they yanked off their clothes and pretty soon were reddening their bare heinies with snapping towels. One of the boys had a thatch of curly black hair. I thought, What is this guy? A freak?

In the middle of this diversion Chick Bramble and the rest of us succeeded in putting on our gym suits without giving up too many personal secrets. Imagine our consternation after class when we learned that we were expected to take off our gym suits and race through a V-shaped shower area, and that a teacher named Mr. Gracey, a man who wasn't even our father, was in charge.

Skinny Bobby Boyle went all the way through in a sideways shuffle. A few of the boys fluttered towels in front of them as though this were the normal way to shower. My own technique was to run so fast that observers would see only a blur. T. George Harris passed me en route.

On the school bus the next morning I heard the sad tale of a shy boy named David Tinning, the only other eleven-year-old in our class. When he'd finished donning his gym clothes, his protective male undergarment was left over. Hey, he called out, where's this go?

A quick-witted classmate identified it as a nose guard. He told Davey, If they issued you one, that means the nurse says you gotta wear it.

The nose guard fit. Davey popped into the gym just as the seventh-grade girls were being dismissed. Their shrieks made him duck out the first exit, which happened to lead into the arms of Miss Christine Morley, an assistant principal who was widely believed to be responsible for the torture and executions of at least six students.

Hold it right there, mister! she said. What's that on your face?

In a muffled voice, David said, Yes, ma'am.

What's that on your face?

Oh, this? He peeled it off and said, This is a nose guard.

And that was how Nose-guard Tinning got the nickname that would follow him into college athletic records and beyond. I haven't checked, but it may be on his tombstone.

3.

At first the teachers at Upper Darby Junior High seemed less than friendly to the prodigal student. Knocking around from school to school, I'd retained all my old limitations and developed some new ones, and in the seventh grade my marks and my behavior began to slip. I managed a B-C average for most of the year, but there were hardly enough numbers on the back of my report card to describe my personal defects. I scored 6 Talkative, 7 Original, 28 Wasteful habits, 8 Careless, 29 Improvement needed, and those were just in math. Other teachers noted 16 Poor examinations, 18 Poor foundation, 24 Poor class work, 12 Indifferent and indolent, 2 Inattentive, 10 Uninterested, and several other numbers.

I also had difficulties in shop courses, a new concept to me. In Electric Shop I shorted the school lights. In Wood Shop I snapped a band-saw. In Metal Shop I banged two hammers together and sent a steel chip into a workmate's eye. There were no hard feelings as he recovered full vision in a month or two, but the teacher gave me a D and advised me never to touch another hammer.

Mother signed my report cards with a painful sigh and a close look into my eyes, as though she were trying to find my missing I.Q. somewhere behind the retinas. I wondered how she and Daddy felt about letting me skip the third grade. I'd never felt too good about it myself.

4.

Sometimes tapioca pudding and butterscotch pie popped up on our dinner table, but Sis and I were given to understand that we shouldn't expect regular desserts even though we'd moved back to the suburbs. It seemed that we'd migrated to Drexel Hill on a slight uptick in the economy but arrived in time for another collapse. It was 1936, the year FDR crushed a weak candidate, Gov. Alfred Landon of Kansas, even though a third of the work force was unemployed. Singing comedians described the situation on the radio:

Why, I read in Monday's paper
That ten thousand men were hired.
Yeah, on Tuesday they forgot to say
Twelve thousand more were fired.

Radio comics told us not to worry about going to the poor-house because there was no room – It's filled with millionaires! A straight man would say, Prosperity is just around the corner, and the comedian would respond, What we'd like to know is which corner? We turned so many corners we're dizzy....

It was another low point of the Great Depression.

Daddy kept us afloat by freelance adjusting for independent auto insurance companies and a part-time job as a mechanic on weekends. He would inspect damaged cars in the daytime, then sit up 'til midnight typing reports with his index fingers to save the cost of a steno. He bullied the keys and brooked no sass. He seemed to have a special feud with the shift key. Long after midnight I would hear comments like I need a capital, ya son of a bitch... Listen, sport, I'll snap ya the hell in half, ya make that mistake again ....

The upright L. C. Smith that he'd bought from Mr. Geldberg came with a red-and black ribbon, and Daddy used the color for emphasis. He made two carbon copies of every letter, as though he expected his words to end up in the Library of Congress, and he cursed and fumed over each correction, rubbing at the paper with a gray pumice eraser and a stiff black brush. Eventually the red and black inks ran together and his words started to come out speckled. In the morning I would see his carbon copies, full of strikeovers and erasures. They looked like modern paintings that had been left out in the rain. As soon as I hit a number, he told me, I'll get me one of them new green ribbons. Daddy was ever an innovator.

I'd always known that he lacked formal schooling, despite his claims to the contrary, but somewhere along the line he'd picked up a slight familiarity with 20th Century Business English. He would type, Replying to yrs of the second inst., letter received and contents duly noted... Myself and ass't inspected said vehicle....

I had to assume that "ass't" was his brother Ralph O. Olsen or another alias. He would type, Your correspondent begs to report that said vehicle will require the following repairs, as follows, to wit....

Sometimes he threw in a "viz" or a reference to this physical year. He referred to himself as "the writer" and to others as "the honorable," presumably including ax murderers. Most of his reports ended with the same flourish: With all due regards, may I respectively say that I remain, Very Truly Yours, R. O. Olsen, Licensed Automotive Inspector, LB. Sometimes he added, Purdue U., 1912. His signature looked like a Chinese ideograph. He blotted it with toilet paper, which he then recycled to the bathroom to the confusion of guests. At the very bottom he added "ROO/dq" to indicate that his girl[40] had typed the letter. Daddy didn't have a girl, but if any of his business contacts inquired, we were instructed to say that his executive secretary was Dorothea Quigley who held a degree in office work from Drexel Tech and was on vacation at Rehobeth Beach.

Every so often Daddy asked what I was learning in school, but I was reluctant to be specific since he liked to correct my teachers and still suffered from the same old tendency to get things a little wrong. He seemed interested in a story I'd heard in math class about the concept of infinity. Later I heard him telling a family friend, You know, Dick, if you put a couple monkeys in a room, they'll have six, eight babies. The babies have babies, and them babies have babies. Dick, it's a scientific fact that if you put a couple monkeys in a room, sooner or later

---

40   Standard 1930s terminology for secretary or stenographer.

they'll write *Hamlet*.

5.

As the Depression widened and worsened, Daddy seemed to lose some of his sense of humor in the struggle to keep us in the suburbs. Sometimes he got the point of a joke and sometimes he didn't. He skewed punch lines worse than Mother skewed clichés. When he heard that an actress had told a telephone caller, "All I have on is the radio," he repeated it as:

Hey, hon, whatttaya wearing?

Oh, I'm just listening to the radio.

If you didn't laugh at his cracks, Daddy would complain that you weren't worldly.

Family members were his favorite victims. Seated around our Philco we heard Joe Penner joke about a duck, a peacock, and a zebra. Later I heard Daddy tell a friend over the phone:

What is the difference between a duck?

Take off them crazy pajamas and I'll show you.

If you corrected him, you were wrong. You were the one who never got things straight. Sis was a straight-A student and the first to suspect brain damage. But not the last.

One of my deepest insights into Daddy's twisted brain-waves came in my second year of junior high. We'd inherited a set of red-leather engineering textbooks from the previous tenant of our duplex on Taylor Avenue. I was taking Algebra 1 at the time and the books were beyond me. But not beyond Daddy. Wasn't Purdue an engineering school? At night he would sit in his corner chair and scribble in the margins, forehead furrowed as he licked the point of his pencil and made occasional erasures while his tongue stuck out the corner of his mouth.

Out of curiosity I pulled down one of the books. Page after

page was marked by his hieroglyphics. At first I thought he'd been using scientific notation that no eighth-grade kid could understand, but after a closer look I realized that he'd invented signs and symbols, written nonsense formulas, shaped letters that weren't English or Latin or Chinese or any other language. A chicken with dirty feet would have made as much sense. Next to a long geometrical proof he'd put a big question mark. Under a section on stress analysis, he'd written "crap" as though he'd re-worked the equations for himself and found errors. Alongside a passage about holomorphic values (whatever that meant), he'd scribbled, I'm from Mo.

I lay in bed pondering this glimpse into Daddy's thought processes. Surely he knew his fakery would be found out – or did he presume that Sis and I would never open these books? Now I knew for sure that he hadn't seen the inside of Purdue University or any other college – or any other high school, for that matter.[41]

6.

In 1937 we had two phones installed: a Bell for the family (Clearbrook 270) and a Keystone (I never learned the number) for an independent adjusting business that Daddy intended to start when he raised some capital. The Keystone system advertised, When the Keystone rings, it's business. Ours never rang.

---

41   It took me years to work up an explanation that made sense, at least to me. Of course Daddy wanted to create an impression of being educated, but I think he also wanted to get the feel of it. He'd left school to play baseball, where formal knowledge didn't matter, and somehow found his way into the business world, where knowledge was king. So he reinvented himself as a man about town who was worldly, knew all the answers, was never wrong, and could step and pitch and drive and shoot craps and pick horses with the best. Did he believe his own mythology? In the end I think he did.

Mother argued that we couldn't afford one phone, let alone two, but Daddy told her that he would be entertaining clients at home and needed to look prosperous. He said, Always remember, Flo. Money comes to money.

Mother said she was waiting to find out.

From the beginning Daddy fought with telephone operators. Listen, girlie, he would say, how many times I gotta tell ya – no more wrong numbers .... Yeah? Yeah? ... Pay attention, girlie! I said no more calls from bill collectors. What? What? Connect me to your boss, and I mean now!

Soon everyone except Howard Ehmke knew our Clearbrook number, and Daddy took defensive measures. We were instructed to inform bill collectors and shysters that the head of the household would return in a few weeks. If they asked how to contact him, we were to say, There's no telephones in that part of Baffin Bay.

Mother asked what *shyster* meant.

Mouthpiece, Daddy said.

Mouthpiece? What's a mouthpiece?

Jeez, Flo, Daddy said, you're the unworldliest person in the world.

When Daddy answered the phone himself, he would lower his voice and ask, Whom shall I say is calling? Then he would say one moment, plee-uz, and return to the line as a tenor, usually Ralph Olsen, Rudolph's brother, who'd just dropped in from Sioux Falls, Iowa. Sometimes he posed as our chauffeur or butler. In these roles he said he would be happy to take a message and see to it that Dr. Olsen received it as soon as he returned from a conference at John Hopkins Hospital in Baltimore. I heard him tell one caller, No, it ain't Johns Hopkins. How the hell many guys d'ya think it's named after?

When these stratagems wore thin, Daddy threatened legal action. I would listen as he worked himself up. Why are you calling me, bud? No, this ain't Drexel Hill, this is Hazleton.... Hazleton, up in the coalfields.... You got your lines crossed, cap'n ... I tol' ya, there's nobody by that name here ... I'm the plumber, that's who the hell I am. Who the hell are you? ....

Sometimes he worked himself into such a lather that he lost track of his own stories. You're calling me a liar? ... No, this ain't Clearbrook 270.... Well, I oughta know my own number! ... You're making a mistake, lady. Goddamn it, this is Clearbrook 270!

Whenever Sis and I were sent to the drugstore, we were instructed to say "charge it, please" and head for the exit. We exhausted our credit at one pharmacy after another, first Doc McCollum's at the end of Taylor Avenue, then Doc Stroup's on Burmont Road, then Doc Hahn's on Edmonds. Our last hope was Doc Raymond, whose all-purpose drugstore in a dreary little plexus at the slow end of Garrett Road carried everything except caviar and rattlesnake meat and was a forerunner of companies like Rexall and Walmart in its own small way.

By the time we started charging at Raymond's, we'd already been cut off at Berry's 5&10, Kahn's Delicatessen, LaRitz Bakery, Wooding's Meats, Scott's Groceries, and the A&P. Every few days Daddy would drive to Springfield, on the far side of Darby Creek, to charge groceries under a fake name and address.

Henry Raymond entered my life as a nondescript little guy in an apron and left it as my No. 1 role model. He first caught my attention when I asked to charge a pint of his creamy homemade chocolate ice cream.

Look, young man, he said, drawing me into a corner where we couldn't be overheard, I don't mind if you charge medicine. I don't mind if you charge your dad's tobacco. But – nobody needs ice cream.

He beckoned toward the upstairs apartment where he lived

with his wife Kathryn and their son Sidney. We can't afford it ourselves, he whispered.

Nothing that Doc bought was one-half as precious as what he sold, and I wanted to stay on his good side. I paid cash for my own purchases and made it plain that the Olsen family's credit problems were none of my doing. Doc seemed to respect my attitude, right up to the sad end of our friendship.

7.

As spring turned into summer on Taylor Avenue, I began to pick up pocket money cutting grass and running errands, just enough to satisfy my growing needs for Tastykakes, Philadelphia's succulent chocolate and butterscotch cupcakes at ten cents for a package of three. I could put away two or three packages between the school bus stop and home. I was hopelessly addicted to every product made by the Tasty Baking Company and remained so for years.[42]

Mother entered into discussions with some of my teachers and neighbors and decided that I was old enough for a regular allowance. Daddy was out of town at the time, so the resolution carried. Of course, I had to hold up my end of the bargain. I had to eat my vegetables (but not asparagus – Mother had made it an exception to avoid mealtime bedlam). I would be expected to dry the dinner dishes, be on time for meals, keep my clothes neat and clean, and not repeat a certain word that Mother had heard me say after I sent away to the Johnson Smith Novelty Co. in Chicago for a Chinese Good Luck Ring and received a package of garlic-flavored gum. I also had to maintain a B

---

42   Tastykake fanciers outside of the Philadelphia area consider themselves in "Tastykake exile." As a twenty-one-year-old cub reporter on the *San Diego Union*, I wrote that a bride had twenty candles on her kake.

average at school and take a bath every Saturday night whether I needed it or not. If I met these conditions, I would be eligible for my weekly allowance, provided, of course, that Mother's purse wasn't empty at the time.

My weekly allowance was ten cents.

Dancing school became the next economic issue. When Drexel Hill boys turned twelve, they signed up at the school on Ferne Boulevard at two dollars per lesson. Daddy saw this tradition as a frippery. What's next? he asked. Walking school? Breathing school?

When I told him that Johnny Reminger and some of my other friends had signed up, he said, Well, I never went to no school, and I know a little about dancing. How 'bout that, Flo? Can I step?

You can step, Mother said, intent on darning a sock.

I'll learn ya myself, Daddy told me. Pay attention. This here's the Charleston.

He crisscrossed his hands in front of his knees. I'd seen Uncle Sonny do a better dance waving off a fart, but I knew better than to criticize.

I said, Drexel Hill kids do the fox trot.

Fox trot? Foxes don't even do the fox trot no more. Heard of the turkey trot?

No.

The black bottom? Flo, can I do the black bottom?

Mother spoke through a needle she was holding in her lips. Yeth, she said. You have danthing feet.

I begged off to do my homework. I knew what a huge success the turkey trot and the black bottom would be at the freshman hop.

A few weeks later Daddy and I had a tense conversation about camp. Nobody went to camp when I was a kid, he said, and look at me – I come out all right, didn't I?

It took me awhile to realize that these discussions were really about money. We had none to spare. So I didn't go to camp. Or to school dances. Or to A's and Phillies' or SPHAS' games, prizefights or wrestling matches, ice hockey games at the Arena, or any event that required tickets or carfare.

Times were bad, but I hadn't realized how bad. It seemed as though half our neighbors owed money to the other half and we were all going to the poorhouse hand in hand. Mr. Scott had taken over the payments on the Romneys' 1931 Oldsmobile but still owed Mr. Romney for the down payment. The milkman stopped delivering to the Temples until Mrs. Temple borrowed money from Mrs. Melson to pay her bill in full. Then Mrs. Melson went broke and the milkman cut her off 'til she borrowed money from the Mackeys to bring her account up to date. Housewives would ask to borrow a couple of dollars 'til tomorrow and pay it back a month later – or move away. Old Mrs. Lumley held one of her séances for neighborhood women, and when the table rose off the floor and the rapping began, the spirit said, Pay Mrs. Lumley the ten bucks you borrowed!

8.

Mr. Bruner lived in the house to our north. A quiet dark-haired man in his forties, he kept to himself, nodded when greeted, and spent most of his time walking around his small property, head down and brow furrowed as though he were studying each blade of grass.

Sometimes I would see his lips moving, and sometimes he would jerk his arm like a baseball umpire and reverse direction. I asked Mother if he was all there.

Yes, she said. He's a good man. He's on a war pension. For shell shock.

It took her a long time to explain. As a young teen in Jersey City, Mother had known an ex-soldier from New Brunswick who was committed to a locked ward and never came out. Mother said she thought that Mr. Bruner was a little better off than her childhood friend. But I wasn't so sure. One night we saw him walking around in a crouched position, firing an imaginary rifle into the hedge. Mother asked Mrs. Bruner about it later and she said he'd been on a reconnaissance mission and was now debriefing himself at field headquarters in the bathtub.

There was a worse case of shell shock in the next block, a bug-eyed little man named Smollie who frequently ran through the backyards dressed only in his undershirt, yelling that the Serbs had broken through on the right flank. He would burst into song:

Beetles here, beetles there

Beetles in your underwear....

Daddy said, Well, he knows his own BVDs best.

Once Mr. Smollie accused our bread man of spying for the Kaiser and challenged him to a duel. After the bread man chose jelly doughnuts at ten paces, the feud blew over. Just when Mr. Smollie seemed to be improving, he parked his 1929 Nash crosswise on West Chester Pike, shouldered his Enfield rifle and started demanding *cartes d'identite*. His family moved to the city to be closer to his room in the asylum.

Joseph Reminger, our duplex neighbor, had fought in the trenches and was a bona fide hero in full control of his faculties. He never boasted about his wartime experiences, but over time he passed a few military tips to his son, and Johnny passed some of them on to me. From Mr. Reminger we learned how to tell mustard gas from phosgene. He said that a Marine never hung back even if it meant advancing straight into enemy guns. A Marine didn't waste bullets. A Marine kept his bayonet razor-sharp and aimed for the soft body parts. If the bayonet stuck in bone, a Marine would give it a sharp quarter-twist, then yank.

I asked Johnny what happened to Marines who got scared and ran. Johnny insisted that there were no such Marines. He taught me Marine war songs:

The first Marine went over the top, parlay vous.
The second Marine went over the top, parlay vous.
The third Marine went over the top
Because he heard a nickel drop.
Hinky dinky parlay vous.

And a battlefront song with a vivid passage:

The worms crawl in, the worms crawl out
In your belly and out your snout.

Thus I was provided with the raw material for years of vivid nightmares.[43]

Johnny's father had made a seamless adjustment to civilian life. A slight soft-spoken man with neat brown hair that he combed sideways, he left every morning for his sales job at Wilkie Buick on North Broad Street. He always drove a brand-new demonstrator, and the Reminger driveway served as a one-car showcase. Daddy had to park our junker on the street since we had no garage, and it was a shameful contrast to Mr. Reminger's gleaming new Buicks with their nickel-chromium grilles, sleek lines, shiny bumpers, and white-walled balloon tires. Every few weeks he would appear in a different model, from the economical Special and the flashy Super to the fancy Century and top-of-the-line Limited. Mr. Reminger told us there wasn't a Buick made that couldn't hold 100 miles an hour on the open highway and eighty on the curves, and if Joe Reminger said it, we knew it was the gospel truth.

For years Buick had advertised, When better automobiles are built, Buick will build them, and Mr. Reminger brought the

---

43   In a flight physical during World War II, an Army Air Corps psychologist asked me if I'd ever seen anyone killed. Yes, I answered. Every night.

proof home. He drove the first two-tone automobiles ever seen in our neighborhood and made us gasp in admiration at cars that were lime on top and sea green on the bottom, or contrasting shades of blue. He drove a streamlined Buick Super that was painted a burnished oxblood with a sand-colored fabric roof. It had so much chrome that you felt like slapping on suntan lotion. The Buick Super lingers in my memory as the all-time great automobile. The Ferrari Testarossa is a close second.

Mr. Reminger had been selling these cars since the twenties and none of us kids could imagine him doing anything else. Then he was laid off. No more two-tone Buicks in his driveway. No more peeps under the hood at the latest overhead straight-eight Dynaflash engine. No more demonstration rides around the block. No more glossy catalogs with pictures suitable for framing. Mr. Reminger now shared the boxy black Chevy sedan that his wife Rhoda used for trips to the market.

It's the Depression, Mother explained to Sis and me.

I never trusted that damn Buick company, Daddy complained.

Husbands up and down our block shuddered. If Joe Reminger could be laid off, whose job was safe? His wife, a pleasant and reserved woman, took a clerking job at Strawbridge & Clothier. Word spread that Mr. Reminger was selling apples, the symbol of abject poverty from the earliest days of the Depression. We were all relieved when Mother learned that the rumor was false.

9.

Not long after Mr. Reminger lost his job, we heard about a shotgun suicide three blocks away. He was a middle-aged man who'd been an executive of a shoe company and now refused to get on his knees and sell them. The Riccobonis were evicted and had to return to the Italian ghetto in South Philly. Bobby Filmer's father, a friendly man who was a favorite of us boys, stole from the Frankford Arsenal to stall off foreclosure on his house and went off to federal prison for a year. Able-bodied young Drexel Hill men signed on with the WPA and CCC, blazing woodland trails from nowhere to nowhere. Teen-aged kids quit school for sweatshop work in the Clifton Heights clothing mills or the clammy old paper mill on U.S. 1 at Crum Creek. College students who couldn't pay their tuitions explained that they were "needed at home" and left school. Shopkeepers lowered prices, lowered them again, then put up signs: Everything must go!! The A&P and American Stores sold Hershey bars for four cents apiece, three for a dime. Two service stations on Burmont Road fought a gas war, and when one owner (Tydol! Veedol!!) lowered his price to twelve cents a gallon, the other shut down for good.

A magazine ad advised, When you buy an automobile you give three months work to someone which allows him to buy other products, so buy a car now – help bring back prosperity. Auto dealers paraded 1,200 used cars up Broad Street and unloaded a few at fire-sale prices. The *Inquirer* quoted Will Rogers: We are the first nation in the history of the world to go to the poor house in an automobile. W. C. Fields complained that the cost of living had gone up another dollar a quart.

During the "Roosevelt Depression" of the middle thirties, Bruno Hauptman was electrocuted for the Lindbergh kidnapping, and millions who couldn't afford the movies appreciated the diversion. The King of England provided more free entertainment by giving up his throne for a woman Nanny described as "that hotsy-totsy from Baltimore."

Aviatrix Amelia Earhart made headlines she never read after vanishing in the Pacific.

Meteor showers convinced pessimists that the end was near. Radio newsmen like Lowell Thomas ("So long until tomorrow") and Boake Carter (he of the English-accent) reported that a foot of dust had fallen on Oklahoma and the whole state seemed to be packing up and moving to California.

In Drexel Hill we became accustomed to the sight of moving vans with sofas and rocking chairs lashed to their rear ends, followed by cars carrying glum-looking parents and sobbing children: suburbia's Joads. I would wake up and learn that another friend and his family had left for the rowhouses of central Philadelphia. Homes emptied and re-rented, then emptied and re-rented again, as the upper class sank into the middle class and the middle class sank from sight.

At home I began to hear the same kind of muffled conversations that had preceded our flight to Jersey City. Would Nanny and Aunt Ronnie take us in again? I wasn't sure we'd be welcome. Where would I go this time? The poorhouse? Part of me was convinced I was headed for starvation. If grown men like Joe Reminger and Ole Olsen couldn't make it, what hope was there for an untalented shrimp who couldn't even learn the multiplication tables?

A blizzard struck, and a man flipped me a dime for digging out his car on Huey Avenue. This convinced me to take my snow shovel to busy Garrett Road and help stranded motorists on the hill above Raymond's Pharmacy. Most of my clients paid me a nickel or dime for the assistance, but some just waved and drove off.

What a fine young man! a woman called out as she rammed her car into gear, pelting me with ice and snow. A man with a walrus moustache got into his Graham-Paige sedan after I'd dug out his wheels and drove off yelling, Good job! I spent two hours clearing a widow's sidewalks and was promised a quarter on Tuesday. When I arrived to collect, I found a for-sale sign and an empty house. I stole a bottle of milk from her milk box, but it was sour. I changed my mind about The Shadow. Crime does pay, for old ladies.

10.

After I finished eighth grade Daddy found me a summer job jerking sodas in the 69th Street terminal. Keep two dollars of your pay, he instructed me, and give Mother the rest for room and board. That's the way we done it in Indianapolis.

Daddy had asked the proprietor to pay me what I was worth and not a penny more. He told the man that the job would be good experience for a ninth-grader, and the salary wasn't important. Daddy was always generous about things like that.

For a week I alternated between waiting on customers and eating Breyer's chocolate chip ice cream, devouring a quart and a half to two quarts a day. On Saturday the owner handed me an envelope. I tore it open in the car as Daddy drove me home. Out fell a two dollar bill, a quarter and a dime.

Daddy stopped the car and counted the money. He said there must be some mistake. Then he found a slip of paper: "$2.35, final wages." He said he would report the man for using child labor. He didn't know about the ice cream. I thought I was well paid.

He promised to find me another job. A week later he said, Ain't nothing out there,

Sonny. I might have to jerk some sodas myself.

I was a poor broke schoolboy again.

One evening I heard Daddy tell Mother that he'd done some figuring and it took forty-five dollars a week to keep us above water in Drexel Hill. He said he was earning five or six dollars less and he didn't know how long we could go on.

So we were on the edge again. I worried about leaving my friends and growing up in a place like Boyd Avenue, and I worried about whether I could ever earn forty-five dollars a week as an adult. What could I possibly do that would be worth that kind of salary?

I remembered Daddy's suggestion about telling your troubles to Jesus. I got on my knees at bedside and prayed, Dear Jesus, just give me a job that pays forty-five a week and I'll never ask for another penny for the rest of my life. Not – one – more – cent. Ever!

I knew I was abandoning my chance to be rich, but it was worth it for the security.[44]

11.

My relationship with Jesus seemed more personal now that I'd finished two months of catechism classes at Grace Evangelical Lutheran Church on School Lane. I'd never understood exactly why it was so important to become an official member of the church since Daddy almost never went and Mother seemed more interested in the Ladies' Aid.

The Ladies' Aid had something to do with the church, but I wasn't sure what, unless it was to spread gossip for Jesus. One night they were meeting in our living room and I overheard Mrs. Elizabeth Mollineux interpreting *Ecclesiastes*, explaining that the preacher meant *selfishness* when he said *vanity*. Then she explained that faith, hope, and *charity* meant faith, hope, and *love*. I wondered why God didn't put down faith, hope, and love when he wrote the Bible, so that some pushy suburban woman wouldn't have to translate. I asked Mother and Daddy but never got an answer.

---

44 Jesus held me to the deal 'til I was 23. And he didn't adjust for inflation.

Ever since I was little, Daddy had told me that every male Olsen was awarded a gold watch for Confirmation. I didn't care one way or the other. I had a Mickey Mouse watch that kept good time except when Mickey's gloved hand scraped against the face. I would have preferred a box of Milky Ways or a Jimmy Foxx baseball bat to any kind of watch, gold, platinum, radium dial or otherwise, but Daddy insisted that I be confirmed in the church of his father and grandfathers and the family tradition called for a gold watch. He pointed out that his only brother Edwin had fathered two daughters and I was the last hope to carry on the family name. I thought, The family name? Is there a shortage of Olsens?

The theme of our catechism lessons came from *Revelations*: Be thou faithful unto death, and I will give thee a crown of life. I had no idea what that meant. I was already alive. I was as alive as any boy in Upper Darby. How many crowns of life did one kid need?

Pastor Wallick preached Lutheran hellfire and the Ten Commandments. He was an intense little Michigander with a stubbly moustache like Hitler's and two gorgeous daughters who caused a few of my friends to commit sins behind their bathroom doors.

I ticked off the Commandments one by one and decided that if God issued report cards, I was probably on my way to a C or a C minus. It was true that I'd had no Gods before him, whoever and wherever he was. I'd used the Lord's name in vain, but probably not enough to make him mad. I wasn't sure about the graven image business because I wasn't sure what a graven image was. I hadn't kept the Sabbath entirely holy, but I would start next Sunday. I gave myself a B at honoring my father and mother, although Daddy could make it difficult. I'd killed, but only fish and bugs. As for not committing adultery, I didn't think I had the necessary equipment as yet. There was no question that I'd broken the Eighth Commandment, although I didn't intend to make stealing a career. I'd never borne false witness against the Remingers, the Bruners, or any of our other neighbors.

The Tenth Commandment puzzled me and I asked Billy G about it. He was as confused as I was. We knew we weren't supposed to covet our neighbor's wife or our neighbor's ass, but as Billy pointed out, the Bible didn't say anything about coveting our neighbor's wife's ass. This was especially unnerving to him as he watched his neighbor Mrs. Rubens undress almost every night, and he was planning to get in touch with her as soon as he figured out how to go about it. I asked him what he would do with her if she should suddenly become available when Mr. Rubens was out of town. He said he wasn't sure yet, but he would probably kiss her and run his hand across her heinie 'til he got bored. I told him I'd already seen one girl's heinie and not to expect much.

Pastor Wallick ordered us to memorize the Commandments whether they seemed to make sense or not. He promised that we would understand everything about Jesus and the Bible when we were a little older. That was his standard answer to any and all inquiries. Daddy told me, You need to get more worldly. The Ten Commandments never hurt nobody. Just don't overdo 'em.[45]

To suit me up for Confirmation, my parents took me to a famous clothing store on Market Street. My eyes bugged out at rack after rack of sharp-looking suits – gabardine, worsted, tweed, sharkskin, mohair, and flannel in patterns of plaid, pinstripes, solids, and checks. In the rear of the store a sign advised, Up One Flight To Save Money. Up we went.

---

45   This advice came from a man who stayed home from church on Ash Wednesdays but applied burnt cork to his forehead because "in the business world I run into a lotta Christers."

My face flushed when Daddy told the salesman that we needed some glad rags for the young whippersnapper here and we were looking for something in a blue-serge double-breasted. We could go as high as ten dollars.

I'd arrived at the age when a school kid could be ostracized for wearing the wrong shade of socks and would hide in the woods all day rather than appear at school in rubbers or unstylish socks.

After I tried on a rack of Navy blue suits, Daddy selected a nine-dollar serge that hung on me like a collapsed tent. I detested it all the more since it came with two pairs of pants and probably wouldn't wear out 'til I was in my forties. I sneaked a piteous look at Mother, but she was looking the other way. She'd fought the clothing wars since Sis and I were little kids, and I think she was shell-shocked herself.

Daddy was so pleased with his selection that he drove us to Fifty-Second Street for shoes. He always bought mine a size or two too large so they would last. The salesman measured my foot with his wooden ruler and brought out several boxes. I slipped into a wing-tip that would have been perfect for a young banker. It had spirals and curls made of a thousand little dots that I figured were for ventilation. They certainly weren't for beauty.

Daddy said, Too tight, huh, Sonny? Let's try the next size larger.

Oh, no, sir, the salesman insisted. He was a skinny little man in a shiny brown suit and patent leather shoes. You don't want them too big, sir. Bad for the boy's feet. Let's take a look.

He led us to an X-ray machine and showed me how to slip my foot in a slot at the bottom. I saw my bones inside the shoe. It was a perfect fit.

Mother came back from the ladies' room and said, Get your foot out of there! She'd always been leery of anything connected with radiation and had refused to let me keep a Johnson Smith "see in the dark" lens that I ordered through the mail. She'd learned from her own mother that the air was full of mysterious rays and gases that could strike you dead at any time.

Daddy said, You don't believe that gadget, do you, Sonny? The shoe's too tight, ain't it?

Yeah, I said. I guess so.

In the end he picked out a four-dollar pair of oxblood "low-cuts" that I detested even more than the blue serge suit. They were two sizes too large and would make my classmates collapse with laughter. At the time, the dress code at Upper Darby Junior High required single-breasted jackets, contrasting pants, and saddle shoes.

Why didn't I argue and yell and roll on the floor? Because it would have been a waste of time. Daddy would have said that I was too wet behind the ears to have a sense of style and I wasn't worldly and anyway double-breasted was the rage these days – the sharpest dressers in town wore double-breasted suits and oxblood low-cuts. How did he know? Why, he was friendly with designers! With tailors! He was in and out of their shops all the time. Daddy wrote the book on style. Who else on our block went to church in matching derby and spats and called it puttin' on the Ritz?

Twice a year.

12.

I took Holy Communion in my double-breasted suit and ox-blood shoes with the thousand holes and received a parchment from the Reverend Lloyd Merl Wallick attesting that John Edward Olsen had professed faith in our Lord Jesus Christ and vowed obedience to His Gospel and was received into full

Communicant Membership in the church by the solemn rite of Confirmation. Now I could join the Luther League and help take up the offering on Sundays, one hand behind my back per a long-standing tradition that showed just how much Lutherans trusted one another.

On the church steps, I ran into smart-mouth Tommy Tenison, on his way to play ball or mug an old lady – you could never be sure with Tom. I showed him the document, and he said, You found Jesus, huh?

Yep.

I didn't even know he was lost.

Daddy came home late that night and sat on the side of my bed. Sonny, he said, I can't get you a watch.

I had to think for a few seconds. Then I remembered the old family tradition. That's okay, I said.

No, it ain't okay. It, it – ain't okay.

He looked away. In a broken voice, he said, I went bust on that suit and them low-cuts.

I'd never seen my father shed a tear. It was a moment of terror. Strong men didn't cry. Major league pitchers certainly didn't cry. Those were the rules. What was I supposed to say?

What was I supposed to *do*?

I reached over to pat him on the arm, but he got up and left. I'd forgotten our rule about touching.

Awhile later I heard the stairs creak and hardly had time to snap my Big Little Book shut and turn off my Boy Scout flashlight. My door opened slowly and I smelled Bayuk Phillies.

Sonny?

I pretended to be asleep.

Sonny boy?

I held my breath.

Oh well, he said. Then he was gone.

A few days later Mother explained what happened to my

watch. A race fixer who was out on parole had given Daddy a sure thing, and Daddy had placed a big bet so he could buy me a better watch than the cheap model he'd picked out. His horse ran second. Someone forgot to inform the winning horse that the race was fixed.

A month after Confirmation, Daddy burst into the house with a big smile. He unwrapped a package and handed me a blue velvet case. I opened it and found a Lord Elgin gold watch, "curved to fit the wrist."

Let that be a lesson to you, Daddy said. It was one of his favorite expressions.

I wasn't sure what the lesson was. Bet the right horse? Don't take tips from crooks?

Daddy was never easy to read.

A few nights later he saw me doing homework and asked why I wasn't helping Mother with the dishes. Oh, I said, jumping up from the desk, I guess I forgot.

You guess – you – forgot?

He slapped me and I fell back against the desk, more surprised than hurt. Sis ran past me screaming. He'd never laid a hand on either of us.

I staggered into the kitchen and grabbed a dishtowel so I wouldn't be slapped again, but the first drop of blood made me feel faint. Mother steered me to the sofa and covered my face. Daddy said, Flo, call the croaker. He looked pale.

The nosebleed had stopped by the time Dr. Borland arrived. He said the patient would probably live.

I was put to bed and didn't see Daddy 'til breakfast. He said, How you was, Sonny? How's the old boy?

He was out the door before I could answer.

Mother handed me an orange slice and said, Your father's not himself these days.

It's okay, I said.

Things aren't going so good.

I told Mother I'd already figured that out.

13.

At school I was starting to develop some literary taste. My pals and I had been reading pulp magazines for a year or so, and the first author who caught my eye was Robert Leslie Bellem: I aimed my own roscoe from the hip. It said: "Chow chow!" and belched two slugs, one in each gam. He spun around and sat down on the floor and got a silly look on his hard-boiled pan.

I thought it was neat the way he wrote *roscoe* for gun, *slugs* for bullets, *pan* for face, and *gam* for leg. As I told my English teacher, Shakespeare could of learned a thing or two from Robert Leslie Bellem.

Mr. Richards had introduced us to the Bard at a time when most of us were still under the impression that Out, out, damned spot! was a book by Albert Payson Terhune.

We were unprepared for words like *forsooth* and *gadzook*. Billy Glossop caused a stir by raising his hand and asking, Does this here word *fardels* mean what I think?

Mr. Richards told him it meant *bundle*.

Not where I come from, Billy said.

Steve Groff was asked to read a passage from a famous Shakespeare play. He began, Romero, Romero, wherefore art thou Romero?

That's Romeo, Mr. Richards said. R-O-M-E-O, Romero – I mean, Romeo.

Right, Steve said. He continued: Romero, Romero, wherefore art thou Romero....

Mary Topham turned several shades of crimson as she stood alongside her desk and read:

An honor! were not I thine only nurse,

I would say thou hadst sucked wisdom from thy teat.

That started the first snickers. The second wave came when Ginny Voss read:

... We sucking on her natural bosom find,

Many for many virtues excellent....

I sat frozen to my seat, wondering what I would have to read aloud, and whether I could get out the window without being seen. Luckily Mr. Richards skipped me.

A few days later we were reading from *The Merchant of Venice*, and I was puzzled by names like Lorenzo, Antonio, Salerno, Bassano. Wasn't Shakespeare English? What kind of Italians drank mead instead of dago red and never played bocce or mora or dined on pasta fazool? Shakespeare should have done a little homework on Boyd Avenue.

Connie Warburton read aloud, Content, if faith, I'll seal to such a bond and say there is much kindness in the Jew.

My hand shot up. I said, Shouldn't that be, uh ... Jewish person?

No, Mr. Richards snapped. He didn't look up from his desk.

My mother said ....

We're reading Shakespeare, not your mother.

That night I took a longer look at *The Merchant of Venice* and found another confusing passage:

I should stay with the Jew my master, who, God bless the mark, is a kind of devil; and, to run away from the Jew, I should be ruled by the fiend, who, saving your reverence, is the devil himself. Certainly the Jew is the very devil incarnate....

I thought, Where've I heard stuff like that?

The light went on in my brain. Shakespeare sounded like Daddy's favorite radio preacher. Sometimes it seemed I could hear Father Coughlin's voice blaring from every other radio on our block. He didn't talk like a Philadelphian or a Jerseyite or any other human being I'd heard. Who wanted to listen to a guy who rolled his R's, said *sol-you-tion* for solution and pronounced both the T's in butter?

I decided not to discuss Shakespeare with Mr. Richards 'til I became more worldly.

14.

The preacher from the Shrine of the Little Flower wasn't the only loudmouth my pals and I were subjected to in the late 1930s. We were bored by the babbling of Mussolini, Hitler, and the other Nazzies. The little German with the black moustache just sounded nuts.[46] I never understood why thousands of people would stand in the rain to hear him gargle. Mussolini walked as though he had a load in his pants. Pally Sally Tanner had been more graceful.

Mother never said much about race or politics, but Daddy observed that it might be time to "crack down on them Jew bankers in Strawberry Mansion.[47] I'm sure he got his ideas from Father Coughlin and some of the old Germans (Daddy called them "Dutchmen") at the Columbia Turners. Whenever he came home from the club, he seemed a little higher on the Nazzies and their leader.

I had no interest in race and religion and was happy to remain as confused as ever on such touchy subjects. A rhyme

---

46 Twenty years later I encountered the same affected style during a short career as a radio news editor. The offender was Walter Winchell, who also said *scupe* for *scoop*. As Winchell snarled his message into the microphone, his right hand sent a stream of dots and dashes over the airwaves via an automatic telegraph key. By that time the U. S. Army and Office of Strategic Services had taught me high-speed Morse Code and I recognized that he was sending gibberish.

47 An affluent Jewish enclave in Philadelphia.

went around our class:

Ikey, Mikey, Jakey, Sam
We're the boys that eat no ham.

I wasn't put off; I just didn't get it. Who cared if Ikey, Mikey, Jakey, and Sam didn't like ham? And I didn't get the joke that Billy G told me in wood shop as I routed out the entrance hole for my birdhouse:

What's the fastest thing on earth?
A kike on a bike in the Reich.

I asked Billy what a kike was and he said he would have to check with his source, William Glossop Sr., but he thought it might be a Jewish person. He wasn't sure why they rode their bikes so fast.

I asked what Reich meant and Billy wasn't sure about that either. I said, What the heck's so funny about kikes and Reichs?

He said, My dad says it's funny, and he's a lot older than you.

Mother always said that the Glossops proved that humor is a funny thing.

I noticed that some of our classmates took to laying an index finger above their lips, mouthing Heil Hitler! and goose-stepping around the halls, but I didn't feel much anger or force behind their mockery. They would just as soon have mocked the Girl Scouts, Eskimos, or men with lisps. To the students of Upper Darby Junior High School, the Fuehrer and his goony side-kicks were ridiculous. And we knew why: They were grown-ups.

15.

My attitude about Blacks, known at the time as The Colored, was also rooted in ignorance.

Except for an occasional servant, we suburban kids had

no contact with Blacks – or yellows, reds, purples or any other color except pale peach. At Saturday matinees we laughed at Rufus, Rastus, Beulah, Sunshine, Mandy, Cowpoke, Lightnin', and the other Blacks who shuffled and stumbled and bumbled around the feet of us superior whites. We laughed as they misspoke their lines: Yassuh, Mr. Benny ... No, suh, bossman ... Ain' nobody here but us chickens ... Well, shut mah mouf wide open... Feet, do yo' stuff....

Ah's regusted....

This was offered as entertainment and we accepted it as such. We were blissfully unaware of racial injustice. The colored stayed in their place and we stayed in ours. If I asked Billy to do something for me, he would joke, Who was your nigger last week? Kids with flashy clothes were called nigger rich. A thick roll of dollar bills with a five or ten at each end was a nigger bankroll. Blacks were always late because they ran on CPT – colored people's time.

When Dummy Davis said my chocolate cream puff reminded him of a nigger's ear, I didn't think it was especially funny, but I put on a laugh. What the heck – everybody joked about Blacks. We didn't think it was wrong. We didn't think about it at all.

16.

Just before my freshman year, sex began to change our lives. Meetings of our boys' testosterone club usually began with the latest wisecrack on the subject. Billy G said, I'm going to Gimbels. Ladies' pants are half off.

Jim Shay said, My uncle works in a bloomer factory. He pulls down forty a week.

Not to be outdone, I made up a sex joke of my own. Why

does the chicken have a one-inch wee-wee?

Wee-wee? Jim asked. You mean ...?

Uh, yeah. Uh, penis.

You mean cock!

Um – yeah.

Beats me.

To get to the other side!

Nobody got it.

In Upper Darby Junior High School, erections were known as boners and were a popular topic of conversation after we caught on that they could be used in several ways, some highly enjoyable. Mine popped up in the bathtub and helped to break the Saturday night monotony. A few of my friends were slow to understand what was happening to them, and Wally Pheth asked his mother to take him to the emergency room. When George Whitefield inquired about boners, Billy G told him they were for opening cans. Billy was the first to discover that if you looked at the statue of William Penn atop City Hall at the right angle, he had a giant wee-wee.

Our thirteen-year-old smart set bestowed a new name on Miss Bonner, an eighth grade teacher. After Mrs. Varro's bloomers fell down while she was delivering a lecture on the Roman Umpire, she was subjected to so many giggles that she moved to Rhode Island.

Mr. Koch's name caused paroxysms of suppressed laughter, and no one dared mention the school secretary, Miss Kunstler.

Sometime between the eighth and ninth grades, we boys began our fixations on words like *whore, snatch, courtesan, dildo, prostitute, concubine, tit, harlot, pussy, strumpet,* and *slut* as they insinuated themselves into our vocabularies one by one. It was quite a job to keep up.

John Dixon told us what *merkin* meant and said he knew a teacher who wore one.

Billy Glossop said, I know her. She isn't bowlegged. She's pleasure-bent.

Tommy Farnaby put in, She only screws her friends and she has no enemies. I didn't understand every nuance of the discussion. To that point I'd had only two or three sexual adventures in my life, none involving another human being. But I read a lot. Copies of dirty magazines were in wide circulation, especially in the boys room. Every story featured half-dressed females. Pornographic comic books were a step up (or down). One showed Mickey Mouse with a ten-inch penis. Another depicted 'tilie the Toiler in sexual congress with Rin Tin Tin. Blondie appeared on her knees doing something to Dagwood that no confirmed member of Grace Evangelical Lutheran Church of Drexel Hill would dream of doing. Jeez, Buttsy O'Neal said, how can he ever respect her? In English class Billy Glossop whispered, How now, fellatio? Luckily his voice didn't carry beyond me and Jim Shay and Lulu Abernethy. I was the only one who knew it was from *Hamlet*.

In after-school discussions there was a lot of hopeful chatter about "fast" girls. I was never certain who was fast and who wasn't and which girls did it and which girls didn't, but it made no difference because I was still a little uncertain about exactly what they did when they did it. On the rare occasions when I was allowed out after dark, I engaged in a little window-peeping to augment my sexual knowledge. Our Taylor Avenue Lorelei was a 300-pounder named Mrs. Candice Lull, who left her shades up when she undressed and gave two performances every Saturday night. As I watched her gyrate out of her clothes, I often found it hard to determine whether I was looking at a large bust or a small heinie.

It didn't take long for most of my pals to become masters of masturbation, but I lagged behind. I just couldn't make it work. Billy said I probably wasn't my type. On the plus side, I wouldn't go blind. I responded to girls in a vacant moony way. I was the far extreme from our class sex maniac, the dentist's son who got a boner from looking at a cricket's leg through a microscope. His father diagnosed him with *penile dementia*. John Dennis admitted that he had a wet dream every night and sometimes while watching girls' basketball. Jack Nokes spent hours in his attic, tracing comic strip pictures which he then altered to show Smilin' Jack and his D-Icers in *flagrante delicto* on an airplane wing, or the Dragon Lady taking on three members of the crew of a junk. In our lewd comic books, homemade or not, spurting semen appeared as tear-shaped globules of a size that might have been emitted by woolly mammoths.

I was glad I didn't have to explain stained sheets to my mother. When the wet dreams finally started, they didn't measure up to the comic books and convinced me that I would never have children.[48]

17.

One teacher towered above the others at UDJHS. Our general science teacher, Vaughn Smith, was a spellbinding lecturer who held our attention even though he constantly inveighed against smoking, pinball, gambling, candy, reading comic books on Sunday, and just about everything else that made a kid's life worthwhile. He was supposed to be introducing us to biology, physics, and chemistry, but he believed it was his duty to witness for Christ, as he put it. In his lectures, Mr. Smith made frequent connections between the laws of science and the Bible even though the school board had advised him to ease and desist. On the last day before each Christmas vacation, no school board on earth could keep him from delivering his own

---

48   At last count I'd had eight.

Sermon on the Mount and trying to convince his students that every word of Genesis was literally true and evolutionists simply didn't understand science.

Nevertheless Mr. Smith was universally admired. The classroom was his stage and he could make a topic like precipitation as dramatic as a fight between Flash Gordon and Ming the Merciless. He was unrelentingly dramatic. If he spotted jaw movement by a female student, he would stop in mid-sentence, throw his arms wide and intone:

The gum-chewing girl and the cud-chewing cow
They're different, but I don't know how.

Mr. Smith didn't seem to mind gum-chewing males, but he was impatient with smart-aleck boys. One day he was describing how farmers repelled moles by sprinkling carbon disulfide around their holes when Roscoe Bardi raised his hand and asked, How do you catch the moles?

Catch them? Mr. Smith asked.

Yeah. So you can put that stuff in their holes.

Mr. Smith's handwritten note informed Roscoe's parents that their son could benefit from a little memory work, perhaps two or three chapters from the Old Testament.

Both parents signed and returned the letter, and from then on Roscoe was on his best behavior even though he could hardly utter a sentence without using the word *begat*.

The rest of us boys kept trying to see how hard we could push. Billy G had always been good at disguising Aw shit! as a sneeze. He fooled Mr. Smith the first time, but on his second attempt Mr. Smith gave him twenty-four hours to copy First Chronicles.

When Billy turned it in, Mr. Smith pointed out that he'd misspelled *Zophrah*. This isn't *Mrs. Godey's Lady's Book*, he told Bill in front of the class. This is – the Bible. The Word of God. Master Glossop, I want perfect copies of First and Second

Chronicles by tomorrow.

After he checked Billy's work the next day, he peered over his lectern and said, Feeling better? No sneezing today?

It was foolish to try to put one over on Vaughn Smith. As he reminded us from time to time, he had five thousand years of science on his side.

18.

I began my freshman year in September, 1938, a year younger than most of my classmates and still a few miles outside of the social loop. I was thirteen, Carolyn had just turned eleven, Mother was thirty-two, and Daddy forty-eight. The "Roosevelt Depression" seemed to be ending, but the recovery was slow to reach our block. We were still going without dessert and wearing worn-out clothes and puttering around in a rackety old sedan that backfired and made poor Mr. Bruner run for the byberry bushes (or "the rear echelons," as he called them).

In my heart I was convinced that our family had never belonged in Drexel Hill, that we were imposters who would be run out of the neighborhood just as we'd been run out of Highland Park. We were hanging on by avoiding creditors, by stealing and lying, and if we ever had to pay the piper, we would be on our way to Jersey City to sponge off the honest poor again. There was no point in fooling myself.

Just before Christmas Mother and Daddy got into a big fight. She told him that she was tired of hiding from bill collectors and had applied for an evening job at the LaRitz Bakery.

Daddy yelled that this would make him look bad. What'll the Remingers think? What'll the Bruners think? What'll I tell 'em at the club?

Mother said, You can tell them your wife needs a new hat.

Daddy stayed away from the house for two days. When he returned, he said he'd slept at the Media Athletic Club. He said he was ashamed to be seen on Taylor Avenue. A week later he stayed out all night again and explained that he'd broken a tie rod coming back from Doylestown and had slept in the car. Mother said, I wouldn't be surprised.

With both our parents working, Carolyn and I would be coming home to an empty house for the first time in our lives. Take care of Sissy, Mother instructed me before her first day of work at the bakery. Act like the man of the house.

It was an interesting challenge for a week or so, but after a while the charm was gone. My sister wasn't a baby, but one day I came home from school to find her sobbing.

Where's Mother? she kept saying. I want Mother! I felt like crying myself.

At first we would find our dinner in the refrigerator with instructions on how to heat it up, but we never seemed to get it right. The liver came off the griddle looking like an arch support; the bacon crackled, sizzled, and caught fire; the canned corn turned into birdshot. One night Sis refused to eat a Salisbury steak just because it looked like a raw wound in the middle.

I yelled, Put mustard on it!

Mustard gives me gas!

We all got gas! What're you, the Queen of Sheba?

A few nights later I got into an overtime table tennis match in Johnny Reminger's basement and forgot that I'd left Mother's ham-and-rice casserole in the oven. Three units responded from the Garrettford Volunteer Fire Department and soaked everything in the kitchen, including Daddy's Media A.C. lumber jacket and an angel food cake Mother had baked for a church bazaar.

When our parents realized that the dining arrangements weren't working out, they started giving us a dollar and a half a day for a hot supper at a family restaurant six blocks away. For a few nights I dined on chocolate whipped cream pie, chocolate cake and chocolate milk, with chocolate ice cream for dessert. Sis ordered from the menu and warned that I was ruining a good thing for both of us, but I was in the grip of chocolate lunacy, a lifelong problem. Even after I began ordering balanced meals, I would eat her dessert on the grounds that sweets weren't good for girls and I was now the man of the house and if she caught malnutrition, I would be blamed.

In the late thirties most families dressed for dinner at home and everyone dressed to eat out. That meant coat and tie for me, a nice dress for Carolyn, and hats for both. Each evening we arrived at Dugan's Home Cooking looking like the top of a wedding cake. After a few days the waiter began giving us funny looks. I would see him standing just inside the kitchen door with the cook, glancing our way and talking behind his hand.

I didn't understand. He'd been respectful and so had Sis and I. As we entered, he would say, Will it be three for dinner, sir? (Sis insisted on dragging along a doll.) In turn, I'd always been polite and friendly to the waiter. I would ask, What's on the dinner? When he served our portions, I would observe that one must be good. I would make comments like: An end slice, please, my good man. May I have a touch more wooster sauce?

Since I still had trouble with percentages, I always left a dime. Better too much than too little. Sis and I had been patronizing the restaurant for almost two weeks when the waiter followed us out on the street. Excuse me, sir, he said, but ... the missus left her gloves.

19.

After Mother's second month on the bakery job, I came downstairs to find her sitting in the kitchen clenching a dishrag. Daddy was on another trip – his absences now lasted longer – and every responsibility was falling on Mother, including bussing me to the credit dentist, bussing Sis to the doctor, working every night at the bakery, and running the house.

I'm okay, Jackie, she said in answer to my look. Just a little tired is all.

We chatted for a while, and I suggested that she take a day off from the bakery. She said, We need the money more than I need a day off. We owe everybody.

She sighed and went upstairs. No one in our family ever said Good night. Until Sis and I were in high school, we were expected to give our parents a bedtime peck on the cheek, but we'd fallen out of the habit.

Sitting at the kitchen table staring at the back of the Wheaties box, I remembered the lump that had stuck in my throat as I sat on Mother's hospital bed after her quinsy surgery. I hoped she wasn't getting sick again. I had no way to get her to the hospital.

I tried to imagine life without Mother. It would be tough enough without Daddy, but without Mother I would curl up and die. I noticed that she'd left her apron hanging over the chair. I sniffed cinnamon buns and bread and wondered whatever happened to her cologne. Baked goods smelled nice, but they were no match for Evening in Paris.

Mother was in the bathroom when I went upstairs, and I slipped into her bedroom to check on the cobalt blue flask. It was in its usual place in the carved wooden box. I remembered how I used to stare at that bottle as a little boy and how it made me pick blue as my favorite color. I touched the bottle and noticed that the crystal stopper was loose.

The flask was dry. How long had Mother been out of cologne? I guessed it was just one more of the luxuries we could no longer afford, along with tapioca pudding, butterscotch pie, ginger ale, and Hap's ice cream. How I missed her lovely smell.

On Sunday I helped collect the offering at church and then joined two other Luther League boys to separate the money in Pastor Wallick's sacristy. Two envelopes were provided for our parishioners: one for donations to our church and the other for Missouri Synod missions. The envelopes were numbered for identification, and we checked off the amounts as we put the money, mostly coins, in a cashbox in the center of the table.

The count was nearly finished when I opened an envelope and pulled out a brand new five-dollar bill. Pastor Wallick was still changing behind the curtain. The Luther League boys were lollygagging. In one unplanned unthinking moment I slipped the envelope into my pocket.

At home I locked the bathroom door and examined my take. It was the biggest haul of my life and by far my most serious crime, but I wasn't worried since I intended to repay the loan as soon as my lawn-mowing business got in gear. The church treasurer need never know about his generosity. I flushed the envelope and went shopping.

The next morning Daddy and I were sitting in the kitchen when Mother came downstairs in her robe. It was such a treat to see her smile.

Ole, she said, did you hit the number?

Daddy looked surprised.

I just noticed it, she said.

Noticed what?

The cologne.

I caught the scent. The smell made me five years old again, burying my nose in her fur coat.

It didn't take long for my smirk to give me away. Daddy said, You little bugger! Where'd you get that kinda dough?

I said, I saved up.

Mother said, Three-ninety-five? It must've taken you ....
Months, I said.
They agreed that they were raising a fine young man.

20.

At thirteen going on fourteen I was spending much of my time
at Raymond's Pharmacy on Garrett Road. It was a five-minute
walk from home and in the middle of a row of shops that had
barely survived the worst of the Depression. Uncle Sam's offered cleaning and pressing and a thimble of arak for special
customers. On summer days beads of sweat formed on Uncle
Sam's hairy chest as cumulus clouds poured out his door. We
would spot him in the middle of the steam, smiling and singing under an American flag that covered half a wall. He was
an Armenian emigre who turned into a super-American like
my great-grandfather Zawadzki. After Fourth of July fireworks,
Uncle Sam would drape himself in red-white-and-blue bun-
ting and run up and down the alley firing his revolver. A stray
bullet pierced a neighbor's bathroom wall and just missed his
young daughter. When the Township police arrived, Uncle
Sam explained, I boom my gun! I happy! I American! Then he
shot out the streetlight.

A mystery man was developing a mystery product in a
storefront lab next to Uncle Sam's. He seemed convinced that
we were out to steal his formula, and if we idled too long in
front of his store he would run us off. We soon learned to hurry
past and look the other way.

There was also a two-chair barber shop, a deli, O'Donnell's
bar, Mary's Laundry ("Don't kill your wife. Let us do your dirty
work"), and a meat market that offered scrapple, Philadelphia's
contribution to the redistribution of inedible animal parts.

Raymond's Pharmacy, crown jewel of our little Cannery Row, occupied a choice spot in the middle. I first noticed how sharp Doc Raymond was when my pal Tommy Frasch and I worked the old telephone prank on him: Do you got Prince Albert in the can?

The next time I saw Doc, he said, Thanks for the call. You saved the prince's life.

I went back home, muffled my voice, and tried another old standard: Is this Raymond's Pharmacy on Garrett Road? Well, you better get off. A car's coming.

That evening Doc said, Thanks, son. We got off the road just in time.

Doc seemed to know what made boys laugh – he had a son of his own, a handsome blond kid named Sidney who worked alongside his father after school and rode the family horse into a lather on his afternoons off. Sid was quiet, but Doc was always good for a laugh. He would buttonhole you at the door and say, Why do bees hum? Because they don't know the words! When we ordered a chocolate bar, he would ask, Male or female? Doc told me and Tommy Frasch about the man who scratched his crotch while ordering a sundae.

Doc asked the guy, Crushed nuts? The man said, Nope, shot off in the war. That was our level of humor, and Doc's, too.

Upper Darby's biggest assortment of penny candy was on glorious display in Doc's glass case. A bagful, a day's supply, went for a dime. Doc's jawbreakers were the size of ping-pong balls; the layers changed color down to a white core that tasted like Sen-Sen. He sold ropes of black and red licorice, sourballs, molasses taffy and saltwater taffy, Jujubes, peppermint sticks, black licorice pipes, chewing-wax tubes filled with colored syrup, candy cigarettes with red tips, bubble gum, false teeth made of chewing wax, candy corn, popcorn balls, jelly beans, sugar candies shaped like unhusked peanuts, Hershey's kisses in their silver jackets, fudge, malted milk balls and horehound drops that he told us he kept in stock "for the surgical stocking set."

In an era when most merchants were content to lock up and go home demoralized, Doc had the energy and flair of the dedicated artist. He stocked everything from wind-up toys to ladies' hose to pencil sharpeners to "rocket" baseballs to shaving lotion, colognes and lipsticks. Doc's was the only place in Delaware County where a kid could buy Bangsite, the powder that made our Johnson Smith cannons explode like Black Tom. It was the only place where you could buy a Trip to the Moon game and replacement pieces. Doc prided himself on offering the thickest milk shakes in Delaware County – ten cents for regular, seventeen for large – beaten to icy perfection on his green Hamilton Beach mixer.

He insisted on making his chocolate shakes with vanilla ice cream. When I asked why, he explained, The vanilla makes it fluff. Mix chocolate ice cream and chocolate syrup and whattaya got? Chocolate milk. You can get that from the milkman.

Doc's soda fountain consisted of five spin-top stools and a slab of gray marble. The faucets produced a steady flow of seltzer or a needle spray that put the head on ice cream sodas. In a back room he concocted hot fudge, butterscotch, and other syrups and sauces and nine flavors of ice cream. He decanted vanilla beans in sherry instead of grain alcohol to produce a different flavor. He used pure malt, not the synthetic Hemo that some of the drugstores were offering. If you bought a shake or a sundae at Doc's, you were served a paper cup of pretzels just to prove that his heart was still in the South Philly neighborhood where he'd grown up.

I used to lurk in a corner of Raymond's Pharmacy that was devoted to Megow's airplane and ship models and the makings. Kits for the Sopwith Camel, Luscombe Phantom, and Spad with a ten-inch wingspan cost a dime; larger planes like the

Douglas Airliner, Fokker Triplanes, and Martin Bomber went for a quarter. Doc carried a lumberyard of balsa, plus wheels, wire, rubberband motors, glue, dope, paper to cover fuselages, decals, propellers, wheel pants, airplane paint. The corner smelled like banana oil.[49]

Across from the models was Doc's circulating library, four shelves of books that he rented out for a nickel a day, three days for a dime. I was an avid reader long before we moved to Drexel Hill, having devoured the Tom Swift series by Victor Appleton, all twelve volumes of the Boy Scout adventure series by Herbert Carter, and a couple of hundred Big Little Books and comic books on Tailspin Tommy, Clyde Beatty's Lions and Tigers, Secret Agent X-9, Tarzan, Chester Gump, Red Ryder, "Mickey Mouse the Mail Pilot," Little Orphan Annie, Dick Tracy, *Treasure Island*, "Frank Merriwell at Yale," "Joe Louis the Brown Bomber," Popeye and the Shadow, plus the CocomaIt Big Book of Comics, and other anthologies. But Doc's lending library elevated my tastes. He talked me into renting works like *The Nazarene* by Sholem Asch, *Christ in Concrete* by Pietro DiDonato, *The Stargazer* by Zsolt de Harshany, *Kitty Foyle* by Christopher Morley, *How Green Was My Valley* by Richard Llewellyn.

One day he handed me a book and said, She wrote this for kids like you.

I stayed up past midnight reading *The Yearling* by Marjorie Kinnan Rawlings by flashlight. When I admitted that the ending made me cry, Doc refused my nickel. 'Til you grow up a little, he advised, maybe you better skip the endings.

Raymond's Pharmacy had four booths by a plate-glass window, a magazine stand, a photo booth and a pay phone that

---

49   During World War II, I took flight instruction in an Army L-2, a fabric-covered Taylorcraft with an 85-horsepower engine. The first time I entered the hangar, I was instantly transported to the northwest corner of Raymond's Pharmacy.

I liked to flush for hanging coins. My biggest take was eight quarters and a dime – evidently someone had tried to call Siam.

The closest Doc ever came to offering a gambling device was a big glass case containing a miniature crane and a junk-pile of prizes ranging from fake jewelry to Ronson lighters. I watched as a man went through a stack of nickels on an attempt to collect a cigarette case. After he kicked the machine and left, Doc said, I don't blame the guy. You couldn't pick up that case with a derrick.

The next day the machine was gone.

Raymond's was the last local drugstore to install a pinball machine, and it didn't take long for some of us to get the bug. Doc confided that some of my friends were spending more money than they could afford and he was thinking of returning the machine. Other pharmacies lured kids by paying off in nickels instead of free games, but Doc preserved his machine's amateur standing. We kids lined up to lose ourselves in the jangles and whirrrrs and clunk-bang-zing-crash-ding-ding-ding-ding when we racked up free games. Pushbutton flippers were a few years away, but we learned how to goose the machine and drive the steel ball upward to register more points.[50] Too light a touch had no effect, too heavy produced a klaxon-like noise and a blinking sign that said "tilt" and brought Doc around the corner from his drug counter to see if Harry LeBoyne was running up free games again by shoving a wire under the glass.

I never needed a wire. It seldom cost me more than a dime or fifteen cents to win enough free games for an afternoon's diversion. Boys gathered to admire my skill: big boys, little boys, boys I liked, boys I disliked, boys who'd bullied or insulted me,

---

50   This technique was called *jostling* (pronounced jozzeling) and I later perfected it at the University of Pennsylvania, where I was considered unofficial pinball champion by me and Florencio Martin, a Puerto Rican girl I was seeing. Unfortunately the university's athletic department neglected to keep records.

boys who owed me money and vice versa, all sorts of boys, and I was the king of Doc's pinball machine and no argument about it. Until I discovered bowling, it was the high point of my athletic career.

21.

For a long time I rationalized that Doc was to blame for my worst fall from grace and it wasn't my fault. As I learned later, this was the typical excuse of lawbreakers. I told myself that the fudge bars had been too big a temptation; Doc shouldn't have introduced them to his customers in a little pyramid right out there on top of the counter. He kept most of his candy behind glass, but the bars were there for the taking: three or four ounces of rich fudge coated with a crust of dark chocolate in a perfect example of sensory overkill. How could I resist?

I couldn't.

I spaced my thefts two or three days apart. Somehow the pyramid remained intact, so I figured Doc was replenishing the display. I fully intended to pay him back right after I repaid the five dollars I'd borrowed from Grace Evangelical Lutheran Church.

Late one afternoon I was sitting at the counter, turning the pages of a comic book and reaching inch by inch toward the fudge bars with my free hand. Just as I snatched the prize, I spotted a pair of eyes peering at me from behind the stacks of Meow's models. Doc shook his head almost imperceptibly. Then he backed out of sight.

For weeks I hung around our house listening for sirens. I tried to build a new social life around other neighborhood drugstores, but it was impossible. Doc Hahn had the personality of a tomcod, Doc McCollum was a grump, and Doc Stroup would let a kid wait fifteen minutes before taking his order. None of them had pinball machines or malts like Doc's or sold a scrap of airplane model material.

After a month I screwed up my courage and returned to Doc's. Maybe he hadn't seen me; maybe I was a victim of my own overactive imagination. I'd no sooner entered than Doc ushered me behind the pharmacy counter and beckoned me to a seat in front of shelves of pills, powders, and a couple of stoppered glass flasks containing brightly colored liquids. Framed diplomas affirmed that Henry Raymond held degrees in chemistry and pharmacology. There was a picture of his pretty red-haired wife Kathryn.

In a low voice Doc told me that he'd always considered me a cut above most boys.

You're college material, he said. I can tell by the books you rent. You're as bright as my son Sidney.

I took that as a high compliment. Then he switched to ancient history. He said I wasn't the only kid who liked sweets and he'd suffered the same temptations as a boy.

Some of his high school classmates had turned to crime and ruined their lives. A childhood friend was stabbed to death in a gang fight. Two others were in Eastern State Pen. Doc said, Listen to me, son. Prison begins with a candy bar.

He said he'd known all along that I was stealing and asked what he should do about it.

I said I would pay him back if he would just let me off.

He said, You'll never learn anything that way.

After a few minutes of silence, he picked up the phone and said, What should I tell your parents?

I didn't know what to say. Daddy was barely bringing home food money. The rent was three months behind. Our Keystone phone had been yanked, and creditors made threatening calls on the Bell. What a blow it would be to him and Mother to learn that while they'd been struggling to raise their kids in a nice neighborhood, their son became a master criminal.

Doc's fingers hovered over the telephone. I made up my mind I wouldn't cry.

Thirteen was too old to be acting like a girl. The overhead light glinted off his rimless glasses.

He said, How many bars did you hook?

I dunno, Doc. Maybe ... four.

I'm short six.

Yeah, maybe six.

Tell the truth, son. Otherwise we're wasting our time.

I wasn't lying, Doc. I, uh ... I don't remember.

Then I realized: you were lying. You're lying right now. What a jerk. You belong in the pen.

He asked what else I'd stolen.

Nothing, I said.

In your whole life?

No.

I left out the five bucks from church. And the chocolate-covered Graham crackers at the Highland Park A&P. And all the swag in Jersey City. I promised myself that if Doc let me off, I would repay every penny with interest.

He pushed the phone aside and said, You'll make good on the candy?

Yes, sir, Doc.

That's six bars at a nickel each.

Right, Doc. Thirty cents.

You'll keep your hands in your pocket?

I nodded. He gave me such an intense stare that I had to look away. He said, Do I have your word?

I thought, After he catches me stealing and lying, he's willing to take my word? I promised and we shook hands. He handed me a paper bag and said, Run this prescription around the corner to Mrs. Lutz. It should've been there an hour ago.

When I returned from Berry Avenue, he opened the candy case and reached toward the Hershey bars. This'll seal the deal, he said. Male or female? I saved my lunch money and paid him back in a week.

–

22.

With summer came the yells and yowls of boys playing baseball on a dozen vacant lots. In the years before World War Two, empty lots were so common in Upper Darby that we used them for tennis courts, vegetable gardens, trash dumps, dog runs, football fields, and neighborhood carnivals and fireworks. There were so many vacant lots in Drexel Hill that many of them went unused, populated only by insects and birds and crisscrossed by boys on their way to play ball in another vacant lot.

In those pre-war years a body of pseudo-scientific thought held that curve balls were an optical illusion and there was no such thing as a drop, inshoot, outshoot, sinker, or screwball. In my case, the theory was correct. Lying in bed at night after listening to a ballgame on my Bakelite Philco, I would do a mental inventory of my pitches. I reassured myself that I had at least ten, counting the spitball. But when Johnny Reminger put on his first baseman's mitt to play catch with me in the vacant lot at Taylor and Morgan Avenue, all my pitches went straight. I twisted my bony wrist to produce a curve ball, but it went straight. I twisted my wrist the opposite way, like Carl Hubbell, and the ball went straight.

I pressed my knuckles against the cowhide to produce a fluttery gasping pitch that would defy all batters, and it went straight. In those days every major league pitcher's repertoire included a "slow ball" to keep batters off balance. I had that pitch down pat.

The terrible truth was that at thirteen I was still an imitation pitcher. I was a pitcher because I said I was a pitcher, because I'd once owned spikes with a pitcher's toeplate, and because my father had been a pitcher. Otherwise I was barely a ballplayer, let alone a pitcher. I was still the shortest kid around, and when we chose up sides, I was usually selected last and assigned to right field, where I would do glissades and pirouettes under fly balls. If there'd been a field to the right of right field, that's where they would have assigned me. If we weren't always short a few players, I wouldn't have been chosen at all.

Parents seldom appeared at our baseball games and didn't waste their free time teaching their sons how to take two and hit to right. Daddy and I had an occasional game of catch, but he had a tendency to overpower me, even though his injury caused him to pitch with a herky-jerky motion that didn't seem to involve the muscles below his waist. He still had plenty of steam. When he pitched to me, he would shake his hand in a little arc if he intended to throw a curve. One evening toward dusk he forgot to signal and the pitch broke my nose. That was our last catch. From then on, Daddy seemed disheartened by baseball. It was as though the Detroit Tigers, the All-Phillies, All-Nations, and his sandlot teams hadn't existed, as though he were angry at baseball and baseball were angry at him.

In the end, that might not have been far from the truth.

In Drexel Hill, our preparations for each baseball season began an hour or two after the last patch of dirty snow melted away, usually in late February or early March. None of us boys on Burley Lane, Burmont and Garrett Roads, Ferue Boulevard and Taylor Avenue had to be told to start taping up bats and balls.

The most important part of our preparation was rubbing neatsfoot oil into our gloves. Daddy had worked the old neatsfoot joke on me when I was seven or eight. He brought home a bottle of yellowish fluid and said, This is for your mitt, Sonny. Just a drop or two. Remember, a lotta neats died for this.

How many? I asked in horror.

Lemme see, he said, holding the bottle to the light. I guess a dozen.

I had nightmares about poor little neats being torn from their mother's breasts to have their feet amputated and spend the rest of their lives crawling on their bellies just so I could keep my glove soft. I asked Daddy if I could use Three-in-One oil instead. He frowned and said that players who didn't use neatsfoot oil were bush.

Most of the empty lots where we kids played baseball were surrounded by houses and streets. If a ball cleared the outfield fence, it would often roll into the front yard of some grouch on wheels who had buckets of confiscated balls in her basement. So our first rule was: Over the fence is out. We rarely had more than one game ball, which consisted of a grass-stained cowhide cover over some thread wrapped around a cork center and enclosed in friction tape. Some of those projectiles weighed a pound and produced sore arms that quarts of Sloan's Liniment couldn't relieve.

Our over-the-fence-is-out rule presented a psychological problem for heavy hitters.

If they held back on their swing, the ball might roll to the fence for a triple, but it also might be caught. If they hit it over the fence, they were out. Our best hitters strode to the plate in a confused frame of mind, and some of them switched to track, pinochle, and psychotherapy.

23.

Just up the hill from Raymond's Pharmacy, Garrett Road petered out and turned into a ghost subdivision – a windblown grid of empty streets and unfinished driveways with weeds growing through cracks in the cement. Doc told me the project was a developer's pipedream that turned to a nightmare in the '29 crash. Off to one side was Mrs. Hasselman's riding academy where energetic boys could saddle up and ride old swaybacks in return for mucking out their stalls. As in most juvenile transactions of the era, no money changed hands.

I worked a few shifts at the stables 'til I began to notice that Mrs. Hasselman always assigned me to Dolly, a spavined old mare with a bad reputation. Dolly seemed to require that her riders weigh at least one hundred pounds; if not, she didn't feel disposed to leave the paddock. I got the feeling that she was saying to herself, Are you up there? Is anybody up there? Go 'way, ya bodda me!

If Mrs. Hasselman smacked Dolly's rump to goad her into motion, the sly old mare had another trick up her withers. Halfway around the track her girth would start to slip and I would be riding sideways. To her credit, Dolly always stopped and waited for me to extricate myself before she gave an insolent twitch of her tail and trotted back to her stall.

Two such incidents were sufficient for me, and I abandoned my equestrian career.[51]

Over the hill from Mrs. Hasselman's stables, the ground sloped to a polluted stream that we kids knew as Darby Crick. It wasn't long before I was drawn to the rushing water as I'd been drawn to Naylor's Run, Cobbs Creek, New York Bay, and

---

51 Sixty years later I was relating my riding misadventures to a childhood friend from Drexel Hill. He said, Oh, you mean Dolly! He'd learned how to counter her trick. When she was being saddled, the sly mare would puff out her stomach so the girth would work loose. My friend learned to punch her in the stomach and simultaneously tighten the strap.

the Hackensack River.

Maybe my watery urge had something to do with seven brothers who'd lived on an island off Denmark.

On a Sunday afternoon I hiked a half-mile down Rosemont Avenue to an old stone bridge and found myself in a streamside village that didn't resemble Drexel Hill in any way.

A stone basin collected water bubbling from a pipe in the earth, and a sign on a small building advertised "Beaver Springs, bottle water for sale." I wondered why anyone would pay for water when they could fill their own containers for free. As I wondered, a car pulled up and a man filled some gallon jugs. I decided that the Beaver Springs bottling company had probably failed in the Depression and left its pipe open as an act of kindness.

Just across the bridge a group of men pitched horseshoes on a patch of level land above the creek bank. One had a twirly moustache, another wore farmer's overalls, and another was barefoot and kept hitching up his denims. As I watched, a fourth man spat a stream of tobacco and took a swig from a bottle. They were all built like sticks. Words like *goddamn* and *son of a bitch* wafted to my ears. I decided to continue downstream on the Drexel Hill side.

After a quarter mile I came to a bend in Darby Creek and an abandoned mill covered with ivy and moss. Two fat sunfish finned in a pool behind a low stone dam. An algae-tinted raceway sluiced an ebb of water toward a wooden wheel that hung loose on its axle. A pond was ringed with cattails and coated with a soupy-green scum. A frog croaked and hopped out of sight. I looked into a dry well and saw the hairless carcass of a cat thirty feet down. Somewhere in the distance a red-winged blackbird rang a doorbell. Everything lay in the shadow of locusts, maples, sycamores, and other trees.

I parted some weeds and wriggled through a broken window into a cavernous room with a saggy floor that looked ready to drop into the foundations. In the faint purple light I saw marks where equipment had been bolted to the floor. The air smelled moldy. I wondered what the mill had been milling when its waterwheel made its last turn. There were no clues on the empty floor.

I spotted a tiny office in a far corner. A webbed canopy covered a gas fixture; my touch destroyed it, and the remains floated to the floor like cigarette ash.[52] I peeked inside a half-open wall safe and found a pay register showing that Lobb, Kelly, and Potter had earned four dollars each for a week's work. It was undated, but the handwriting was flowing and old-fashioned, a little like my father's.

I was sitting on my haunches turning the pages when I heard a sound. A short bearded man appeared in the greenish light that filtered down from the wooded hillside to an open door. He held something that looked like a rifle or shotgun.

Get outa there, he said.

I was too scared to move.

He said, Get out now!

I weighed my choices. I could try to reason with him, or I could sprint across the weakened floor and do a jackknife out the window, probably breaking a few bones in the process.

As I inched toward him, I said, Don't shoot me, mister. I was just ... looking around. I didn't take nothing.

There's nothing to take! You goddamn brats stole us blind. Get outa here before I call the cops.

He gestured toward the door with the rifle. Apparently my freedom depended on running past him. At the door he raised the gun and knocked me down with one blow. His rifle turned out to be a crutch. As he stood over me I saw that he was old

---

52 I learned later that it was something called a Wellsbach mantle, designed to glow white-hot in a gas flame and increase illumination.

and bald, maybe fifty-five or sixty. One eye was a reddish slit and his mouth was a dark hole.

He raised his weapon again as I scrambled out the door. I ran toward a narrow uphill trail and passed a stone hut with the door open. I couldn't imagine what he was watching or who hired him. Maybe chasing kids was his hobby. Maybe he'd lost his eye in a mill accident and couldn't get another job. Maybe the job kept him from being bored. I didn't stop to inquire.

Just before I reached the rim of the Darby Creek gulch and Mrs. Hasselman's riding ring, I burst through a patch of rhododendrons and saw a rock quarry. Marks in the stone showed where workers had pried big stone slabs from the wall and cut them to size on the quarry floor. A half-loaded wagon with a broken tongue stood next to a hand-lettered sign: No Dumping. Trash and junk stood six feet high.

I knew I would never return to the mill. But the quarry was tempting.

24.

Before my first class on Monday morning I asked my homeroom teacher, Mr. Brown, if he knew anything about a mill near the bottom of Rosemont Avenue. He said that a member of the faculty was studying the history of Darby Creek and planned to write a book. Go see Miss Morley, he said. I'll give you a hall pass.

I said, Not, uh ... Miss Morley? I could feel the blood drain from my face. Christine Morley had become school disciplinarian after our principal, Mr. Wallace Savage, proved too kind-hearted. Miss Morley had no such problem. As assistant principal she turned mischievous boys into quivering blobs of Jello. She was a slight woman with a prune face and graying hair that she wore in a tight bun. Rimless glasses magnified points of light that glittered like ice crystals in her eyes. If she ever smiled, it must have been in private. She didn't use instruments of torture, raise her voice, or lift a hand. Her favorite question was: Do you have anything between your ears or are you as stupid as you look?

So far in the school year, only one of my close friends had been ordered to Miss Morley's snakepit. Jim Shay had been overheard reciting a poem in the boy's room:

> Mary Mary quite contrary
> How does your garden grow?
> With silver bells and cockleshells
> And one goddamn petunia.

After his session with Miss Morley, Jim didn't return to class. He said he had to go home to change his clothes.[53]

That's okay, I told Mr. Brown. I don't need to know about the mill.

Scared of Miss Morley?

Who the heck isn't?

She's actually a very nice lady.

So's the Dragon Lady, I said.

Tell Miss Morley I sent you, he said as he scribbled out a hall pass. You'll thank me.

I shook my head. How did I get myself into a situation where I had to see the nastiest teacher in the Upper Darby School System and I hadn't done anything wrong?

Mr. Brown: Go! You want to find out about the mill, don't you?

No.

He nudged me out the door.

---

53 Two years later, as a senior in high school, 240-pound Jim Shay was named All-State football tackle. He told me that every time he set up at the line of scrimmage, he saw Miss Morley's face.

I knocked at the torture chamber, and a thin voice said, Come in.

I opened the door and found myself in a small office as warm and inviting as a casket. Stand up straight! Miss Morley snapped. Who sent you?

Mr. Brown.

Mr. Brown? Nice Mr. Brown?

I kept shifting my weight from one foot to the other. Stand still! she snapped.

It's the old mill, I blurted out. The one at Darby Creek. The one....

Which old mill? Be specific.

I thought I saw a softer look come over Miss Morley at the mention of the word "mill." When I said I was referring to the one at the end of Rosemont Avenue, she beckoned me to a chair and asked, Why do you want to know?

I was inside the other day. By accident. It's just — it's, uh — interesting. A man hit me with a crutch.

After that, I could hardly get a word in. I learned that early in the 17th Century, Dutch adventurers had dropped anchor in the Delaware River below the present site of Philadelphia, poled through the Tinicum swamps and rowed up a creek that the Lenni Lenape Indians called Mukruton. The first explorers were followed by waves of Swedes and then some homesick Englishmen who renamed the creek Darby.

Miss Morley described Addingham, the village along the creek, as a collection of abandoned mills and stone houses inhabited by the descendants of a water-power culture that went back a dozen generations to immigrant weavers, cord-winders, papermakers, spinners, and ordinary laborers.

Did you see the Swedish cabin? she asked. It was built in the 1600s.

No, ma'am.

Don't be so lazy the next time. Walk a little farther down-stream.

Miss Morley told me that early grist mills had used Darby Creek waterpower to grind wheat, rye corn, and buckwheat into flour. Bolting mills sifted the flour from the grist mills. Slitting mills made nails. Blade mills turned out scythes, axes, cleavers. Oil mills squeezed linseed oil from flax. Fulling mills spun cotton into yarn, and carding mills combed the yarn into cloth. For a hundred years the Tuscorara milled paper, cardboard, and finally cotton. Darby Creek mills like the Bee Hive operated even earlier, some in the 1700s.[54] The New Caledonia had so many workers they fielded their own baseball team.

Miss Morley explained that the original Addingham was a village in England; a few locals still spoke with a trace of a Yorkshire accent. Once there'd been forty stone tenement houses along the creek. One old building had been pressed into use as an insane asylum. Steam power had put most of Darby Creek's mills out of business and stranded the workers and their families. Some remained, as suspicious of outsiders as West Virginia mountaineers.

Miss Morley warned me to stay clear of Addingham boys. They seemed to regard every inch of land around Darby Creek as their personal property, deeded by God in perpetuity. They used visitors for target practice. Their warrior chief was a head-strong young man named Delos "Tut" Culver, who'd lost an arm in a childhood accident but could ride and shoot like Buffalo Bill.

I told Miss Morley that I'd run into bullies in Jersey City and had no desire to meet more in Upper Darby. I asked if the quarry behind Mrs. Hasselman's stables was safe territory. She hesitated, then said, I would call that No Man's Land.

---

54   Kent Mills, a few miles downstream from Drexel Hill, was still turning out woolen suits and coats during World War Two.

After this inspiring talk, I asked around our neighborhood and found that many older residents considered the Addingham children forest animals. They didn't attend school, cussed, smoked, and ran the woods like Indians. Doc Raymond told me about hiring a young Addingham man to jerk sodas. He quit after a week, explaining, I can't do this no more. I'm an outside person.

Every once in a while an Addingham girl would hike over the hill, knock on a back door, and ask if she could do chores for a dime or a quarter. My classmate Nick Malebranch made the mistake of kidding one of the girls about her flour sack dress, and she knocked him down, slapped his face, then outran him to the woods. Nick said she didn't wear underpants. That made Addingham even more enticing.

25.

My preoccupation with the moss-covered mills and the abandoned stone quarry made me more bored than ever by my school subjects: English, Spelling, History, Geography, Mathematics, Printing, Art, Music, and Phys. Ed. Mr. Vaughn Smith's science class was the only one that held my interest. Our virtuoso teacher taught us how to identify sedimentary, igneous, and metamorphous rock. When he offered a leatherbound copy of the New Testament as a prize for the best collection of local minerals, nothing could keep me out of No Man's Land.

My first big discoveries weren't minerals but man-made treasures salvaged from the piles of trash on the quarry floor. Lids from vacuum-packed coffee cans became a special prize. I would flip them sideways and send them spinning out over the gulch, gleaming in the sunlight as they floated down toward Darby Creek. I imagined them sinking to the bottom of the water to advertise Maxwell House and Chase & Sanborn to passing minnows.

What I hadn't imagined was a howl and a yell from far below. Cut that out up there!

Had I roused the warrior chief?

I heard someone thrashing up the hill. I sprinted across Mrs. Hasselman's field and didn't stop 'til I reached Garrett Road.

I returned to the quarry the next dawn but avoided the temptation to throw lids. I was hovering between a B and C in General Science and needed to rack up an impressive mineral collection. Armed with a screwdriver and tack hammer, I scrambled up the quarry wall to a shallow cave and began chipping away. The rock face was broken by patches of glittering micaschist, feldspar, gneiss, and saltpetre, all of which I could identify, courtesy of my training by Mr. Smith. I pried off a few quartz crystals and saw streaks of iron ore and something that looked like decomposing granite or marble with a few specks of fool's gold.

Or was it ... *real* gold?

I'd nearly filled my Johnson Smith knapsack when something embedded in the micaschist caught my eye. It was a tiny dark nugget in a broken crystalline shape. I chipped it out and held it up to the morning sun. It glowed a dark red and made me wonder if I'd found a ruby. I dug in and exposed three or four more, one of them a well-formed crystal about half the size of my pinky nail.

I looked around. No one was in sight. The only sound was the tinkle of the stream below. I heard one of Mrs. Hasselman's horses neigh and decided not to cross her corral with my treasure. Someone might be out riding. I'd read what happened at Sutter's Mill when a prospector panned up a nugget of gold and started a rush of greenhorns. Miners had been killed for a pinch of gold dust. I decided to keep my discovery a secret.

At school Mr. Smith congratulated me but told me I couldn't have found rubies. The Lord saw fit to provide Upper Darby with many wonders, he informed me, but he chose to share precious stones like rubies and diamonds and emeralds with his children in other parts of his kingdom.

I told him that my nuggets were too pretty to be common minerals. If they weren't rubies, they were something else valuable – maybe a rare jewel that hadn't even been named.

Mr. Smith smiled and told me to bring them in. The idea made me nervous. Instead I went to the school library and pulled down a book on mineralogy. The answer jumped right off the pages. I'd discovered a cache of Garnets!

Everything I needed to know was in the book. Garnet was the January birthstone, the jewel of choice for the second wedding anniversary, the symbolic stone of Capricorn. Its name came from the Latin *granatus*, meaning granular. The Romans found it nestled like little grains in other minerals just as I'd found it nestled in micaschist. Garnets came in every color except blue – I thought I might have seen a fleck of green in the quarry – but the dark blood-red specimens were the only ones used in fine jewelry.

Dark blood-red like mine!

I returned to the quarry the next morning and the next and the next. I discovered a crack in the back of the shallow cave that would have been too small for most of my classmates. I squeezed inside and shone Daddy's flashlight on a wall of stone and micaschist that looked as though it had never felt a hammer or a chisel. I forgot all about Mr. Smith and his classroom assignment. I stopped worrying about Tut Culver and the other Addingham boys. If they hadn't spotted me climbing the quarry wall, they wouldn't see me inside the cave.

With every layer of micaschist, I exposed more precious stones. Most of the garnets were slightly decomposed, edges chipped or splintered, and some were crusted with dirt and clay. But there were a dozen or so good specimens and two or three that were almost perfect. I imagined how they would gleam after polishing. I knew from Mr. Smith that raw diamonds came out of the earth looking like bits of flint, and pure gold looked almost black.

Why should garnets be any prettier in their wild state?

26.

I hid my Cocomalt jewel chest under a stack of magazines in my closet and kept my mouth shut at school. Mr. Smith didn't bring up the subject. I was bursting to reveal my secret at least to my family – but I didn't want to turn into a modern Johnny Garnetseed with the whole ninth grade following me to my trove. Whenever Tommy Frasch or Marshall Main or my other friends asked me to come out and play, I made an excuse and sneaked off to the quarry.

By the time I'd filled the Cocomalt can, I couldn't resist dropping a few hints around the house. Mother, I said, how much are beaver coats?

She said she had no idea.

How about your fox stole?

Oh, that. I think he paid forty dollars.

I bet you'd like another one.

She gave me a funny look and said, Saving your allowance?

I might surprise you someday.

Never mind the stole. Pay off our debts.

I said to myself, Yeah, starting with Grace Evangelical Lutheran Church. That'll be easy. Maybe I'll buy Pastor Wallick a new altar.

Instead of reading at night, I lay in bed planning our future.

Mother could quit her job at the bakery. Sis would have the royal blue satin dress that she'd seen in the window at Frank & Seder, plus a whole set of Shirley Temple dolls. Our family would dine out again, and there'd be no more liver, scrapple, or those 16-ounce cans of salmon that cost twenty cents and stretched over two meals. I would buy Daddy a pair of prescription glasses to replace the fifty-cent models he kept buying and breaking. I would pay the back rent, pick out a new wardrobe for school, load up on balsa wood from Doc Raymond's model airplane department, and send Nanny twenty bucks to spend at the day-old Horn & Hardart. I had my eyes on a balloon-tired Schwinn, ballbearing roller skates that laced up the ankle, and a two-man toboggan for winter fun at the Hi-Top Golf Course.

For the Olsen family, the Depression would soon be over.

27.

On a Saturday morning I got up at dawn and jogged toward the quarry. I would need every ounce of energy. About ten feet above the shallow cave that I'd pretty much mined out, I'd spotted a promising shield that looked as though it might hold garnets and tourmaline, if not rubies and sapphires. I wished I had a confederate, like some of my heroes in the Tom Swift and Frank Merriwell books, but I didn't want to share my secret.

This was a job for the intrepid loner who'd pioneered explorations in the Hackensack marshlands, Lehigh Valley freight yards, and the shores of New York Bay. Maybe I would find some Iceland spar to go with my garnets!

The sun hung just below the treeline as I trotted across the field behind Mrs. Hasselman's barn. I imagined Dolly in her darkened stall, ears straight up as she listened to my footfalls and worked out new ways to humiliate me. Four monarch butterflies flew by in formation. The knee-high weeds were beaded with dew, birds twittered in the brush, an owl's last hoot of the night trailed away in the upper branches of the maples and sycamores, and a soft cool breeze blew from the direction of the Delaware River, twenty miles to the southeast.

Just before the path slanted downhill toward the quarry, I spotted a pair of brown eyes peering from the lower branches of a tree. I almost jumped out of my sneakers before I realized they were buttonwood balls. I told myself to stop acting like a sissy. I was hot and thirsty, so I took a short detour to Indian Basin. Our history teacher, Mr. Donald Coulbourn, had explained that Lenape Indians chipped out the bowl-like depression to collect spring water.

I cupped my hands Boy Scout-style for a drink. A luna moth as big as a baby sparrow flew off the underside of an interrupted fern. The water in Indian Basin didn't taste like the stuff that flowed from our taps in Drexel Hill. Mr. Coulbourn had told us that spring water was full of healthy minerals like iron, magnesium, and calcium. It tasted like wild soda pop.

I dipped my hands into the stone basin, splashed a few drops on my face, and took a deep breath. As I leaned over the little pool for a final slurp, a woman's face stared back from the water. She had long white hair and a big nose.

I stood up slowly. She was watching me from the rock above. I thought my heart would spin out of my chest and soar away like a Chase & Sanborn lid.

It's okay, I blurted out. I'm just, uh ... I'm just on my way to the quarry.

I wasn't sure, but I thought I heard her say, We know. Her voice was old and scratchy. I didn't see her move, but all at once she was gone.

I wondered what to do. Would she follow me? Was she ... alive?

I scrambled through some greenery that I hoped wasn't poison ivy and caught a glimpse of a bony figure slipping into the woods twenty yards away. She wore a dress and was barefooted. She walked unhurriedly, as though enjoying a morning stroll. She vanished in a tangle of laurel.

I picked my way back up the trail, making sure to avoid twigs and loose rocks. As I walked I tried to rein in my imagination. Maybe the woman hadn't said, We know. Maybe she'd just said Good morning or Hello or Hi. Who's afraid of a barefooted old lady anyway?

I felt safer when I reached the quarry. The shield above the cave was just catching the sun, and patches of micaschist glittered. Garnets! I said to myself. Where there's micaschist there's garnets! I'll pry out enough to buy every Big Little Book in Kresge's and every comic book in Woolworth's and spend the rest of my life eating veal loaf sandwiches and chocolate ice cream and drinking seventeen-cent malts at Doc Raymond's. I'll make Mother and Daddy as rich as Freas B. Snyder and Van Leer Bond and John McClatchy and all the other Upper Darby millionaires put together.

28.

As I started my climb, I was glad I was traveling light. I'd stowed a tack hammer and screwdriver in the pockets of my corduroy knickers. If anyone saw me, I was just a kid fooling around in the rocks.

It took a minute or two to scramble up the loose shale to my cave. I paused and looked toward Darby Creek. Nothing moved. The only sound was a faint gurgling. Higher!

Soon one of my Keds rested on the top edge of the cave opening and I was only three or four feet below the promising shield. I pressed my eighty pounds against the rock to hold my position, took a few deep breaths, then wriggled up. I discovered that the shield wasn't as smooth as it looked from the bottom. The surface was layered with a frosting of grit and seemed to steepen. It was like climbing against tiny ball bearings.

I thought about turning back. The rock face smelled of sulphur and I flicked off a caterpillar that turned out to be saltpetre. I'd heard that saltpetre shrank big boners, but at the moment that wasn't a problem.

I rested 'til my heart slowed. Then I made a mistake. I looked down. There was nothing between me and the quarry floor but air.

I decided to lower myself a little to prove that I was still in control. I found that going down was harder than going up. The cracks and bumps that had passed in front of my eyes as I climbed were now four or five feet below my line of vision, and I had to feel for them with the tips of my sneakers. I kept missing. Pebbles bounced down the face. A swallowtail butterfly flitted above my head.

Suddenly I started sliding. I jammed my stomach and hips and chest and everything else including my face against the wall and slowly ground to a stop. I looked down again.

My feet were five or six feet above the top of the cave. When I tasted blood, I said, Help!

No one answered.

I began to feel sorry for myself. I thought, Why should anybody help such a dope?

Pastor Wallick had told our catechism class about God's punishment for sinners: locusts that would sting like scorpions for five months. I thought, That's unfair! Why not fire and brimstone? I hated bugs.

I looked down and yelled, Help, help! Somebody get me outa here!

The stables were probably open by now, but my voice wouldn't carry over the rim.

The sun warmed my back. A buzzard made some commas in the sky. I hoped he'd had an early breakfast.

I decided to renegotiate my deal with God. I informed him that I would like to cancel the $45-a-week deal. If he just got me off this wall, I would settle for $30 a week, $20, even $10. I would settle for one good meal a day. I would settle for nothing at all. Not only that, but I would give up pinball and Tastykakes, study the Bible religiously, and not skip the begat chapters or make wisecracks about turning water into wine, which any kid could do with a Gilbert chemistry set. I promised to memorize the Apostles Creed and the Benediction and the 23rd Psalm – no, I would memorize all the psalms. I would go to divinity school and become ordained. O Lord Jesus Mary and Joseph, please get your servant down! I realized that I'd forgotten someone. You too, Holy Ghost....

After a while it hit me that God had better things to do. My only hope was that one of his children would spot me and send for help. But I didn't see how the Garrettford fire department's rescue equipment could get down to this quarry.

I thought about Uncle Bill Johnson. They can kill you but they can't eat you. I guessed he didn't know about buzzards. I wished he was here with his Popeye arms. But he couldn't save me. Whatever happened was up to me. I had to do something, even if it was wrong.

I relaxed my pressure against the wall, dug in with my toes and fingers, and tried a controlled slide, inch by inch. I hated to imagine what would happen if I fell into the loose rock thirty feet below.

I slid a little and dug in again. A fingernail tore. Now I was bleeding in two places. I said to myself, This won't work. Your foot'll miss the cave and kick around in open space and you'll get tired and fall.

I yelled 'til I was hoarse. Birds and mice were probably the only creatures that could hear me. I'd climbed into my own outdoor coffin.

As I pressed against the wall, I saw a dot that might have been a garnet. I added another promise to Jesus: I'll give up garnets! I'll give my collection to the missions in Missouri!

I waited for divine inspiration, but none came. My strength was ebbing. In my early-morning lust for jewels, I'd skipped my Wheaties. It was time to let go and leave the rest to Jesus. Maybe I would fall between the sharpest rocks.

I heard the voices before I saw them. Hey! What're ya doing up there?

I twisted my neck and looked down. Three boys approached the rock pile. They looked seventeen or eighteen. One carried a rifle. When he aimed it in my direction, I saw that his left arm was missing.

Tut Culver.

I started to pray. God, you're not gonna let him snipe me off the wall? I know he doesn't like Drexel Hill boys, but....

I heard a scraping sound. They were on their way up. Culver went first and climbed twice as fast as the others. I saw his rifle, propped against a boulder below.

Get me off, I pleaded.

Get your own self off, Culver said. You got yourself up, didn'tcha?

He began issuing orders. Move to your left! More. More! Lower your right foot an inch. One inch! Feel that crack? Dig your foot in. No, stupid. Your right foot! Now ... slide.

Slower. Slower! ... Whoa!

I pushed inward with my toe and felt empty space. I'd reached the top of the cave.

Culver said, Now ... let go!

No! I'll fall.

Let go, damn it!

I'll, I'll ... hurt myself.

I heard them whispering. Then Culver said, Bye.

I screeched, Don't leave!

You're one of them Drexel Hill punks, right? You're so smart, get yourself down.

Please. I tried. I can't.

Then do what you're told and quit bawling.

When I hesitated, he yelled, We're right below you! Let go, goddamn it!

I slid another inch or two. I could feel my feet still dangling in the air.

He said, Keep coming! Down, down.

I dropped another foot and felt something brush the toe of my sneaker. He yelled, Now ... drop!

I held my breath, shut my eyes and let go.

Two and a half pairs of arms caught me and lowered me to the floor of the cave as gently as a bird feather. My chest pumped like an accordion. I couldn't feel my hands and feet. I tasted blood.

Culver said, What the hell were you doing up there?

Something told me not to mention garnets.

I said, I was ... exploring.

Don't come back. Tell your friends.

It took me a few minutes to catch my breath. The rescue party backed down to the quarry floor. I watched as Culver shouldered his rifle with his one arm. Move it, he said.

I slid to the bottom on the seat of my knickers. Everything hurt. As I touched my bloody lip with my bloody finger, Culver waved the barrel toward the path that led out of the quarry. He yelled, Get outa here! Now!

I picked my way through rocks and trash. I felt as though I

was scraped to the bone.

I'd wobbled and limped about twenty feet when I heard a sharp hiss. I spun around.

I'm shot! I yelled. I'm shot!

The one-armed boy lowered the rifle. Where'd I getcha? he asked.

My heinie!

The three boys laughed. Tut Culver said, Get back to Drexel Hill or I'll shoot ya again. Higher.[55]

I limped up the trail and broke into a gimpy run across the pasture. No horses or horsemen were in sight. When I reached Garrett Road, I pressed my knuckles against the seat of my corduroy pants to stanch the blood. I wondered how far the bullet had penetrated. Did it hit an artery? I stuffed my khaki Boy Scout handkerchief down my pants and pressed it against the wound to keep my insides from oozing out like our Samoyed dog in Highland Park.

When I reached home I heard familiar noises in the basement and realized that Mother was doing a load of wash. I rushed to the bathroom and unbuckled my belt. What would I tell the police? The ambulance driver? My parents? PHOT #3

I peeled my underpants away from the wound. The pain

---

55 Many years later I learned that Delos "Tut" Culver had grown up in the nearby Tuscarora Mansion. His redoubtable mother Annie was one of the first females to hold the post of postmaster and used part of the mansion for the Addingham Post Office. After her death, her one-armed son expanded his self-appointed role of protecting the property. In the early 1940s, a few years after he saved me from the wall and shot me, Culver used his knowledge of birds to rid the Philadelphia City Hall of pigeons. (His method remains unknown but may have involved broadcasting recordings of feeding hawks.) He was active in the Delaware County SPCA and later turned the Tuscarora property into a bird sanctuary, protecting it from developers who threw up rows of ticky-tacky homes above Darby Creek after World War II. In 1971 he helped to create a program called Give Wildlife a Brake and was photographed accepting a plaque from President Richard Nixon. (His body was angled away from the camera so his empty sleeve wouldn't show.) To his death Culver kept a shotgun loaded with rock salt and occasionally fired it in the vicinity of trespassers. It was reported that an Upper Darby schoolteacher took a load of salt in his buttocks but was too embarrassed to complain to police. Old ways die hard.

had turned to a dull throb. I wondered how hard it would be to pry out the bullet and whether I had the guts to do my own surgery with a kitchen knife. I hadn't shown my bare heinie to Lulu Abernethy and I didn't want to show it to a bunch of strange doctors and nurses. How could I explain what happened without giving up the secret of the garnets?

I lowered my shorts and a copper BB fell to the floor. I twisted around and saw a tiny red dot in my left cheek. It looked like a mosquito bite.

I cleaned up my blood lip and fingertip and decided not to discuss the incident with anyone. I was sure my parents had been expecting the worst ever since Jersey City. I doubted that they expected me to be shot, but Mother probably wouldn't be surprised.

Nanny had told them about the street fights and probably about my stealing, too. I couldn't blame her. It would have been a disservice to everybody to pretend that I'd behaved myself.

I decided to avoid Addingham for a few months. The garnets wouldn't be weren't going anywhere.[56]

29.

By now I'd made good friends in my neighborhood – Johnny Reminger, Marshall Main, Bobby Filmer, the doctor's son Dick Coffey, Tommy Frasch, Doc Raymond – but my secret was still too important to share. The Olsen family's future depended on the jewels that I kept in a Cocomalt tin in an old steamer trunk

---

56   Years later my work as a journalist put me in the company of famous alpinists like Lionel Terray, Gaston Rebuffat and Riccardo Cassin in mountaineering meccas like Chamonix, Grindelwald, and Lecco. Despite their friendly suggestions, I never made another rock climb. I bracketed the world's greatest faces in my mind: the Eiger North Wall, the Dru, the Walker Spur, the Civetta Wall, Piz Badile, and the quarry at Addingham.

in our attic.

Then I spotted a streamlined Schwinn bike in the window of a 69th-Street store and decided that I couldn't live another day without it. What would it hurt if I sold one of my garnets? There were plenty more. Tut Culver couldn't keep me away from that quarry forever.

The next morning I showed my collection to Mr. Vaughn Smith.

Interesting, he said.

He handed the can back and returned to some papers he was correcting. I thought, Oh, my God, they're not garnets! I mis-identified them! Mr. Smith was an expert on local minerals. He'd identified every stone in my collection and awarded me a B+.

I said, Aren't these, uh – garnets?

Yes, Jack, he said. They're garnets. He didn't look up.

What're they worth?

He took the can back and poked inside. Maybe a quarter, he said.

I said, Two bits?

That's right.

Apiece?

No.

When he saw my jaw drop, my favorite teacher informed me that garnets were as common as flint in Delaware County quarries, that these specimens weren't even close to jewel qual-ity, and that most garnets were labeled industrial and used for grinding. He told me that Noah used a garnet lantern to help navigate the Ark. It was true that garnets could make the Olsen family rich, but only if I found about ten trainloads.

Going home in the smelly school bus, I sat alone in the back row and thought about the ups and downs of the busi-ness world. No wonder Daddy had so much trouble earning a living. I started out with radishes and ended with garnets, and both businesses fizzled. I decided that whatever I took up next, it wouldn't be red.

30.

It was white. Tons of snow fell in that winter of 1938-39, and I trudged all over Drexel Hill with a shovel on my shoulder. As usual, my best customers were ladies of fifty and up, some of them widows. Girls my own age looked right through me, but old women were a pushover. I worked my charm to the limit. Why, hello there, Mrs. Yeager. It's so nice to see you on this wintry day. I see you haven't shoveled your driveway. May I be of assistance?

The trick was to avoid asking for money. If the customer asked how much I charged, I would flick my hand lightly to suggest I was only interested in her friendship. I would take longer than necessary with the walkway. I would scrape and hack at nonexistent patches of ice. Then I would turn up at the front door, huffing from my exertions, and gasp that I was finished and it had certainly been a pleasure to clear a path to such a lovely home. She would ask, How much do I owe you? and I would say, Fifteen cents.

Some of my clients would pat me on the head and chuckle. Some would turn away and daub at their eyes. Some would invite me in for Bovril or hot chocolate. But none would pay me fifteen cents. They would dig in their purses and come up with pirates' treasures like fifty-cent pieces and, more than once, paper money.

One snowy day I called on Mrs. Stephanie Boris, who was getting on in years and used an ear trumpet that resembled a megaphone. She greeted me with a bundle of fur nestled in her arms. The dog seemed smaller than the pink bow that seemed to grow from its head.

Oh, I said, how cute. What kind is it?

Mrs. Boris looked at her watch and said, Quarter to four.

It took me an hour of dramatic effort to clear her sidewalk and chip the ice from her birdbath, downspouts, and statuary. Now and then I would glimpse a curtain moving behind her window.

When the job was finished, I was taken by a brilliant idea. If asking for fifteen cents brought in half-dollars and dollars, how much more would I make if I asked for ... nothing?

I dragged my tired carcass to the front door and told Mrs. Boris that it had been a pleasure working for her and I hoped to have another opportunity.

She stroked her pet and said she would certainly keep me in mind.

Thank you, ma'am, I said. It occurred to me that it might be a good idea to pet the dog. When I reached out, a set of needle-sharp teeth drew blood from my index finger. Mrs. Boris said, You shouldn't have touched her. Daisy's so sensitive. Then she shut the door.

Mother told me there were plenty of Mrs. Borises in the world and not to let them get me down. Remember, she said, you've got to walk before you crawl.

Daddy pointed out that every new business suffered setbacks. He told me to go out and find a couple dozen more customers like Mrs. Boris. What you gotta look for, he said, is volume.

31.

That winter I began hanging around with a new kid in the neighborhood, Taylor Klein, a member of a vintage Philadelphia family that appeared to be passing through Drexel Hill on its way down the social ladder. In my memory Tay comes across as a double for the Roaring Twenties novelist Scott Fitzgerald, with the same strong nose that bespoke instant admission to Skull and Bones or Porcelain. He read magazines like *College Humor* and *The New Yorker* and spoke a variety of English that he'd learned at an upper class prep school called Penn Charter.[57] His parents had lost their Germantown mansion, retreated to Drexel Hill, and enrolled their only child in Upper Darby Junior High School.

I liked Taylor even though he was different. He didn't *know* things; he *presumed* them. Instead of saying *now*, he referred to *this particular time.* He ended sentences with So to speak, As it were, If you will. The first time I heard him say If I may, I said, Well, sure, Tay. Go right ahead.

I wasn't put off by his aristocratic airs because they seemed so natural to him, and I was pleased that he enjoyed my lower-class company. He was a star tennis player and more than my match at ping-pong, Chinese checkers and Parcheesi, but he wasn't pushy about his skills. He was the only boy I knew who didn't want to start a fist fight every time I cheated him at poker. He was impressed with Daddy and tried to draw him out about the Tigers, but as usual my father no spikka da English on that subject. Mother told me that Daddy suspected Taylor Klein was Jewish.

That word.

By now I'd been told that Jewish people were different, but all I'd noticed was that the women were bigger in the chest. My classmates Harriet Simon and Jules Holberstam were Jewish, and they were both good students, polite, friendly, nothing unusual. My only source of information on the subject was

---

57 At a football game a few years later, I heard their fight yell: Penn Charter, Penn Charter, Fight Harder, Fight Harder, which crossed the field as Penn Chodda, Penn Chodda, Fight Hodda, Fight Hodda. It was a little like being back on Lembeck Avenue with the O'Burls.

Daddy's favorite radio preacher, Father Coughlin, and he was as boring as ever.

One day Taylor Klein and I were flipping baseball cards in my living room when Daddy turned on the floor-model RCA radio that came with our furnished house. I recognized the singsong voice that I'd first heard when we lived in West Philly. The radio priest was asking if the world wanted to go to war for six-hundred thousand Jews in Germany who weren't American or French or English citizens but citizens of Germany.

Then he rattled on about economics and capitalism and a few other big words.

Taylor and I continued flipping cards. When the sermon was over, Daddy turned off the radio and left the room, shaking his head.

If I may say so, Taylor said, he certainly has some nutty ideas.

He's okay underneath, I said. You gotta getta know him.

Get to know him? I'd rather get to know a skunk.

I started to tell my pal to pipe down before it hit me that he was talking about Father Coughlin, not Daddy. Oh, I said, he don't bother me.

Taylor said, My old man says he should be censored.

I didn't know what censored meant. Well, I said, it's okay with me.

At dinner I mentioned that the Klein family didn't think much of Father Coughlin.

Daddy said, No, I guess they wouldn't.

A few nights later Taylor told me he couldn't come over to work on our science project because he had to go to a church supper with his parents.

Church supper? I said. Aren't you...?

Oh, no, Taylor said. I daresay everybody makes that presumption. We're just plain old-fashioned Episcopalians.

I brought Daddy up to date at breakfast, and Mother asked him what on earth gave him the idea that the Kleins were Jewish.

I dunno, Daddy said. I just ... heard.

When she was tucking me in, Mother said, Sometimes I wish your father would turn up his hearing aid.

Daddy didn't wear a hearing aid. She must have been thinking of old Mrs. Boris.

32.

A hot summer began and I was invited to spend two weeks in the Pocono Mountains with a new kid in the neighborhood. Billy Kaselman was a blond-haired boy with a slightly snaggled tooth that gave him an endearing smile. We'd met after a Saturday matinee showing of *Kid Galahad*, with Bette Davis, Humphrey Bogart, and Edward G. Robinson.

My cronies and I usually went to the Waverly to propel Jujubes and paper clips into the light from the projector and create our own meteor shower. If I found myself sitting next to a female classmate, my entire attention would shift from the plot of the movie to the possibility that our arms might touch – and she might not pull away. But she always did, and who could blame her? I was the shortest kid in my homeroom, didn't date, didn't dance, and had a line of patter that was tailored to women with blue hair. In my entire thirteen years I'd had one planned date, but I'd made the mistake of telling her to meet me inside the theater. We never spoke again.

Kid Galahad was a boxing film, and when we boys spilled into the daylight, nothing could keep us from staging a prizefight. Somebody put gloves on me and Billy Kaselman and I decked him with a tap to the forehead in the first round.

I leaned over him like the gallant Kid Galahad and fanned him with my boxing glove. He opened his eyes, winked, and shut them again. I caught on right away. Boxing was fun, but there was no point in hurting each other. Later we shared a laugh at our acting ability. It didn't hurt my reputation when word flashed through the neighborhood: Jackie knocked Billy cold with one punch!

The Kaselmans' summer invitation presented a problem for my father. This time there was no doubt: Billy's stepfather Jack was the brother of Cy Kaselman, the star of the SPHAS' basketball team, and the SPHAS were as Jewish as Moses, as Daddy put it one night when he didn't think I could hear him talking to Mother downstairs. It wasn't a long conversation. Mother said, So what? Jackie'll fit right in. Daddy said, Why? Because he's circumcised?

Mother told him she didn't care if the Kaselmans were Jews, Holy Rollers, or Baptists. She said that Sis and I had never gone to summer camp and this was my chance to have a wonderful summer vacation.

I did. From our first day in the low green mountains, the Kaselmans gave Billy and me free rein. We sneaked into a traveling circus at Mount Pocono, flattened pennies on railroad tracks, picked buckets of blueberries, snagged trout in a hatchery pond, went on a hayride with some kids from Stroudsburg, sliced golf balls on a driving range, played tennis, badminton and croquet, swam and canoed and bashed water snakes with a paddle, and giggled with some Scranton girls in swimsuits, not knowing what to do about the faint stirrings in our shorts.

One day Billy and I returned from a hike to find a Packard convertible with leather seats parked outside with the top down. Packards cost $10,000 and were backed by a proud slogan: Ask the man who owns one. I noticed a golf bag on the jump seat.

I'll be darned, Billy said. Uncle Cy's here. Whattaya bet

there's a girl with him?

Under a rack of horns on the living room wall, a blonde with a chest like one of Petey Dallesandro's roller pigeons sat on the arm of Cy Kaselman's chair as the basketball star chain-smoked cigarettes and discussed stocks and bonds with his saturnine brother Jack. I was googly-eyed. The SPHAS' star didn't look much different from the skimpily dressed young man I'd seen five years earlier sinking one free throw after another in a pregame warmup at the Broadmoor Hotel and then drilling a two-hand set shot that beat the black invaders from New York in the final seconds. He still wore his kinky waves tight against his head. He was a striking specimen of manhood in his open-collared sportshirt, gabardine slacks, and black leather basketball shoes.

After a venison dinner and the first halvah I'd ever eaten, the vacationers straggled out to the stone veranda. Mrs. Kaselman sprayed with Flit and dabbed Billy and me with citronella. The Kaselmans and Cy's girlfriend drank highballs and Billy and I took a few sips and tried to look grown-up. A chorale of spring-peeper frogs was in rehearsal, and in the distance the Lackawanna's night freight moaned and clanked as it chugged around an uphill bend. The Kaselmans treated Billy and me like short adults and even told a few off-color jokes. Hey, Cy asked, do you guys know the definition of a virgin in South Philly? A girl under ten that can outrun her brother.

I was so giddy that I asked if it was okay if I repeated a joke I'd heard at school. It's a knock-knock, I said, and quickly added, Don't worry. It's not dirty. Mrs. Kaselman said, Hey, this is Liberty Hall. She was a heavy-set woman with a big laugh.

Knock knock, I said.

Mrs. K. said, Who's there?

Lena.

Lena who?

Lena a little closer, honey.

The women laughed the loudest. Jack Kaselman managed a smile and said I'd better clean up my act before I hit the Orpheum circuit. It was a high point of my childhood career in comedy.

I lay awake for hours. For the first time I realized what Daddy meant by worldly. I thought, There's a lot of great stuff going on outside of Upper Darby. I hadn't yet learned the word *epiphany*.

Before Cy and his blonde drove off in the morning in his 12-cylinder Packard, he gave me an autographed picture and a piece of advice: Don't smoke, kid. It stunts your growth. If you gotta smoke, don't inhale. If you gotta inhale, make sure your insurance is paid.

I didn't know if he was hinting about my size, so I just said, No, sir, Mr. Kaselman. I'd never smoke. I wanna grow up to be like you. He lit another cigarette and drove off.

At home I told and retold the details of my Pocono vacation 'til Daddy said he'd heard enough. I decided that his feelings were hurt because the Kaselmans had shown me a good time and he couldn't afford to send me to camp, dancing school, or anything else that cost money. A few days later he said he had to admit that they were pretty good people for Jews.

Mother corrected him. Jewish people, she said.

33.

Later that summer of 1939 we took the Black Horse Pike to Atlantic City, and for once I was allowed to visit the Boardwalk unescorted. I was trying to choose between saltwater taffy and frozen custard when I heard orchestra music coming from deep inside the Steel Pier. It was being piped from the bandstand to a loudspeaker over the entrance. I stood with my hands on the iron bars and stared into the kaleidoscopic colors as the dark-haired bandleader introduced a pretty singer named Helen Forrest and a song called "Comes Love."

Comes a rain storm, put your rubbers on your feet.
Comes a snowstorm, you can buy a little heat.
Comes love – nothing can be done.

The bandleader named Artie Shaw gave her another down-beat and she swung into her next song:

Day in, day out,
The same old voodoo follows me about,
The same old pounding in my heart
Whenever I think of you
And darling, I think of you
Day in and day out.

Then Helen Forrest did a little switch and sang about "Day out, day in." I'd never heard anything so neat. When she finished singing, she perched at the side of the bandstand and tapped her high heels as the orchestra banged out some instrumentals. A tousle-haired young drummer pounded so hard on a song called "Traffic Jam" that I was sure his sticks would snap.[58] Once in a while a stubby sax player[59] would set his instrument aside and belt out a novelty like "Indian Love Call" or "Prosschai." His voice put me in mind of Doc Raymond's milkshake mixer.

In almost every number the bandleader played a solo on his black clarinet, and some of the dancers stopped to watch and listen. With his wavy dark hair and high cheekbones, Artie Shaw looked like a movie star. His orchestra played with such a steady insistent beat that I imagined an invisible metronome ticking out the time in the background. I gripped the bars as

---

58 I met Buddy Rich in Chicago a quarter century later and he told me I was right. He broke plenty of sticks and some drumheads, too.

59 Tony Pastor.

though the Steel Pier might float out to sea, but I couldn't keep my lower half still. It was a wonder I wasn't arrested.

I didn't know how long I'd been in a hypnotic state when Artie Shaw cued his final selection. From the opening phrase I recognized it as a song that I'd been hearing on my favorite Philadelphia stations, WFIL, WIP and WDAS, and on two New York stations that came in at night, WOR and WJZ. I tightened my grip as Helen Forrest sang:

When they Begin the Beguine
It brings back the sound of music so tender,
It brings back a night of tropical splendor,
It brings back a memory ever green ....

After she finished, every instrument in the orchestra slammed in at top volume, with Shaw's clarinet squealing higher and higher 'til I was sure he would reach G above high H and break every light bulb on the Boardwalk. My ears were still ringing when the orchestra swung into its spooky closing theme. Dancers drifted toward the bandstand, and I relaxed my grip on the iron bars and headed back to our rented room in a daze.

All night long the music played in my brain. Now I knew why Johnny Reminger practiced his clarinet. If I could play like Artie Shaw, I would give up chemistry, astronomy, minerals, Tastykakes, girls, and wet dreams. I remembered my primitive musical urges in 1936, when we lived in West Philadelphia and I heard Henry Busse and Clyde McCoy. Back then I'd yearned for a trumpet and ended up with a ukulele.

I started lobbying for my Christmas present early. I wanted a slender silvery trumpet that I'd seen in the window of a music store on Township Line. In a black leather case with green satin liner, it reflected the streetlight in iridescent gleams and sparkles.

I worked my parents carefully. Mother, I said, every house

needs music. I wish I had something to play for you. Maybe ...
a trumpet?

Mother said we couldn't afford an expensive instrument
right now and Johnny Reminger was already supplying us with
all the music that any six pairs of human ears could endure.

I switched my attack to Daddy. I told him that I intended
to be a swing trumpeter when I grew up, but I had to get started
on the instrument or the other kids would beat me out.

Trumpet? he said. Ain't no money in that.

I told him that I'd read in *Downbeat Magazine* that Harry
James made a thousand bucks a record.

Oh yeah? Daddy said. Well, I seen *Downbeat* at the bottom
of a outhouse. Don't believe everything you see in a magazine.

But then he made a stunning reversal. On a trip to Newark
he hit a three-horse parlay and telephoned home with the news
that he'd found the perfect instrument for a future jazz great.
And because I'd been such a good boy, I wouldn't have to wait
'til Christmas.

The gift of a lifetime arrived in a cheesy cardboard case, but
I didn't care. I didn't need a black leather case with a green satin
liner. It was the contents that mattered.

As Daddy, Mother, and Sis looked on, I opened the snaps,
lifted the lid – and tried not to gulp. Inside lay an ugly hunk of
brass tubing. It looked like a trumpet that had been sat on, fat
and bulbous and half the normal length. The valves, tubes and
bell were jammed together to give the impression of a miniature boilerworks. The instrument was a dull yellow color, like
unpolished brass, and reflected no light.

I pushed what turned out to be the spit key, blew into the
mouthpiece and produced my first note as a swing musician. It
sounded like a wet fart.

I'll catch on, I said. I was trying to smile.

Daddy said, I knew you'd like it, Sonny. I always wanted a

cornet when I was a kid.

For three months I slogged through lessons from the school's bandmaster, Maestro Michael Dotti, at two dollars a session, an expense I split with my parents. I gave up when we came to grace notes and triple-tonguing. I lacked the fingers and heart and had only one tongue.

With my classmate Chick Bramble, a fine jazz drummer himself, I was making 5 a.m. trips to the Earle Theater at 11th and Market to be first in line to see Glenn Miller, Gene Krupa, Tommy Dorsey, and other swing bands, and I realized that I would never catch up to trumpeters like Harry James, Roy Eldridge, and the two Billys, May and Butterfield. It wasn't happening fast enough for me; nothing ever did. I was still the kid who took stairs three at a time. My stubby cornet ended up in pawn.

34.

By ninth grade I was wearing long pants, but they only made me look shorter. I tried out for baseball and came afoul of a coach who judged talent by the ability to catch fly balls. He sent us candidates out to deep center field and began lofting fungoes that were higher than Billy Penn's boner. I never got within twenty feet.

After he cut me, I tried to explain, I'm a pitcher, Coach. Pitchers don't catch flies.

On my team, he explained, everybody shags flies.

I tried to figure out what had gone wrong. The Olsens were a baseball family and I'd blown my first try at making a school team. I should have put more effort into learning the game on my own instead of depending on Daddy. My job had always been to watch him play. Maybe he wanted me to become a good ballplayer, but he never got around to showing me how it was done. I explained this to my pal Billy G. A poor excuse, he said, is better than none.

In a few days my failure had company. My friend John Zutch had made the team but was cut because he was allergic to the number 16 and the coach wouldn't let him change jerseys with Sil Sivonius even though Sil quit because he considered the number 99 demeaning to a player of his ability. Mike Chalfant was cut because he couldn't stop crying after he was picked off first base. Ronnie Estes was dropped after he skipped practice for a cello lesson. Greg Mesmer was cut for biting an umpire who called him out on the hidden ball play.

Failing to make the school team didn't keep us losers from playing ball. We formed the Drexel Hill Stars, an informal group whose role in the world of amateur sports seemed to be to provide practice for good teams. The old line about not winning or losing but how you play the game had no meaning to us. We took the field expecting to lose. The only variable was the score.

Not that we didn't have goals. Manager Dick Coffey used to give us pep talks before the games: Come on, gang, let's score a run today! Hey, let's hold 'em under ten! We can do it!

But we seldom did.

Our toughest competitor was Drexel Manor, a scrappy bunch of kids from a bluecollar neighborhood whose residents carried a chip on their shoulders about us plutocrats up on the hill. The Manor players wore uniforms and competed in the Connie Mack Conference. Their home field, upgraded from a vacant lot where over the fence used to be out, featured a backstop made of chicken wire and a wooden refreshment stand. The batting boxes were lined with lime, the bases were held in place with spikes, and the infield was raked 'til it was as smooth as a pool table. Their best pitchers were lanky Gene Weinert, who could throw every pitch in the book[60] and a stubby kid named Lee Griffiths who could fire a baseball through the side of a panel truck. Our hitters stood in the batting box in a C position, our rear ends waving outside the lines. I once asked the Manor catcher when Lee Griffiths intended to pitch the ball. The catcher said, He just did.

Drexel Manor had a hundred or so regular spectators who lined the foul lines for every game and kept up an incessant racket with dippy chants like, We always win – in the Drexel manner. At least once per game they would go into their chant:

D-R-E-X-E-L

Drexel, Drexel, Fight like – Heck.

That was their idea of clever, and maybe it was, the first twenty times you heard it.

Manor players held after-school practices, unheard of in kid baseball. We Drexel Hill Stars employed a more relaxed approach. We would head for the ballfield and hope to find some action, even if it was only work-up. In our scheduled games, we had trouble fielding nine players and had to borrow from our opponents, usually their worst player. Some of us didn't own spikes or use neatsfoot oil. Harper Alexander played in his uncle's golf shoes.

Our playing techniques were a disgrace to our town and our nation. We nicknamed our third baseman Inert. If the ball was hit at him, he would stab at it, and once or twice in a game he would be credited with an assist if he didn't throw the ball over the first baseman's head. In a practice game against the Garrettford firemen, he set a new Upper Darby township record with four errors in one inning. Nobody was counting, but Inert blabbed about his achievement for weeks. Imagine that, he would say, thirteen years old and already in the record books.

Our second baseman Jeff Pratt was known as The Waver

---

60   And was the son of Phil "Lefty" Weinert, former Phillies pitcher.

because of the way he fielded hard-hit grounders. We kept him on the team because he owned two baseballs and a Chuck Klein bat with a nail in it.

Our right fielder Pat McGrady was subject to daydreams and had been known to wander off to the drugstore in the middle of a game.

None of our outfielders understood the concept of the cut-off man. They felt it was sufficient if their throws reached the infield on the first or second bounce. Who cared? We had no respect for hidebound old baseball tradition. We thought baseball was about laughing and jumping around and having fun. Drexel Manor, on the other hand, won ninety percent of their games and never smiled. When their captain and manager Bill Kribben accepted the trophy for winning the township championship, I thought he would start bawling. Abe Lincoln was happier on the way out of the Ford Theater.

Daddy never attended our games, and I didn't discuss the Stars with him. He wouldn't have understood.

At school I tried out for basketball and scored a driving floor-length layup in my first intramural appearance. After the game, Albert Paul and I got into a shoving match. He asked what kind of dope would dribble the length of the floor to score two points for the other team, and I told him that I was the best dribbler on the team and I could teach him some moves. He said I was the best dribbler, all right, but in the wrong direction. I said, Oh, yeah? He said, Yeah!

Such was the high level of repartee at Upper Darby Junior High School.

Mr. Hudson issued us sixteen-ounce boxing gloves so we could settle our differences in the gym. Albert won on a TKO when I developed a leg cramp just before the opening bell. He promised to give me a rematch but we never got around to it. We didn't understand boxing traditions either.

35.

The Great Depression still hadn't gone away, and we junior high school kids had to take our pleasure where we found it, as long as it was free. We rode our bicycles to Long Lane, scrambled up the huge collapsible gas tank[61] and pedaled away like six-day bike racers when the watchman showed up. We would sit in the driver's seat at the wrong end of the Red Arrow reversible trolleys and push the lever that sprayed sand under the wheels. Santa brought me a No. 15 Gilbert chemistry set and I nearly asphyxiated myself by burning raw sulphur in our attic. I also brewed up a batch of hydrogen sulphide and produced a rotten egg smell that drove us to Fairmount Park. In the morning the milkman asked if the fumigation had been a success.

Pocket money was where we found it or earned it or hooked it. I caught Japanese beetles in kerosene traps and was recompensed by my parents at the rate of a penny a dozen, which added $1.32 to my treasury before the last beetle flew back to Tokyo for the winter. I mowed lawns and ran errands, but the payoff was meager. My flower sales had long since dropped to nothing, and radishes were a rosy memory.

Without a ready supply of spending money, my friends and I looked for cheap new ways to have fun. Don Craig Peterson and I pitched pup tents in our backyards and spent hours trying to read the codes sent out by lightning bugs until we were advised by Mr. Vaughn Smith that such flashing messages could be decoded only by other lightning bugs.[62] J. W. Tracy came up with the idea of putting his mother's Greek vase on his phono-

---

61 The tank from which Birdy leaped in the novel by William Wharton.

62 A conclusion which was verified by scientists who followed in our footsteps years later.

graph turntable, pressing a needle against the spinning surface and retrieving the ancient potter's comments. We were still at an age when we believed that anything could happen if you wished hard enough. We were surprised when this experiment failed on the first attempt.

On the second, we broke the vase.

Sometimes we turned to Mother Nature for inspiration. Like Highland Park, most of Drexel Hill was wooded over by locust, maple, hickory, chestnut, walnut, oak, and sycamore trees. There was a flowering mimosa in our back yard, a Japanese maple in front, and a gingko next door. A military line of stiff poplars separated our duplex from the backs of houses on Rosemont Avenue, and seventeen-year locusts took up residence high on the trunks. They whirred like Buck Rogers' Disintegrators all day, then split out of their skins and disappeared for another seventeen years, leaving husks that were useful in shaking hands with girls.

36.

In our sophomore year, my schoolmates and I began to find high comedy in the process of elimination. That was when I first heard venerable lines like Shit plus two is four.... The shit hit the fan.... You don't know shit from Shinola.... Shit runs downhill.... What a crocka shit....

The punchlines of jokes from Upper Darby Junior High School still reel across my mind, sometimes in the middle of funerals and weddings. You wouldn't shit me, wouldja? .... Me gotta move now, teepee fulla shit .... Be careful, Reverend, that ain't second base! .... It looks like moose shit, it smells like moose shit, it tastes like moose shit – but it's good! .... Not right now, ma'am. I wiped my ass on a moon beam .... The dog dined Mexican ....

Billy Glossop still blurted out Aw shit! when he sneezed, and he'd broadened his repertoire to include Big hard-on for Beg pardon. If you asked him a question, he would mumble, I dunno. Ass ol' Charlie.

Billy taught the little Brannon twins that the official Cub Scout oath was Shit, piss, and corruption. He'd quit Scouting after learning that there was no merit badge for smoking. It was bad enough, he complained, they wouldn't let me cuss. The high point of his first thirteen years of life seemed to be running into Babe Ruth on the parking lot at Shibe Park after the A's had walloped the Yankees. Billy said he stepped right up and asked, Can I have your autograph, Mr. Ruth.

The slugger said, Eat shit, kid.

Our conversations at that age were more like competitions, with ritual responses. If you scratched your backside, some wiseguy would say, Going to the movies? I see you're picking your seat.

If your fly was open, they would say, It's two o'clock in the waterworks.

If somebody said, I'm done, you responded, Then wipe yourself.

If you were asked where you'd been, you replied, Down at the rabbi's picking up tips.

The correct answer to the question, Got a match? was Sure, my ass and your face. If a friend wanted to borrow money, you responded, How ya fixed for shirts and underwear? The correct answer to Got the time? was Yeah, you got the nerve? If you asked a stupid question, you were told, You tell me and we'll both know. On the school bus someone could always be trusted to call out, Hey, driver, could you stop the bus and let my brother Jack off?

Farts brought ritual comments like Who dropped a rose?

... What crawled up your ass and died? ... Cut him up and see what he eats ... Deliveries in the rear, please ... The waiter did it ... The dog did it ... The teacher did it ....

We spent hours classifying gaseous emissions. A high-quality assbuster would draw sharp comments like Hey, go get fitted for a new asshole. Ask for size 48! "Doggy farts" were the quiet kind that could be blamed on pets. "Wet ones" (as in, Was that a wet one, Bill?) required a dash to the nearest bathroom. A "seven-come-eleven" fart meant that you'd taken a chance and lost. Squeakies were emitted by sissies and girls. "Dreadnoughts" were so strong that other people couldn't avoid reacting, all the better if they were female teachers. "Bathtub farts" were self-explanatory and the most rewarding. There were few moments in the life of an adolescent boy more satisfying than sending up bubbles and practicing gearshift techniques at the same time.[63] That's what was usually happening when our mothers demanded to know, What on earth are you doing in there? Mother asked the question so many times that I was tempted to yell, I'm trying to jerk off, but so far I only farted.

We junior high school kids were certain that our jokes and wisecracks had never been heard outside the township limits. If a boy seemed too pleased with himself or his joke, someone would say, Well, smell you! Another would add, Ya can, too. At the mention of the seventh planet from the sun, we convulsed. We sang about girls who didn't wear pants in the southern part of France and how Sadie lay under an old pile of lumber. Our rallying cry was sung to the tune of "The Stars and Stripes Forever" and began:

> O the monkey wrapped his tail around the flagpole
> To see his asshole ...

To the tune of "Humoresque," we sang:

---

63 This activity diminishes with age and may be expected to peter out around fifty. Or seventy-five.

Gentlemen will please refrain
From flushing toilets while the train
Is standing in the station.
I love you.

We sang:

Oh what does a Scotchman wear under his kilt?
A whang, a whang . ...

Our version of "Dark Eyes" began: Aw piss on ya ...

No one could deny that my buddies and I were almost ready for the stage, if not the silver screen. If Groucho Marx, Woody Allen, and Victor Borge had been in our ninth-grade class at Upper Darby Junior High School, they probably would have become successful humorists.

I was almost fourteen when my parents finally got around to having my teeth fixed.

Assisted by his loquacious wife and nurse, Dr. Osborne did fillings for three dollars each in his ratty office above a store on Garrett Road. The Osbornes were good with children, uttering encouragement and aphorisms in lieu of novocaine and gas. By the time you figured out their trick, your backside was a foot off the seat.

Nothing to like about it, Doc would say as he drilled a hole the size of the Addingham quarry in my jaw. His favorite line was, A hundred years from now you won't know the difference.

I said, Doc! It hurts now!

Mrs. Osborne was the first (but far from the last) member of the healing arts to tell me that the pain was all in my mind and would go away if I thought nice thoughts. I thought about Lulu Abernethy's bloomers, but my mouth still hurt.

Dr. Osborne's practice didn't include extractions, and when my impacted molar had to be yanked, he referred us to a dentist in West Philadelphia. On a cold and rainy night Daddy and I parked in front of a dark house on Chestnut Street. The dentist greeted us with a clammy handshake. He was his own assistant, and both of them were as charming as Frankenstein's Igor.

After he settled me in a black leather chair, I asked, Will this hurt?

Instead of answering, he turned around and leered. For a second I wondered if he intended to strangle me. I repeated my question, and again he ignored me. I would have fled if Daddy wasn't waiting in the anteroom. The gas cup smelled like an inner tube. I prepared for my last few minutes on earth.

I woke up with a mouth full of blood and a granite jaw. I was so limp that Daddy had to carry me to the car. I didn't even complain when we passed Hap's Ice Cream Parlor without slowing down.

A week later my eye was caught by a short item in the *Philadelphia Evening Bulletin*. A man had died of a heart attack in that same dental office. An investigation absolved the dentist of blame. I just wished they'd asked me a few questions. A man who scared people to death was probably in the wrong business.

I mentioned my discovery to Daddy. Yeah, he said, but he only charged five bucks.

38.

My life took a radical new course soon after my brush with death in the dentist's chair, and a pocket mirror and comb became my most important school supplies. A year earlier I wouldn't have cared if my hair looked like a yucca plant. Now every strand had to be in place. It wasn't a case of wanting to look handsome; it was a case of not wanting to look ugly. Using Kreme, Vitalis, and Wildroot – and sometimes all three – I secured my various cowlicks and created a pompadour that looked like a perfect wave at Atlantic City. Daddy said I would never have to be checked for nits or lice because they would drown.

My pals and I were now old enough to attend major league baseball games together. I tried to avoid Shibe Park, the Philadelphia A's home at Twenty-first and Lehigh, because my allegiance was to the Detroit Tigers and I refused to dilute my loyalty by rooting for another team in the same league. But when the New York Yankees came to town, I joined with boys from all over southeastern Pennsylvania to shower the Bronx Bombers with contempt. They won the pennant every year from 1936 to 1939, but that wasn't all that we disliked about them. They acted as though they *deserved* to win the pennant – and then they went out and won it! After they'd beaten the Cubs four straight in the '38 World Series, one of their players was quoted in the newspaper: "We came, we saw, we went home." He sounded bored. Nanny would have said, How bad he feels. New York sportswriters called the '39 Yanks the greatest team in history, which reminded me of another of Nan's expressions: self-praise stinks.

When our squatty field announcer Babe O'Rourke lifted his megaphone to announce the Yankee lineup, 33,000 Philadelphians would rise to hurl insults and bottles. Even the fans in the quarter seats on rooftops across Twentieth Street stood up and booed.

After the Yanks beat the Athletics by a composite score of 39-2 in a doubleheader, I lost all interest in the A's and shifted my allegiance to the Phillies. They were even worse, but they didn't play the Yankees. Their home field was Baker Bowl, a wooden bandbox that was the smallest in baseball. The seating capacity of 18,000 was more than ample; average attendance was about 4,000 as the Phils struggled year after year to rise into seventh place. It was said that the statue of William Penn atop City Hall had faced north until Billy turned away in disgust at a botched double play. A scoreboard ad proclaiming that the Phils used Lifebuoy was defaced by a semi-permanent graffito: "And they still stink."

Newspaper photographers fired their flash bulbs along the foul lines amidst cries of "Down in front!" The view improved after the Phils fell eight or ten runs behind, usually by the third or fourth inning, and the fotogs fled along with most of the paying customers. At the end of some of the games it seemed as though there were more humans on the field than in the stands.

Baseball fans in other cities cheered for great players like Babe Ruth, the Waner brothers, Ted Williams, Ducky Medwick, Heinie Manush; but at Baker Bowl we made do with Don Hurst, Gibby Brack, Eddie Feinberg, Cap Clark, Kewpie Dick Barrett, Alex Pitko, and Art Rebel. My personal favorites were Ham Schulte, born Herman Joseph Schultehenrich, a sure-handed little second-baseman who never let a ball get past him except when he was batting, and pitcher Kirby Higbe, a South Carolinian who kept a big chaw in his cheek and had a losing record until he was traded to the Brooklyn Dodgers and won twenty-two games in his first year, just to be perverse.

39.

One summer day in 1939 I returned from Baker Bowl just in time to be ordered to Raymond's drugstore to pick up Daddy's Lucky Strikes. Doc handed me the soft green pack and beckoned me behind the Megow's models. Son, he said softly, don't take this wrong, but please tell your dad I can't carry him anymore.

I'd seen this day coming. Night after night Daddy would send me to Raymond's for a pack of cigarettes or a can of pipe tobacco and expect Doc to put it on the arm. I'd become so sensitive about our bill that I stopped playing Doc's pinball machine and walked six blocks to a drug store near the Waverly to drink milkshakes that tasted like drainwater compared to Raymond's seventeen-cent specials that fluffed.

Doc looked uncomfortable. He said, I'm sorry, son. It's been five months. If he could just pay a little on account ....

I understand, Doc.

I have bills, too.

Daddy was sitting on the front porch when I got home. My face must have given me away as I handed him the soft green pack of cigarettes. What happened? he said.

Doc Raymond says no more credit.

What?

We can't charge.

Raymond told you that?

Yes.

Daddy yelled, Son of a bitch!

I was afraid the Remingers would hear us through the thin glass window that separated our porches. Mother came out of the kitchen in her apron and asked what the yelling was all about.

Daddy said, The little kike cut us off.

I was stunned. Mother said, Who?

Raymond.

Doc? He would never cut us off.

Daddy's face was red. Well, he did, he said.

You get too excited, Mother told him. Let dead dogs lie.

Daddy thought this over and said, Yeah, I guess you're right. No mockie druggist is worth a heart attack. We'll take our business elsewhere.

Sure we will, I said to myself. Where? Erie?

I went upstairs and tried to make sense of what had happened. I knew that words like *kike* and *mockie* were intended to ridicule and hurt, like *nigger, shine,* and *Polock.* I'd heard Daddy use them all. But was it fair to call Doc Raymond a kike when he wasn't even Jewish? My mental picture of male Jews hadn't changed since our eighth-grade class stumbled through *The Merchant of Venice.* They were darkish men like Shylock, with wiry black hair and hook noses. My hero Morrie Arnovich of the Phillies fit the description. Cy and Jack Kaselman came close. Doc didn't. He and his wife Kathryn were a different species. Doc had a button nose and brownish hair, and his wife had thick red hair and looked like Mother. How could they be Jewish?

A few weeks after Doc cut us off, I saw him walking on Garrett Road with his son Sid. I turned into a vacant lot before they spotted me. I was so ashamed. Doc hadn't heard Daddy call him those names, but I was afraid my guilty expression might give something away if I talked to him. I was a thirteen-year-old suburban kid of northern European Christian background, and I was just beginning to get an idea of how race could come between friends.

Later that year Daddy begged and borrowed and maybe stole enough money to start a small company of his own, Underwriters Service Bureau. He hired a few unemployed adjusters, brought in a failed businessman with whom he played pool and poker at the Columbia Turners, and hired a secretary who threatened suicide after two weeks of taking his dictation. He printed up business cards showing a big bare foot and the slogan A Step in the Right Direction above the notation: R. O. Olsen, Manager, Grad. Univ. of Indiana, Indianapolis, Magna Cum Loude. His company promised to maintain a roster of free-lance adjusters to lessen the payroll load on small insurers.

USB prospered long enough for us to flee our furnished duplex on Taylor Avenue and move to a larger rental six blocks away on Turner Avenue. This placed us in the orbit of two drugstores on State Road, and Daddy immediately opened up new charge accounts. I saw Sid Raymond at school, but I never saw his father again.

seven

Turner Avenue: Drexel Hill

1.

Our latest move should have improved my parents' shaky marriage, but instead it made matters worse. At night I would hear Daddy's rants, followed by inaudible responses from Mother. He would yell that he'd picked her out of an alley and could put her back. Then he would accuse her of not being worldly. It was the same old argument year after year.

One night I heard him say, I should of left ya in Jersey City where ya belong. Next came the sound of glass, followed by his yell, Two can play at one game! I looked for scars in the morning, but they both seemed healthy.

I sought refuge in the upper reaches of Darby Creek. I'd bought a cheap fly rod on the laughable theory that I could catch trout in a warmwater stream a mile from home. I hooked up with a boy named Dudley Beyler, a straight-A student who lived in the next block of Turner Avenue and knew every fish in Delaware County by name. Together we fished Darby Creek and Naylor's Run and more remote streams like Ridley, Wissahickon, Octararo, Crum, White Clay, Chester, and the Brandywine. We used our bikes, public transportation, and our thumbs, and often found ourselves twenty or thirty miles from home at the end of the day. Some kind motorist always picked us up, and many of them delivered us to our doors. Drivers were trusting in the years just before World War Two, and two Huck Finns standing alongside the highway in hip boots and empty stringers never had long to wait.

Like other southeast P-A stream fishermen, Dud and I were almost always skunked, but the real pleasure, as any angler knows, is in the anticipation. I can't recall a fishing trip when we caught our limit or came close. On a typical excursion we would flail the waters from sunup to sundown and catch between zero and one trout. Not apiece – between us.

We kept going back. We were under the impression that we

were having a good time.

I was fascinated by moving water and always imagined that a wily trout or a musclebound bass was waiting for my hook just behind a rock. Sloshing through the shallows, I realized that I was looking at H2O molecules that would never pass this spot again. Not one drop of the water running over my boots was connected to any of the drops that had gone downstream a second earlier. I mentioned this concept to my teacher Mr. Vaughn Smith and he said, What does that say to you? As he often did, he answered his own question. It says that God is good.

I nodded. But to me it just meant that God was confusing. And he wasted a lot of water.

Mr. Smith was more forthcoming on the subject of Darby Creek geology. I'd always wondered where and how such a fine stream got started. There were no mountains for miles, no steep hills, just gently rolling countryside. On our bikes Dud and I tracked the creek ten miles upstream to a trickle about six feet wide and an inch deep, surrounded by dairy farms and corn fields. And yet it maintained a steady flow twenty-four hours every day and never came close to running dry 'til it ran all the way to the Tinicum Swamp and the Delaware River.

Think of the land as a sponge, Mr. Smith explained. It absorbs rain all year around, but it's always being squeezed by a big hand. Think of gravity as the hand. It wrings out drips and drops and they combine into rivulets and they combine into brooks and they combine into a creek. The creeks become rivers, and the rivers flow into the sea ....

I realized that he'd circled back to *Ecclesiastes* and his eternal reference book. If you could read between the Bible verses, Mr. Smith could teach you a lot of science.

Dud Beyler and I were bait fishermen at heart and took pains to offer gourmet meals. We'd passed in and out of the artificial lure stage in about a week, or as long as it took to learn that a Parmacheene Belle fly cost a quarter and a River Runt plug a buck. One of our neighbors believed that the only reason he didn't catch trout on a given day was because he'd selected the wrong fly. Dud and I weren't so naive. The real reason was that sensible trout preferred real food. We offered grubs, crickets, grasshoppers, helgrammites, crawfish, minnows, red worms, and nightcrawlers. (Mother didn't like me to keep worms in the Frigidaire, so I hid the nightcrawler jar behind Daddy's Limburger in the back of the cheese drawer.)

In fly-fishing streams like the privately held Wissahickon, we used cheap flies, tipped our hooks with a half-inch of worm, and kept an eye out for the Colonel Blimps in their twenty-dollar L.L. Bean fly vests, thrashing the water to a froth with their silly snippets of feather and fluff. If the warden came into sight, we whipped our line back and forth 'til the worm broke off. If it didn't come off, as on one embarrassing occasion, we were treated to a lecture on the wages of sin, ushered out to ponder our criminal ways, and banished from the sacred waters forever. To Dud and me, "forever" meant 'til the next time we sneaked in.

Somehow we always returned to Darby Creek, remembering to steer clear of the Tuscorora Mill, its watchman, and its one-armed sentry, Tut Culver. The old millstream was too warm to hold trout, but it had other charms. Bottom-feeding suckers would nibble at my worm for tantalizing minutes before inhaling the hook. In the rapids, silvery chubs and fallfish rose to doughbait like brook trout. The creek's long pools held a subspecies of smallmouth bass that were full-grown at eight or nine inches, perhaps because of pollution. They put me in mind of the asterites in the Buck Rogers comic books. These mini-bass seldom weighed as much as a pound but seemed as dense and powerful as their big cousins. One jumped clear over my split bamboo rod and broke it in half as I tried to horse him to the bank. I imagined him thumbing his fin at me as he swam back under his rock.

2.

One dawn I was fishing for creek chub at the head of a rapids below the State Road bridge when an eel passed over my head. I was as surprised as the eel and watched as he wriggled through the wet grass atop the bank, advanced six or eight feet and splashed back into the water.

As usual Daddy didn't believe me. You seen a garter snake, he insisted. Ain't no eels in Darby Creek.

I found an encyclopedia in the Drexel Hill library and learned that I'd spotted an American eel toward the end of a journey that began in the Saragasso Sea near Bermuda, continued in the Atlantic to Delaware Bay, then up the Delaware River to the Tinicum Swamp and up Darby Creek past Fels-Naphtha and the Kent Mills to State Road. On the way they wriggled out of the water to bypass spillways and dams.

Daddy was still from Missouri. I decided that the only way to prove my point was to invite an eel home. My friend Dud, master of all things wet and fishy, told me he'd once met an old man from Addingham who ate eels that he caught in a trap. He skinned them, soaked them in milk, and cooked them over a spit like hot dogs. The best bait, Dud said, was a ball of old nightcrawlers, the smellier the better. I hid a bottle of defunct worms under a bush behind our house and waited a week for the August heat to do its work. It took me three mornings of fishing in the same pool to catch my eel. He hit like the Blue Comet and kept the tip of my flyrod vibrating like Daddy's Shick electric razor.

After a thirty-minute battle I slung the eel over my back,

jumped on Sissy's bike, and pedaled madly toward home. I had to stop five or six times to unwind the eel from my size-12 neck. I thought about tapping him on the head with a rock, but something told me to keep him alive. Dark ideas were forming in the back of my mind.

Mother was at the bakery and Daddy was at his office when I got home. I put my eel in the bottom of Mother's work-sink in the basement and added a few inches of cold water. I could hardly wait to show Daddy my "garter snake," but Mother dragged in first. Stay away from the basement, I told her. Have I got a surprise for you!

A few minutes later Daddy arrived and opened a bottle of Esslinger's. He sounded disturbed that his dinner wasn't on the table, but Mother's attitude toward him had been stiffening since we moved to Turner Avenue, and she told him to fix his own meal if he was in such a hurry.

It was a pleasure to head off the latest ugliness before it got started. Hey, Daddy, I said, I got something to show you.

I led him down the cellar stairs and pointed to the washtub. Take a look, I said.

He stuck his nose in and said, Another damn frog?

Wait, I said. I turned on the overhead light.

Okay, Daddy said, what's the joke?

Whattaya mean?

This here tub's empty.

We searched for the eel 'til bedtime. When the Vergers' tomcat visited our back porch, we grabbed him and smelled his breath. Daddy spent the evening with his pant legs rolled up. Mother slept on the porch. Sis had an army of girlfriends and we didn't see her for two days.

At daybreak Mother used the Smiths' toilet next door. Daddy left for work earlier than usual. I hid under my covers 'til noon.

Dirty clothes accumulated for three days before Mother began unloading her big wicker basket and stared back at a pair of eel eyes staring out the trapdoor in Daddy's BVDs. She screamed and ran upstairs to call the SPCA, but they told her they didn't do eels. A slight odor convinced us that it was too late. The Olsens had lost another pet.

3.

Until I left Drexel Hill for good, Darby Creek was my favorite hangout that didn't include girls. At first glance there was nothing special about the creek.[64] But in its 244-square miles of drainage, there were constant surprises. In winter I pressed my ear against the frozen surface and listened to the Alka-Seltzer underneath. Spray created a feathery rime of ice along the shoreline.

Now and then I would run across the ruins of a creekside farmhouse that might have been two centuries old. Stands of maple and oak grew where colonial farmers had cleared fields for their first crops in the new world. Ancient foundations showed up as darkened rectangles in the earth, as though someone had roughed them out with charcoal.

A few fieldstone structures were ready to collapse. My friend Reed Clayton pried a stone from a canted wall and was buried under a ton of rock. He recovered after a long stay in the hospital.

In my explorations along Darby Creek I came to ruined

---

64 Local historian Thomas R. Smith described it as "playing a commoner role among commonplace streams ... merely a part of the whispering and dripping, wondrous landscape."

mills[65] and broken stone bridges that had been used by workers who died before my grandfathers were born. Next to a deep pool I found a frazzled rope-swing that looked as though it had been untouched for years. In quiet water behind the leaky old dams, coffee bugs whirled like the Dodg-'em cars at Woodside Park, and water striders created six perfect circles as they skated on the surface tension. Crawfish inched along the bottom like miniature lobsters and reminded me of my success as a Hackensack crabber. Dragonflies buzzed my lips 'til I waved my hands to show that I required no darning at the moment. Crane flies scared me half to death 'til I learned that they were just big harmless bugs and not monster mosquitoes with hypodermics. Red-bellied turtles started to run, then turned to rock at my touch.

On the creek bank alongside the New Caledonia mill I spotted a snake with a leopard frog in its mouth. Without thinking, I grabbed the snake's tail and cracked it like a whip. The frog flew out, croaked twice and hopped into the water. I wondered what he would tell his wife when he finally got home. Hon, you're not gonna believe this, but ....

4.

In that sophomore year in Upper Darby High School my academics remained on a par with my athletics. I tried out for baseball, football, and basketball and never made it past the first cut. An indulgent track coach tried to show me how to throw a discus so I could earn my purple-and-gold letter. I wore my

---

65   In 2002 I viewed the largest and last of Darby Creek's ruined mills when I drove past the old Fels-Naphtha plant, downstream from Drexel Hill. The big soap factory had long been empty, its windows broken out by vandals. No algae grew in its millpond. Still polluted, the water's surface was a bright orange-yellow color and resembled molten metal.

worn-down baseball spikes while practicing the throwing motion, and my feet slipped out from under me in wet grass. The coach sprinted in from forty yards away, yelling, I heard it snap, I heard it snap!

I felt so proud as the ambulance drove me a hundred yards to the Delaware County Hospital. I'd broken my wrist for old U.D.! At last I'd accomplished something athletic. I was full of painkillers when Daddy rushed into the emergency room with a stricken look. You okay? he asked.

Fine.

You sure?

He's okay, Mr. Olsen, the doctor said. It was a small bone.

Daddy looked relieved. I thought, I'll get a milkshake out of this, maybe even a buck or two.

Sonny, he said, I told you to stick to baseball. Ain't no money in track.

5.

My report cards continued to resemble losing cards in a bingo parlor – I consistently scored 10 (careless), 16 (poor test grades), 17 (late in handing in assignments), 13 (unprepared) and 12 (frequently absent). One of my role models was the most popular student in school, Frank Videon, whose family's mortuary had embalmed most of the Drexel Hill dead. Frank was a practicing hedonist. He showed up for class when he was in the mood, never missed a dance or party, kept teachers and students in tears with his wit, and advanced the science of lollygagging to new frontiers. He was repeating his junior year even though he was brighter than most of his classmates. To me Frank Videon was proof that a smart kid could have a fine time in high school without wasting energy on homework and books.[66] I decided it had something to do with formaldehyde.

My No. 15 chemistry set and fond memories of Doc Raymond convinced me to switch my own ambition from pitching and stargazing to mixing bright bubbly potions, and this in turn required the study of German, since international cartels like I. G. Farben had cranked out so much untranslated research. I quickly learned that my language aptitude didn't extend to German. In retrospect I would like to think that my aversion had something to do with Hitler's public gargling, but it was more likely my sense of economy.

On our first day in class, Miss Grunberg explained that every German noun took the masculine article (*der*), feminine (*die*) or neuter (*das*), and the only way to sort them out was to study vocabulary lists 'til you were *blau* in the *gesicht*. Actual gender meant nothing; one of the first words we learned was *madchen*, the German word for maiden. It was neuter. As Billy Glossop said, The Germans knew their maidens.

In class I asked our German-born teacher to explain this contradiction and she said she didn't feel it was her responsibility to justify a usage that went back thousands of years to the Saxon tongue and anyway I should stop acting like a *dummer Esel*.

Since I didn't know the meaning of *dummer Esel*, I persisted. Are German maidens neutral? I asked courteously.

Neuter.

That's what I said. Neuter.

In Cherman, za maidens are feminine, but za word for zem is neuter.

Scanning my first vocabulary assignment, I learned that a woman (*Frau*) was feminine, but a young woman (*Fraulein*)

---

66   In later years Videon, a millionaire car dealer, was named by *Time* as one of the twenty top salesmen in the U.S. Approaching eighty, he still attended the '40, '41, and '42 class reunions.

was as neuter as a *Madchen*. Lips (*Lippe*) and nose (*Nase*) were feminine, the eye (*Auge*) was neuter except when it was masculine (Blick), the head (Kopj) was masculine, and hair (Haar) was neuter.

Etcetera (*und so weiter*).

In class I told Miss Grunberg that she was losing me. I said, Every day you make us memorize a list of new words, right? And then we gotta figure out how to pronounce 'em? And then we gotta figure out which is masculine, feminine or neuter?

Ja, Herr Olsen, das ist richtig.

Well, it wasn't *richtig* for me. On our latest vocabulary list we found the word *abschied*, which meant "leave." Germans didn't go away; they took leave. The problem came from the pronunciation, Op-Sheet, which rapidly became Ape-shit and the most popular insult in Upper Darby High School. We had Miss Grunberg to thank for something.

After two more weeks I decided to drop German before German dropped me. Friends advised that French employed only masculine and feminine. But there was another problem. In speech, the French swallowed all terminal consonants except C, R, F, and L except, of course, when they didn't. This would require plenty of memorization, but less than German. Hadn't I learned to live with the silent R in Jersey City? I tried to make the switch, but my advisor, a phys. ed. teacher, reported that the French classes were full. He said that I might as well face up to the gender problem since it existed in other languages.

What about Latin? I asked.

Same.

What about Spanish?

I think it's the same.

What about Mexican?

He said, Isn't that Spanish?

I concealed my surprise and asked, Canadian?

He looked at his list and said, We don't offer Canadian.

I hated every split-second (*Augenblick*, masc.) of my German classes. My relationship with Miss Grunberg consisted almost entirely of watching her shake her thin brown bangs in anger and declare, I giff you a F in wed ink!

I was on-track for a solid failure when I hit on a master stroke of deception. A fellow chemistry student had come across a German pamphlet that described the polymerization of certain plastics. I copied it, inserted an error or two, and submitted it as my term paper.

Miss Grunberg took one glance and drew a big F in wed ink. Then she dumped my report into the trashcan. I ended up studying German for three years in high school and one year in college. Someday I intend to learn it.

6.

By my middle teens I was also having sporadic trouble with English and showing no signs that I would ever earn a living as a writer. I found literature and poetry a bramble of confusion, and so did some of my companions.

What the hell's so rare about a day in June? Billy G. asked as we waited in the cafeteria line. Chrissakes, there's thirty-one of 'em, ain't there?

Thirty, I said.

Billy said, Thirty, huh? as though this was news to him. Is thirty supposed to be rare?

I said, That poet should of wrote, O what is so rare as a day in February.

Why?

There's only twenty-eight days. Except in leap years.

How many in leap years?

I dunno, Billy. I think maybe twenty-nine.

Jesus Christ, how're you s'posed to keep up with crap like that?

I was beginning to wonder myself.

My grammar remained on a par with my mother's ("myself and Mrs. Smith went shopping") and somewhat better than my father's ("how ya was?"), but far short of the standards of Upper Darby High School. My English teacher, Miss Bock, tried to help me with a technique called diagramming, in which sentences were laid out in horizontal, vertical, and diagonal grids as though they were exercises in plane geometry.

Mechanical drawing had always been my worst subject, but I applied myself diligently and learned to place the subject of a sentence above a straight line, followed by a vertical line and the predicate, followed by the object or the predicate nominative. Prepositions trailed off at an angle. Dependent and independent clauses were more complicated, but I was beginning to get the idea when Miss Bock chose to embarrass me in front of the whole class. I was standing at the blackboard trying to diagram a sentence of my own: I would of gone if I wouldn't of changed my mind.

I asked Miss Bock, What part of speech is *of*? A verb?

She said she couldn't believe I would ask such a question in a high school English class.

I was stunned. What was next? Oh, Jackie, why don't you just sit down?

Miss Bock explained that *of* was a preposition, and that it had no place in a sentence like, I would of gone if I wouldn't of changed my mind. She told me that I was confusing *of* with *have* and should have got this straight by the third grade.

Yeah, I said. I guess I should of.

I sat down amid titters.

I'd been taught not to argue with my elders, especially the

ones who might determine whether I attended summer school, but I was my father's son and therefore convinced that I was right and Miss Bock was wrong. I'd heard the word *of* used as a verb a thousand times. So many adults couldn't be wrong.

That night I pored through my grammar text until I finally got a handle on the problem. It was clear that *of* was a gerund.

After this latest confusion I decided to salvage a passing grade with an essay so impressive that even Miss Bock would recognize my language ability. She'd ordered us to write 1,000 words about something that had a major impact on our lives, something that aroused our passions and interest.

In my life, what could that possibly be? Baseball? Daddy? The Tigers? Exploring? Minerals? Fish? They were important, but all were overshadowed by – Wheaties.

Except during my infancy and my nine months in Jersey City, Wheaties had been the basis of my existence. I began and ended each day over a bowl of Wheaties with Grade-A milk and three tablespoons of sugar. A life without Wheaties would have been no life at all.

I looked in the school library and found no books on the subject. The librarian tried to help me with a fifteen-minute lecture on the Dewey Decimal System, but my math was too weak.

I composed a letter to General Mills, asking for information on their most important product. In a week I received a packet from Minneapolis. My experience with Miss Grunberg had taught me that it was unwise to copy exact phrases, so I set about digesting the information and regurgitating it in my own words.

I wrote, "Wheaties is...," and stopped.

That couldn't be right. There was certainly more than one Wheatie or Wheaty in each box. There were thousands. If ever a word was plural, it was Wheaties. I crossed out "Wheaties is" and wrote "Wheaties are."

But then I thought, It's just one product.

I turned back to the publicity material and learned that the original Wheaties were the result of a mistake. In 1921 a nutritionist was mixing wheat and bran gruel when he spilled a few drops onto a hot oven and discovered that they sizzled and fried into tasty flakes. The result was called Nutties, then Gold Medal Wheat Flakes, then Wheaties, Breakfast of Champions. This was fascinating information but no solution to the problem of singular or plural. I would have to use my native intelligence.

I wrote my first draft in pencil and typed my final version on Daddy's L. C. Smith, making sure to include the required number of words. The finished product was a masterpiece of fairness and balance, my first major coup as a writer.

To catch Miss Bock's eye, I typed the title in black capitals:
MY LIFE WITH WHEATIES

And my subtitle in red:

Jack Armstrong Never Tires Of Them And Neither Will You

I rewrote my opening 'til it just sang:

Wheaties has had as much influence on my life as my mother, Florence M. Olsen, my father, Rudolph O. Olsen, and my preacher, the Reverend Merl Lloyd Wallick of Grace Evangelical Lutheran Church, Edmonds Avenue and School Lane.

Ever since I was little, my trusty bowl of Wheaties have been at my side ....

My next sentence began, Wheaties is.... My next reference was in the plural. Then back to the singular. And so it went in perfect alternation for a thousand well-chosen words. What could be fairer in a democracy?

Miss Bock gave me an F but upgraded to D after I explained my method. She shook her head and told me that singular or plural would have been acceptable, but I should make up my mind, for heaven's sake. In other respects, she said, my paper was almost good enough to be considered below average. She asked what I wanted to be when I grew up.

A chemist, I said.

She said I'd made a wise choice.

7.

As I entered my middle teens I discovered that other matters were more pressing than school: the crick, the war between my parents, pinball, baseball (playing now, not just watching), ping-pong, chess, minerals, stamps, Indian head pennies, telescopes, microscopes, hitchhiking, chocolate malts – and girls.

I was propelled into this last interest by a sudden tendency on the part of old friends like Billy Glossop and Jack Nokes to talk about nothing else. To hear their conversations, you'd have thought they spent their spare time kneading 40-inch breasts. They would spot a pretty girl, nudge each other and make sophisticated comments like I can have her anytime I want, and She's begging for it and one of these days I'm gonna give it to her.

If the subject's face didn't measure up to their high standards, they would make cracks like You can always throw a sack over her head, and They all look the same when you turn 'em upside down. They regarded redheads as sexiest and would make sharp comments like She can put her shoes under my bed anytime, and I wouldn't kick her out of bed. They insisted that black women would change your luck and you weren't a man 'til you split a black oak.

Our friend Joey Stiles liked to sit by himself at the Waverly. I felt a little sorry for him 'til I noticed that he always brought a paper bag. I bet you'd like a little of that Mae West, Billy told him as we walked out of the theater.

I just had some, Joey said.

As always, Billy was ahead of the pack. When the love song "Dolores" came along, he offered his own version at junior choir practice:

> From a balcony above me
> She whispers Love me
> And drops a rose ....

Our choir director said, I think you'll find it's *throws* a rose.

Billy said, You don't know Dolores.

My cronies' everyday vocabularies now included a four-letter word that I remained too shy to use. To the tune of "The Isle of Capri," they sang:

> 'Twas on a pile of debris that I met her.
> 'Twas on the top of an old garbage truck.
> O how she sighed when I lay down beside her.
> Censored censored censored censored censored fuck.

They sang:

> Hooray hooray
> The first of May
> Outdoor fucking begins today.

When Virginia Jones allowed Billy to walk her home from school two days in a row, he bragged that they called her virgin for short but not for long. He also said, She was only a photographer's daughter but oh how she developed, and She was only a jockey's daughter, but all the horse manure. Billy had a dozen of 'em.

I wanted to contribute to the drollery, but I was a year younger than my classmates and still not up to speed on female body parts. Ever since I'd discovered that Lulu Abernethy's bottom was about the same as mine, I'd tended to evaluate females by their hairdos and faces. But now I found my gaze lowering inch by inch. Breasts were appearing on girls I'd known since grammar school, and my classmates and I kept score.

Didja pipe Betty Lou today?

Yeah, she's getting a good pair. Any change in Samantha?

Maybe a inch.

At that stage of my sexual development, my idealized woman combined a waspish waist with a four-foot bust. I looked for her in the corridors of Upper Darby High School, in the shopping center at 69th Street, in the cars of the Red Arrow Line, in the pews of Grace Evangelical Lutheran Church, and everywhere else except the boys' locker room. But how to tell where truth ended and falsehood began in an era when a girl and her clothes were never parted? Jack Nokes said they all wore padding. He had a rash on his hands and claimed it came from Vera Thompson. He swore she used steel wool.

We had a collection of synonyms for our favorite female part: jugs, attractors, tomatoes, bayonets, headlights, apples, melons, pontoons, water wings, life preservers. Our most serious students of mammography knew the significance of the tiniest signs. Was there a hint of movement under her shirt? Did a little more flesh fill that frilly blouse than the day before? Were things firming up under that tight-fitting sweater? A little too firm to be real?

Our studies were enhanced by revealing pictures in *Life, Look, Click,* and *Pic* and stories in pulp magazines like *Spicy Mystery, Spicy Adventure,* and *Spicy Detective.* In each spicy story, the hero would manage to see or touch or feel a woman's breast. The titles were inflammatory: "Two Hands to Choke." "Passion Killer." "The Barbarian." "Vengeance is Mine"... Covers showed snarling men tearing the dresses off busty women and standing over their half-dressed forms with knives or clubs. Girdles were a favorite prop, as were garter belts and petticoats, usually ripped. Perusing alumni bulletins years later, I was surprised to discover that our class had produced no serial rapists or sex murderers.

Some of my pals spent so much time studying these magazines that they ended up knowing more about lingerie and the female figure than the clerks at Lit Brothers and Strawbridge & Clothier. Jack Nokes was the first to tell Amanda Rigi that it was time for a B-cup. He was our expert on everything mammary. He was the first member of our group to recognize that Barbara Stanwyck was "straight up and down," Mae West's bust was ordinary, Myrna Loy had small breasts with upturned nipples, and Jean Harlow and Bette Davis were "built." I asked Jack how he knew so much about the female body. I just know, he explained.

With our standards changing every day, I was forced to lower certain flat-chested girls a notch or two in the pantheon of females I would like to see naked (if I didn't have to get naked myself). Girls I had once admired dropped off my list. New ones were added. I wished I'd taken an accounting course.

Daddy chose this confused period of my life to provide the obligatory lecture on sex. I could tell from his first words that he was just going through the motions, probably at Mother's instigation. This was the man who snapped off the flashlight when we encountered two nightcrawlers heading in each other's direction. Sex had always been the most closely guarded secret around our house. After Billy G had described the act in full detail, I kept telling him, My mother would never do a thing like that! I tried to discuss the subject with the brightest person on our block, but Mary Teresa Elrich just walked away.

Daddy sputtered and stumbled as he warned me that any contact with the female breast would jeopardize my future in sport. Don't touch their t-t-t-titties, he said. Don't even look. They just make trouble.

He seemed to be endowing the female bust with the same qualities as coral snake venom or curare. I didn't bother to point out that my sports career was hardly worth mentioning and that I was still looking for my first girlfriend. I also didn't tell him that campus beauties like Elaine Hooven, Eleanor Bassett, Edna Stratton, and Virginia Knight, my personal favorite, made me weak in the knees when I passed them in the halls. I couldn't imagine their breasts playing the slightest role in my future.

Daddy lectured for five or ten minutes but added nothing to what I'd learned in *Spicy Adventure.* I couldn't help but notice that his presentation omitted any connection between sex and the crotch. If I didn't know better, I would have thought that girls got pregnant when you touched their nipples. His lecture at an end, he lowered his voice and said, Just between you and I, Sonny, ya seen two ya seen 'em all.

8.

As I entered my junior year my tastes underwent still another change. Big breasts remained an obsession, but my interest extended to legs. My list of desirable girls had to be reshuffled again. My busty classmate Amanda Rigi dropped two notches because of her skinny legs and Jean Statzell moved into first place on balance because her legs were spectacular and the rest of her rated "good." Eleanor Neider's knobby knees forced me to erase her name. Peggy Beecher of the adequate face and Betty Grable legs came from nowhere to take the No. 2 spot behind Jean Statzell. I still didn't count brains and charm in my ratings, or Barbara Sawyer would have beaten out everybody.

No matter how often I revised my lists and read my spicy magazines and mentally undid Ginger Rogers' brassiere straps at the Waverly moviehouse, my bathroom activity remained unproductive. At an age when some of my friends were engaging in circle jerks and a few were hot and heavy with girls, I was still trying to learn the art of self-abuse. I found that the stroke was nowhere near as easy as the tennis backhand or the volleyball serve. I asked my friend Jack Nokes if he had any tips. All's I know, he told me, is think about Joan Crawford in her step-ins and whack away.

So that was the problem. I'd been using Kay Francis. Trust me to pick the wrong woman. I asked him how long it took him to get results and he told me it depended on Joan's mood.

Miss Crawford didn't work for me, and neither did Mae West, and neither did Clare Trevor, and neither did Miss Miles, the math teacher who showed the tops of her stockings when she sat down. Billy G said I should try other celebrities 'til I found one that clicked.

Listen, he said, Kate Smith might be worth a try. Or how about Rin Tin Tin?

I reminded him that Rin Tin Tin was a male.

He said he'd read that there were three of them and they were all female.

I told him I would think about it.

When I was fifteen and finally getting some height, Billy decided that our little group of sex maniacs should pay a visit to the Troc or the Bijou. One look at Ann Corio's headlights, Billy told me, and your troubles are over. Be sure to bring a newspaper.

I pointed out that high school kids weren't allowed in burlesque theaters, but Billy said that kids went all the time. As long as the Depression was on, cashiers would sell tickets to kindergarten kids and chimpanzees.

The next question was which burleycue we should attend, the Troc or the Bijou. I thought of a song we used to sing to the tune of "Heigh Ho, Heigh Ho," from *Snow White and the Seven Dwarfs*:

By-joe, By-joe,
It's to the Troc we go
We pay two bits
To see two tits
At the By, By-joe.

Both strip joints were in the Tenderloin section of Philadelphia, but the Troc was older and bigger and probably had
fewer cockroaches and child molesters in the audience. Margie Hart was on the bill, and Dummy Davis said she'd once
dropped her G-string to prove that her red hair was natural. I
knew about A, D, F-sharp, and B from my ukulele days, but I'd
never heard of the G-string. I assumed that Margie Hart did
her act with a violin.

Tommy Frasch said, Why don't we wait 'til Gypsy Rose
Lee's in town?

Dummy said, Nah! Gypsy Rose Lee is a tease.

Jack Nokes, ever our expert on naked females, said he read
somewhere that Margie Hart's performance was so hot that
Mayor LaGuardia ran her out of New York for showing her
thallopian tube. Hey, Billy G said, my girlfriend shows it all the
time.

Five of us traveled to the Troc via the Red Arrow trolley, the
El and a short walk to rundown old Arch Street. We breezed
inside, but a problem arose after the first act. A man stepped in
front of the stage and held up an assortment of candies. Dummy whispered, That's the candy butcher.

I said, The what?

You better look away. He's gonna slaughter a Hershey bar
right in front of us.

After I'd blown my last buck on a stale chocolate bar with
liver spots, the lights lowered and a man with a hesitant walk
took a seat four or five rows in front of us. In the dark he put
me in mind of Daddy. The hair was the same, so was the height

,and so was the walk. While Margie Hart was cavorting around, I was staring at the back of his head and trying to figure out how to slip away without being seen.

Toward the end of the act the man yelled, Take it off! in a strange high-pitched sissy voice. I was relieved and turned my attention to the stage just in time to see the last few inches of Margie Hart's scarf as she pranced offstage. I never got a look at her thallopian tube.

On the El ride home I brooded about Daddy while my friends reprised every joke by the fat comedian who'd identified himself as the titular head of state. He'd asked the stage nurse, What's a girl got two of that a cow has four of? and answered his own question: Legs! The nurse asked the difference between a good little girl and a bad little girl. That's easy, the comedian said. The good little girl says, Gee, but it's hard to be good. The bad little girl says, It's gotta be hard to be good!

Billy was impressed that the comic had threatened to give the nurse a good spanking "in the shedhouse." That's a terrific line, Billy said. In the shedhouse.... I was sure he would work it into his repertoire of obscene sneezes.

9.

Lately Sis and I didn't know what to expect of Daddy. When he was home he would sit in his chair and stare into space, or swing on the glider on the front porch and watch the passing cars. He developed a twitch in his nose and a droop at the corners of his mouth. He would disappear for a few days, come home for a week or two, then leave again. He wasn't around for his fiftieth birthday in 1940 and I was the only one who seemed to notice. Mother always claimed that he was on the road, working, and then she'd change the subject. I kept his mitt soft and supple with neatsfoot oil, but it went unused.

He acted like a boarder while Mother took care of the house and sold baby clothes at her new job at the Pink 'n' Blue Shop on Garrett Road. I thought of the day I'd spotted him on a bench in Black Oak Park with a woman. I'd been wrong then and I was wrong at the Troc. It seemed as though I only saw my father when he wasn't there. A novelty song was going around:

Last night I saw upon the stair
A little man who wasn't there.
He wasn't there again today.
Oh, how I wish he'd go away.

That was Daddy. I just wished he'd come home to stay. I didn't care that he could be a problem sometimes. He embarrassed me in public, tried to clothe me in outmoded styles, ran up bills he couldn't pay, and got things a little wrong, but he was still my dad. His hair was graying now, and he'd lost some teeth, and he was bent from his mystery ailment,[67] but I still pictured him striking out hitters half his age, skipping over the foul line on his way to the dugout, reminiscing with his major league buddies on how they'd handled batters. In my mind I always saw him (and still do) with the Old English D on his cap. He may have been only a reliever, but how many kids could say that their fathers ever set foot onto a major league field? How many fathers showered with Ty Cobb and Harry Heilmann and had bull sessions with Herb Pennock and George Earnshaw? Whatever the twists and turns of my dad's life, nothing could take that away.

And then he came home to make my life miserable again.

---

67 The ailment was to remain a mystery. Daddy never discussed the subject, and Mother claimed that he hadn't confided in her. Medical friends suggest that he probably suffered an inguinal hernia, a condition in which the intestine pushes through abdominal muscle in the groin. The truss holds back the lump. A simple surgical procedure would have solved the problem, but Daddy had always been terrified of the knife.

It was the summer of 1939 and I was about to turn fourteen. A pretty redhead named June Braddock had invited me to my first co-ed party. Among her other talents, June played accordion and skipped double-Dutch. Daddy asked me confidentially if we were "courting."

No, I said. We're just in the same homeroom.

Don't touch her titties.

I didn't tell him that June and I had brushed forearms at the Waverly when we should have been giving our full attention to Douglas Fairbanks Jr. and Mary Pickford. I was pretty sure that she liked me, and I knew I liked her. As a runt who wasn't worldly, I had to make the most of this opportunity if I ever wanted to catch up with Billy and my other pals.

June's house was a mile and a half from the nearest Red Arrow trolley stop, so Daddy drove me in the Hudson Terraplane that he'd bought after falling for an ad about the "Electric Hand" gearshift. I downed a half package of Sen-Sen in case June offered me my first kiss. It was Jack Nokes' suggestion, and I was pleased that the little black pellets went down like aspirins, with just one gulp of water. I didn't get into my supply of Juicy Fruit gum as I'd discovered that it attracted bees. A light mist was falling and Daddy made me put on my rubbers.

On the way, he asked, What nationality is this jane?

June, I said.

Right. This jane June.

I said I didn't know. I almost said I didn't care, but that would have caused trouble.

Plays accordion?

Yeah.

Any good?

She takes lessons. She plays at assemblies.

She must be Eye-talian. Your wops, they all play squeeze box.

I don't think she's Italian, Daddy. Not with a name like Braddock.

They change their names.

I didn't care. Italian, French, Polish, Chinese — what difference did it make? And why did he call them names? Did people call us squareheads or Nazzies or Polocks? Who cared how June got to be June?

I told him she was pretty and had long red hair. I said, Italians don't have red hair, do they?

They use peroxide. Can this June step?

Huh?

Is she a good dancer?

I don't know, Daddy.

I didn't remind him that I was the only kid in our neighborhood who hadn't gone to dancing school. How would I know if she was a good dancer?

Stay outa trouble, he said when he dropped me off. I know what goes on at these parties.

It was seven o'clock. I tripped on the front steps and skinned both knees. Daddy looked out the car window and shook his head.

At five minutes after nine, a few of the guests were starting to dance when I heard a familiar voice at the front door. He waited on the porch while I pulled on my rubbers. Then he took me by the hand and led me toward the Terraplane. June followed us to the front porch. So long, Jack, she said in a querulous tone.

Yeah, I muttered. So long. Uh – thanks.

Halfway home, Daddy asked, Nice party? I said, It was just getting started.

Nine o'clock. That's plenty late for a thirteen-year-old.

I wished he would hit the road again. And stay away.

10.

And so he went away again. Uncle Ed and Aunt Freda came to town on a moviehouse inspection trip for his new employer, Paramount. They were sorry to hear that Daddy hadn't been heard from in almost a month, but they didn't seem surprised. My father's younger brother was an ex-schoolteacher and insurance adjuster who'd lost his balance when he was fired in the Depression but now was his old self. Aunt Freda's role in life seemed to be to adore her husband. The two of them held hands in our living room and discussed my missing father while I sat at the top of the stairs and listened.

They explained to Mother that Daddy had always behaved erratically and they weren't surprised that he hadn't changed. He'd had a twisted childhood, and Uncle Ed couldn't understand what kept him out of the penitentiary all these years. Long periods of his history were blank. Their mother Louisa died when Daddy was six and Uncle Ed was two. A stepmother tied Daddy to a basement pipe and whipped him with a chain. He ran away frequently but was always caught and returned home. He quit school in the fourth grade to sell newspapers, turning over his income to the stepmother (except for a five-dollar gold piece received accidentally while selling "extras" about President McKinley's assassination in 1901). When he was fourteen he beat up the stepmother and was sentenced to a boys' reformatory. He was paroled to another Ed Olsen, my great-uncle, who was superintendent of the Indianapolis Gas & Electric Company. Daddy bridled at Uncle Ed's rules and left town for good. In Jersey City a railroad bull kicked him off a flatcar. A kindly doctor set his broken ankle and returned him to the streets.

I heard Uncle Ed say, That's just about the last we heard 'til he married you in '24, Flo. We got penny postcards, but he never came back to Indianapolis.

Mother said, I guess he got busy with baseball.

He loved to play ball and he was pretty damned good, Uncle Ed said. I saw him win a doubleheader when he was thirteen. Both games! Then he wanted to play another one!

Mother said she was sorry that she'd never seen Daddy pitch for the Tigers.

Uncle Ed said, The Detroit Tigers?

Aunt Freda said, Rudolph pitched in the majors?

Mother said that's what she'd always been told. When the three of them fell silent, I eased my door shut and wondered why on earth Daddy's own brother didn't know about his major league career. Indianapolis wasn't far from Detroit on the map. If I ever made the majors, it would be big news around our house and our neighborhood. I decided that things must have been different in Daddy's day. Maybe it was because he was just a relief pitcher.

In the morning my aunt and uncle drove off to inspect Paramount theaters in South Jersey for toilet cleanliness, lobby decor, gum under seats, employee courtesy, projection equipment, and other items on the lengthy checklist that Aunt Freda showed me. In the goodbyes, I couldn't bring up Daddy's baseball career without admitting that I'd eavesdropped the night before.

Not that I had any doubts about my father. He'd been featured in every Philadelphia newspaper. He was friendly with Howard Ehmke and Whitey Witt and other major leaguers. He threw a mean curve ball even after his injury kept him from bending at the waist or using his leg-kick. Daddy might have had his faults, but he was major league through and through.

Some of Uncle Ed's other comments stuck in my mind. A fourth-grade education! How nervous Daddy must have felt in the business world. No wonder he acted like a know-it-all and scribbled nonsense in the engineering book. I felt so sorry for him, I didn't care about his lies. Lies were just Daddy. It had been a long time since anyone in our immediate family believed he was a graduate of Purdue or the "University of Indiana, Indianapolis," or even attended college.

Shortridge High School was the Olsen family school – my Indianapolis cousins Dorothy and Helene were the latest graduates – but when Shortridge was mentioned at our dinner table one night, Daddy acted as though he'd never heard of it. The only school reference I could recall was his story about playing in a kid baseball game and nearly being killed by a "buncha shines." The umpire held the ten-dollar pot in a sack behind the pitcher's mound, and when Daddy struck out the last batter he grabbed the money and ran. He climbed up a tree and kicked at his pursuers with his spikes 'til he drew blood, then held tight 'til the police arrived. That incident was one of his justifications for believing that "niggers" and "jigaboos" were all thugs. I considered it another proof that experience is the worst teacher.

I kept hoping that Uncle Ed and Aunt Freda would swing back through Drexel Hill so I could ask them for more details about Daddy's childhood, but they headed north. I wished I could find a box score from one of the games Daddy pitched for Detroit in the 1920s. I would mail it to Uncle Ed and make him proud of his big brother.

11.

One morning I noticed a familiar figure hurrying along Turner Avenue toward the Red Arrow station at Shadeland Avenue. It was our next-block neighbor Jack Ryan, a sportswriter on the *Philadelphia Evening Bulletin*.[68] Mr. Ryan always left home at the same time, walked fast, and wore sports slacks, sports jacket, and

---

68   Among other journalistic achievements, Jack Ryan bestowed the enduring label *Wilt the Stilt* on Wilt Chamberlain, the superstar basketball player.

porkpie hat. He wasn't a tall or bulky man, but he was an inspiring figure to us boys and sometimes made me think about becoming a sportswriter if I ever learned how to use the gerund "of."

I caught up and politely asked if his newspaper kept a file of old box scores.

How far back? he said. He didn't slow his pace.

I dunno. Maybe nineteen-twenty.

Well, I'm sure we've got the A's and Phillies.

You got the Tigers?

You want to look Swede up?

Maybe.

As we approached the station, the trolley from Sharon Hill was just pulling in. Mr. Ryan broke into a lope. Come see me at the paper! he said over his shoulder. Then he swung himself aboard the old brick-colored car.

I took my pal Dud Beyler along because I was intimidated by the *Bulletin*'s fancy building on the Schuylkill River. With its columns, broad plaza, and classic facade, it looked like some kind of temple, Grecian or Roman, maybe Armenian. Mr. Ryan told us how to get to the morgue and said, Tell 'em Ryan sent you.

The morgue?

That's our library. Don't worry. I'll tell Swede where to pick up the body.

When Dudley and I introduced ourselves, the elderly librarian said, My, my, the cubs are getting younger every year. He'd chewed the end of his cigar into soggy flakes and was pulling them off as though preening a canary. The place smelled like a dustbin. He flipped tobacco bits into a brass spittoon and motioned Dud and me to a table scarred with coffee cup stains and cigarette burns.

The Bulletin was a broadsheet, and the bound volumes were as heavy as pine slabs. We'd just opened a book marked "Jan

1920" when Dud said, What're we, stupid or something? Nobody plays baseball in January.

That was why Dud was on the Honor Roll and I was getting Cs and Ds. We turned to the April book and found crackly old box scores of A's exhibition games. We checked every pre-season game with the Tigers, plus each of the twenty-two games in the regular season, home and away. There was no Swede Olsen. No Ole Olsen. No Olsens or Olsons.

We returned the 1920 book and asked the librarian for 1921. The result was the same. Let's start over, I said. We might of missed it.

We hadn't. We moved ahead to 1922. I felt a little sick. Dudley said, You sure you got the right years?

I started to say that nothing was sure about my father, but I kept quiet. Dud was my best friend and could keep a secret, but if Daddy's name didn't show up in these box scores, I would probably hitchhike to San Francisco and ship out to the Fiji Islands and spend the rest of my life digging coconuts.

A voice said, You boys finding what you want?

I looked up and saw Mr. Ryan. I told him what we were looking for and he laughed and said we were doing it the hard way. Wait here, he instructed.

He returned in a few minutes and plopped a thick green paperback book on the table. I'm on deadline, he said. Return this to the librarian. It's got stats on every major leaguer that ever played.

Lemme look, Dud said, grabbing the book from me. You got St. Vitus dance of the hands.

My pal knew his way around reference books. As he opened to the table of contents, I prayed to myself, O Lord, Let Daddy's name be there. I will never miss another church service if you help me out just one more time.

Dud showed me the page. Never in doubt, he said, a

phrase we used when we were shooting pool. Large black type screamed out "Ole Olsen."

Hot damn, I said, slapping my pal on the back. What a dope I'd been to doubt my own father.

The first line read: Bats right, throws right.

See that, Dud? I said. That's Daddy!

His height was listed as five-ten and his weight as 163 pounds. It seemed a little small, but he'd had twenty years to put on weight. I was getting bigger myself, five-nine, 120 pounds, catching up to my classmates.

The next line listed middy's date of birth: September 12, 1894. They'd made a mistake there, not that it mattered. Daddy's birthday was May 19, and I'd always been told that he was born in 1890. Maybe he lied about his age to impress Ty Cobb, the nasty player-manager who used to spike his opponents on purpose. Daddy had taught me that a lie was sometimes necessary.

I skipped ahead to his pitching record. In 1922 Daddy had made thirty-seven appearances, or one out of every four of the Tigers' games. Not bad, huh, Dud? I said.

The book showed that Ole Olsen had won seven games and lost six, racked up 52 strikeouts in 137 innings, held opposing batters to a .281 average, and finished with an earned run average of 4.53. I knew of A's and Phillies pitchers with worse records, and some had held on to their jobs for years.

Daddy's 1923 numbers were disappointing. He'd won one game and lost one, pitched in 17 games and struck out only 12. His ERA jumped to 6.31 and opposing teams hit .290 against him, high numbers for a reliever.

I turned to the 1924 statistics. Daddy's name was gone. That was the year he showed up in Jersey City and married Mother. The figures clicked. He'd had a short career in the majors, but he'd been up for two seasons. What a relief.

Hey, Dud was saying, lookee here.

He pointed to a short biography and asked, Is your old man's name Arthur?

It's Rudolph. Or, uh ... Ralph.

Not ... Arthur?

Arthur?

The Tiger pitcher was Arthur Olsen.

Jeez, I thought, another mistake. You'd think these statisticians could get a man's name right even if they screwed up some of the numbers.

Lemme see, I said.

I read that Arthur "Ole" Olsen had graduated from Cornell University in 1918, pitched for the Tigers in 1922 and 1923, and was a member of the Cornell Hall of Fame. I thought, Why didn't Daddy tell us about this? Why all the jabber about Purdue and the University of Indiana? And didn't Uncle Ed say that Daddy quit school in the fourth grade?

My head was swimming. I was afraid to keep reading. But then I realized I didn't need to read another word.

Arthur "Ole" Olsen was born in Connecticut.

He wasn't Daddy.

He was another Ole Olsen.

What's the matter with you? Dud asked as the El train rattled into the 69th Street Terminal. Maybe they made a mistake. It's not the end of the world.

I said, Yes, it is.

12.

It took me a long time, but I finally worked out a plausible theory based on a few known facts. There had been an Ole Olsen and he had pitched for the Tigers. Daddy would have been thirty-two in Arthur Olsen's first major league year, not too old for a savvy relief pitcher. He could have pitched for Detroit .... But he hadn't.

In my mind I reconstructed a pivotal scene in the hoax. Swede Olsen has just finished pitching a game in Coatesville or Media or somewhere else on the Pennsylvania sandlots. An elderly baseball fan ambles up and says, Ole Olsen? Swede? Weren't you with the Tigers around twenty-two, twenty-three?

Daddy is caught short. He thinks about the question for a few seconds and then nods. He didn't set himself out as a major leaguer, but what was the harm in going along with the old guy – at least for the moment?

Word slowly spreads in Philadelphia sporting circles and soon reaches the ears of locals like Eddie Gottlieb and then up the ladder to major leaguers like Mickey Cochrane and Connie Mack. It becomes accepted: good old Swede pitched for Detroit for a year or two. You could look it up, but why bother? Plenty of talented ballplayers came up to the majors for a cup of coffee, then returned to the minor leagues, the semipros, and oblivion.

Communications were bad in those days.

Now I thought I understood why Daddy never wanted to discuss his major league days, why he cut off discussion about the Tigers, why he didn't want me to root for the team. His Detroit connection started as a misunderstanding, turned into a lie, and then was set in stone – or type. Daddy chose to let it stand.

I wondered how he must have felt at the baseball banquets, the festivities, awards, sandlot and exhibition games when he'd been introduced to the crowd as "former Detroit Tigers hurler." I opened my scrapbook to a 1932 banquet story in the *Philadelphia Public Ledger*: Swede Olsen, former big-league ballplayer and now active in independent circles in this section, extolled

Mr. Nugent for the interest he always has displayed in the semi-pros. Olsen said the Phillies' president was ready at all times to do anything possible for any "backlot" team.

I thought how nervous the fourth-grade drop-out must have been as he stood in front of 800 baseball executives, sportswriters, fans, ballplayers, and ex-ballplayers, any one of whom might jump up and expose him in an instant. In that audience there must have been a few who'd played against the real Ole Olsen from Connecticut. How his heart must have pounded!

I thought how frightening it would be to go through life as something you weren't and to pretend to know everything so that no one would find out how little you really knew. Poor Daddy. As he sat in his chair scribbling nonsense in the margins of our engineering textbook, as he typed "yrs of 8th inst. received and contents duly noted," as he asked the waiter for the soup *du jour* of the day, as he bluffed and blustered his way through fifty years of life, he must have been shaking inside.

13.

I was slouching through my junior year of high school when I accidentally found my own niche in sport. As a ninth-grader I'd been exposed to bowling in the basement of the Garrettford Fire Station, using a 12-pound cork ball to score a surprising 155 in my first and only game. It seemed so simple. If you didn't knock the pins down on the first try, you got another chance. The milk-bottle concession at the carnival in Jersey City had been tougher. Bowling seemed so easy, in fact, that I found it boring and lost interest after that first game.

I might have gone through life with a permanent 155 average if Playhouse Bowl hadn't opened in an old theater building on Garrett Road, three blocks from home. A Pinboys Wanted sign went up and I was one of the first to apply. The pay was four cents a game, but the owner, an affable gambler named Jack Robbins, assured me that a hardworking boy might find himself earning a nickel or even six cents a line in a few months. On league nights I could count on a solid sixty cents for two hours of work, plus another dime or two in tips. It was indoor work, and it beat shoveling snow or selling radishes.

Mr. Robbins apprenticed me to Ed Leuthy, the houseman, a sly gnome who weighed about a hundred pounds and had half a head of stringy black hair, four or five teeth, a Pinocchio nose, a gray complexion and a permanent aroma of chaw tobacco and earwax. For thirty years Ed had set pins in emporiums like Walnut Bowl and Hudson Lanes in Philadelphia, and in the twilight of his career he was generous with his advice. He was also an experienced bowler who could teach me the game.

On my first day of work Ed led me down to the pits. The place smelled like fresh shellac. He showed me how to grab four pins at once – two in each hand, crisscrossed at the necks and set them on the retractable metal nipples that popped out of the floor when you stepped on a pedal. After I got the hang, he showed me a few tricks of his own. Sometimes he set the five-pin just in front of its proper position so that the pins would mix better and produce more strikes, shortening the game. He taught me to stand in the corner of the pit instead of sitting on the back bench and proved that it wasn't dangerous by bowl-ing a couple of balls while I cringed and held my position. It worked like a magic trick. By the time the ball reached the back row, its energy had dissipated and the corner pins toppled gen-tly against my calf. The 10-pin, the most stubborn in bowling, fell every time because Ed taught me to lean into it. The bowl-ers couldn't tell from sixty feet away.

As I learned the trade, my customers began to bowl faster and score higher. I developed my own clientele, bowlers who would ask for the skinny dark-haired kid. They sensed that they scored better with me in the pits. The high game of Playhouse Bowl's first full season was a 266 in which the customer threw eight straight strikes. My knee took out the 10-pin in three of them.

In the afternoons when business was light, pinboys set pins for each other and bowled free. It took me about three months to raise my average to the 170s. I was racking up fifteen or twenty lines a day, six days a week, and learning the alleys. They were slicker in the mornings after my friend Ed oiled them with a rotary machine that sometimes broke away from him and skittered into the gutters. They were stickier in the evenings after the oil broke down and a layer of grit and dust had settled. When the honey-colored alleys were "fast," I twisted my wrist to give my ball more spin. I cut down on the curve as the day progressed. I knew how to handle the lanes at 10 a.m. and 10 p.m. and every hour between.

I was becoming The Young Master of Playhouse Bowl.

Jack Robbins took notice. The owner-manager was a portly man of about forty, a graduate of Ursinus College and a compulsive gambler like Daddy. I liked him because he was fair about working conditions and had a kid's sense of humor. He would greet us pinboys with, Good evening, Mr. and Mrs. Bate, and how's young Master Bate? When he saw me at the urinal, he would say, Leave it alone, it'll grow. He fit right in with me and Billy Glossop.

I found out that Jack had begun watching my afternoon sessions from the balcony.

Pinboys like Johnny Bucceroni and his little brother Sal and I had become so skilled from non-stop practice sessions that we learned to duplicate some of champion bowler Andy Varipapa's trick shots – throwing two balls at a time, making them curve across each other in mid-lane and knock down the

7 and 10 pins in the corners. Or we would plant a pin halfway down the alley, knock it across the divider to take out the 7 in the adjacent lane while the ball rolled on to topple the 10. We learned how to spin the ball *a la* Frank Merriwell so that it would curve in two directions before hitting the head pin. They were gimmick shots, of course, easier than they looked, and we pinboys had plenty of time to work them out.

One afternoon Jack Robbins beckoned me into his cubbyhole office. He said, How'd you like to bowl in our sweepstakes? He snaked a little finger into his ear, scrutinized the contents, and looked disappointed.

I said it sounded fine to me. A sweepstakes was an evening event with cash prizes, open to anyone with the entrance fee. Fifteen-year-old kids didn't bowl in sweeps at the Playhouse or anywhere else; they couldn't afford the fee and they couldn't compete with veteran bowlers. A typical sweepstakes winner might score 600 or 650 in a three-game set. I was a year or two away from that level, but I was consistently bowling in the 170s and my high single stood at 236.

Jack offered to pay my sweepstakes fees on one condition. You gotta promise not to win.

Huh?

You like to bowl free, right?

Sure.

You like competition?

Yep.

Be here tonight at eight. I'll get somebody to set up in your alley.

At first I didn't understand what was going on, but as I competed in one sweepstakes after another, placing as high as third and collecting a little prize money, I realized that our slick proprietor was up to something. I suspected that he planned to win a bundle in a horse race. And I was the horse.

14.

I wasn't directly involved in his hustle, but I knew enough about gambling from watching Daddy, and I pieced Jack's scheme together with a few hints from our houseman Ed Leuthy.

Every night a group of spectators sat in the same seats. They were mostly older men, dressed in gray fedoras, huddled in their topcoats, laying down blue-gray smokescreens with Coronas and Swisher Sweets. They kept up a constant chatter, making new bets, laying off old bets, settling accounts, wolfing at one another. I would hear comments like, A buck no strike ... Two to one against the split ... Gimme twenty pins and the tall guy ... Three to one blue shirt don't strike out.

Jack Robbins was doing a steady business with the gamblers.

Now and then hustlers would appear at the Playhouse and fleece the locals. I learned later that this was known as "picking up the rubes by their pockets." The bowling con worked like the famous pool hustles that would be exposed in books and movies twenty years later. An inconspicuous stranger, often wearing work clothes and renting house shoes, would select a battered old ball, bowl a few practice games in the 130s and 140s, then lose a couple of money matches. When the bets edged high enough, he would start winning by small margins to keep the sucker on the hook. When the bet got high enough, he would strike. And strike, and strike. That was how our neighbor Mr. Rizzo lost $200 on a Thursday evening, and another Playhouse customer forfeited his motorcycle.

A month after I appeared in my first sweepstakes at Jack Robbins' expense, my average had climbed to 180. In an afternoon session with my colleague Johnny Bucceroni in the pits, I put together seven straight strikes for a 239. I followed with a 226.

Jack called me into his office again. Take a little off that hook, he said. High school kids don't bowl that good. You're scaring off my fish.

I knew better than to argue with the golden goose. Night after night of competitive bowling was any pinboy's dream, and every now and then Jack would slip me a buck or two. I planned to join the bowling club at Upper Darby High and make my name as an athlete. Bowling wasn't an official school sport, but club members competed against schools like Lower Merion, Haverford, Abington, and Radnor. Sometimes the newspapers printed the scores. Upper Darby usually lost. I planned to improve our record.

Our mark arrived one afternoon in a vested business suit and a neat woolen tie. His wingtip shoes were shined and his rimless glasses caught the fluorescent lights. He looked like Uncle Ed on a field trip for Paramount. He stood behind the three rows of seats and watched the afternoon action, made idle conversation with Jack Robbins and the regulars, and rented a pair of shoes. He said he hadn't bowled in years but wanted to try his luck.

His first attempt went into the gutter – a "poodle." So did his second. He turned to the gallery with a wan grin. Then he pulled himself together and resurrected a 128. I was setting the pins and noticed that his ball had plenty of natural spin. Such "working balls" could be devastating in the 1-3 pocket. But first you had to be able to hit the pocket.

The man returned the next day, told us his name was Al Rowe and he was a construction engineer. He said he'd carried a 151 average back in Altoona, but that was years ago. He was overseeing a project in nearby Yeadon and might join one of our leagues if he could get his game back in shape.

After his scores improved, he began to stir up a little action with the locals. He won some and lost some and began to aggravate everybody with his snotty tone. He told Ed Leuthy that he bowled like a girl. He told Jack Robbins he'd seen better alleys at the YWCA. He told me to quit leaning into the ten-pin or he'd use me for a dust rag. I was glad to oblige. That only meant that the jerk's scores would drop.

But they didn't. They climbed into the 170s and 180s and he won a few bigger bets. When the locals realized that he was better than he'd looked, he started offering handicaps, twenty or thirty pins per game. Still he took their money.

Jack Robbins let the situation go on for a few weeks and then told me he'd accepted a challenge from Al Rowe on my behalf. He didn't say whether a bet was involved, but of course there was. I learned later that Jack had employed his own style to goad the goader. He'd told the "construction engineer" that he knew a high school kid who could beat his ass. Rowe responded that there wasn't a teen-aged punk on earth who could beat him in a scratch[69] match and why didn't Robbins put up or shut up? They agreed that Rowe and the punk would bowl three games head to head across two alleys. I didn't know the stakes.

15.

We met on a hot July night. The Playhouse wasn't air-conditioned and I was sweating as I picked up my house ball, a black Brunswick numbered 83. After I warmed up with a half dozen lackadaisical efforts on an empty alley, Rowe threw two balls straight into the one-three pocket, his curve hooking perfectly. He beckoned the pinboy that he was ready. He seemed to be saying that two free balls were all the practice a man needed to humiliate a boy.

The spectators quieted. Sweepstakes action continued in

---

69   No handicap.

the other six lanes, but some of the bowlers glanced our way. As I chalked my fingers for the first frame, Jack Robbins gave me a thumbs-up. I was surprised that I wasn't more nervous. If I won, Jack would slip me a few bucks. If I lost, life would go on. What's to worry?

I opened with two strikes. It was almost nine o'clock, the alleys were slow, and my hook was breaking without effort.

Rowe opened by leaving the ten-pin on a perfect hit – a spectator yelled, It's part of the building! – and missed the spare when his curve broke too sharply. I wondered if he was trying to "push" the bet. A star bowler could go a whole season without missing a tenpin spare.

In his second frame he converted a four-ten split, one of the hardest in the game for a righthander. Then he began a string of strikes. By the 'eighth frame, he'd caught me. He spared in the ninth and struck out in the tenth to win by 11 pins. The hustler had thrown a total of eight strikes to my five. I had two games to catch up. I saw Jack standing in the balcony. He didn't look concerned.

Rowe easily won the next game and took a 34-pin lead into the final game. I told myself I would stage a great comeback. Coming from behind was my style and these were my alleys.

We matched strikes for the first three frames of the final game. I struck in the fourth but he ran into another solid ten-pin and settled for a spare. In the fifth frame No. 83 got away from me – I'd neglected to chalk my sweaty thumb – and the ball crossed to the Jersey side.[70] When the wood finished swirling around, the ten was still standing, but a loose pin rolled all the way across the deck and nudged it into the gutter. On a bad throw and a stroke of luck I'd almost pulled even. And I was working on five strikes in a row. The crowd buzzed. Bowlers

---

70   The left side of the headpin was almost universally known as the Brooklyn side. But Philadelphia bowlers called it the Jersey.

drifted over to watch. Up in the balcony, Jack Robbins' pate was beginning to look like my radishes. Little Ed Leuthy stood next to him, a hand over his heart. For a second I wondered how much Jack had bet on the match.

I threw four more strikes in a row. Rowe matched me through the sixth, seventh and eighth frames and then missed a five-seven split by the thickness of a coat of paint.

As I stepped up for my final frame, I'd bowled nine straight strikes and was well ahead in total pins. The hustler was working on a strike and had a slight chance to catch me, but I would almost have to break a leg to lose.

I took a deep breath and let fly. The ball rumbled along the right gutter, broke two-thirds of the way down the alley, and curved into the one and three pins for a strike.

That made ten in a row and Rowe was out of the match. We'd hustled the hustler. But I still had unfinished business. Playhouse Bowl was a year old and had never recorded a 300 game. The closest was 279 – nine strikes and a spare in the final frame. Ed Leuthy had bowled that one and put his own name on the bulletin board. I was two strikes away from perfection.

I told myself to stop thinking and just throw the darn ball. I tried to ignore the ribbons of smoke in the overhead lights or hear the pinfall or the rumbles of other balls. I slipped my two fingers and then my thumb into the three holes, lifted the ball to my chest, rocked a few inches from toe to heel to loosen up, and glided toward the foul line. The hit was light, but every pin fell. A cheer went up and quickly subsided. I needed one more strike.

The gallery went silent. Playhouse Bowl turned into the Videon funeral parlor. Pinboys drifted out of their pits and lined up along the walls. I thought, That's just the distraction I need. Thanks a lot, pals ....

I dried my hands on the towel, chalked my fingers, and

hefted the ball. As I stepped to the backline, I decided to throw this last shot a little harder. It was ten o'clock and the surface was slow. I didn't want to cross to the Jersey side and pray for a lucky pinfall. I didn't want to leave this game up to Jesus. I wanted to leave it up to me.

I pushed No. 83 away from my chest and began the five-step delivery that Ed Leuthy had taught me. I added an inch or two to my backswing and released the ball with a sharp twist.

As soon as it left my hand, I knew I'd thrown too hard. The ball would never get up to the pocket. It curved a few inches, straightened out and rumbled toward the right side of the set-up. My God, I thought, will I miss the head pin? After eleven straight strikes?

Halfway down the alley, the spin took hold and the ball curved toward the pocket.

There was a loud clatter and every pin disappeared. I blinked and took another look. The deck was clean. I felt silly and giddy. I thought, At last, at last! I won the doll for Sis! Butch Bucceroni ran up the gutter swinging a towel over his head. Tears ran down Ed Leuthy's craggy face. Bowlers lined up to shake my hand. I was an athlete.

Daddy's maroon Terraplane was parked in front of our house. For a change, I was glad he was in town. I heard his snoring when I let myself in the front door. It was almost eleven o'clock. He and Mother let me stay out late to set pins.

I was working on my second helping of Wheaties when he came down the stairs in his bathrobe, rubbing his eyes. Daddy, I said, I bowled a perfect game.

You ... what?

I bowled three-hundred. Twelve strikes.

He turned to go back upstairs. I ain't surprised, he said. Not with all the time you spend at that place.

16.

The article in the *69th Street News* was headlined "Perfect Game." I found out later that Daddy bought extra copies.

Jack Robbins seemed annoyed when I saw him the next day. Goddamn it, kid, he said, why didn't you leave a coupla pins? Why'd you go and get your name in the papers?

I said I had no idea who'd spread the news, but I suspected my mother. She'd already sent to the Brunswick-Balke-Collender Company in Chicago for the blue-and-gold pin they awarded to 300 bowlers.

Jack said, Why didn't you hire a skywriter? Jesus Christ, kid, we had a good thing going. Now even Jim Murgie[71] wouldn't bowl you for dough. He handed me a twenty-dollar bill.

Holy smokes, I said. How much did you win?

More than a buck, he said. Less than a grand.

Later Ed Leuthy told me that the house had formed a pool to spread some of Al Rowe's action around. Jack made a three-hundred-dollar killing and Ed hauled in forty bucks himself, a week's pay. Playhouse Bowl had taken the hustler for six-hundred-and-some bucks. We never saw him again. I guess he went back to Altoona.

17.

A rangy classmate named Howard Umberger and I won a few doubles matches against other Delaware County High Schools.[72] Then a Playhouse habitue named Joe Barnes, a lanky Drexel Hill boy who commuted to West Catholic High School

---

71 A local star. He was famous for throwing three consecutive perfect games at 69th Street Bowl.

72 Howard wrote in my yearbook, "Someday we will bowl again." He was killed in action in World War II.

in the city, showed me a newspaper clipping about two students who claimed the Philadelphia high school doubles championship. What the heck, Joe said. Let's take 'em on.

Jack Robbins agreed to sponsor us and issued a public challenge to the champs, Hank Lipinski of Northeast Catholic and Duke Bilyeu of West Philly High. On our own alleys in the first five games of the home-and-home match, Joe and I ended up with a one-pin lead. I was high man with a 988 series, just under a 200 average. But when we traveled to Walnut Lanes, home of our competitors, a raucous crowd of Bilyeu-Lipinski fans scared me half to death. I asked Joe how he could bowl in front of an audience that was booing us and calling us names. He told me not to take it personally. At West Catholic, he said, we're taught to act like Jesus in all situations. Jesus would be calm.

In the end, Jesus and Joe made up for my stage fright with five steady games in the 190s. The three of us became the high school doubles champs of Philadelphia, P-A.

I was surprised that my alma mater didn't declare a holiday in my honor or award me a purple-and-gold UD, but the athletic staff was unimpressed. Joe's school acted as though we'd won the Olympics. I was nervous about going onstage at West Catholic High. I passed the big stone building every time I took the El into Philadelphia, and it looked like a design by Charles Dickens. The athletic field was dotted with somber-looking men walking around in black skirts and staring at their black shoes. Joe said the teachers were good guys, but they cracked a lot of knuckles. He warned me to watch my manners when we went onstage.

We were met at a side door by a young priest who led us through spooky corridors and torture chambers to the wings of an auditorium. I peeked out and saw hundreds of boys sitting in silence. I thought, If this was Upper Darby High, the air would be filled with spitballs and you wouldn't be able to hear yourself breathe. Is this a school or Eastern State pen?

I'm a little nervous, Father, I said to our robed escort.

Brother, he said.

Brother?

We're called Brother.

I'm a little nervous, Brother.

Take a deep breath. Act like a hero. You're a big man at West Catholic.

Yes, but I'm a Lutheran, Father ... uh, Brother.

Our Lord doesn't expect perfection, my son.

I could see that he was trying not to laugh. Have some fun, he whispered as he nudged me toward the stage. Try not to pass out.

The hoots and cheers and clapping surprised me. Except for Nanny and the Tanners, Catholics had always seemed distant and cold, their priests a collection of talking statues who blinked like owls and wore jewelry. Daddy had warned me not to marry a mackerel-snapper unless I wanted to spend the rest of my life arguing about how many angels could dance on the head of a pin. The answer, he said, is none. They'd fall flat on their ass. The good losers Lipinski and Bilyeu were ushered in from the opposite wings and received a loud reception. The principal lifted a silver trophy above his head and shook it like a winning boxer. He said it was emblematic of the Philadelphia High School Doubles Championship and would make a worthy addition to West Catholic's trophy case. He told the students that they could thank their own Joe Barnes and a talented young man from Upper Darby named Jack Olsen. An icicle slid down my back. I'd never heard my name called out in public except when Miss Grunberg lost her temper and awarded me a F in wed ink. I slid behind Joe, who was three inches taller.

The principal pointed at me and said in a stern voice, Come

out from behind your partner, Mr. Olsen! West Catholic wants to see a champion.

Mr. Olsen! I thought, If I make another mistake, he'll crack my knuckles.

A roly-poly priest marched onstage and said something in Latin that made the students laugh and whistle. I couldn't believe my ears: a Latin joke! A comedian priest! I wondered if he knew how to say shedhouse in Latin.

The chubby little Brother nodded toward Joe and began to speak. When our Mr. Barnes teamed up with young Mr. Olsen, he said, clapping me on the shoulder, Mr. Olsen wanted to know if it mattered that he was a Protestant. Mr. Barnes told him, Not if you can make the six-seven split!

The audience went into hysterics. I still couldn't believe what was happening. Behind me were silken embroideries and holy statues and the trappings of a solemn religion, and the congregation was acting like a fight crowd while the teachers told jokes. It occurred to me that Daddy had been wrong again: Catholics weren't mackerel snappers. They were just Lutherans in robes.

18.

Living in my tight little world of bowling, baseball and C-minus report cards, I wasn't even sure what my father did for a living anymore. Underwriters Service Bureau had folded and Mother told me that he was inspecting wrecked cars. When war industries began springing up, he went from Kellett Autogyro to a place called Empire Ordnance and then a shipyard and then Westinghouse.

He can't get along with people, Mother explained when I asked why he kept changing jobs. He talks his way in, she said, but he always gets fired. I don't know what we'd do if we had to depend on him.

Daddy seemed like a boarder these days.

At Playhouse Bowl some of the pinboys and I decided to press our luck with a teen-age team that would challenge other high school kids. Our first problem was wheels. There were six of us, counting Eddie Wales, our Bible fanatic with the 140-average, and we were all too young to drive. We would have to bowl in strange alleys as far as ten and twenty miles away. At first we traveled on our thumbs, but few drivers wanted to stop for a gang of scruffy looking kids.

Since we competed under the name Playhouse Bowl, Jack Robbins stepped in and solved our problem. A junkyard in Clifton Heights was about to flatten a 1925 Lincoln hearse, and Jack talked the proprietor into lending it to us for the season. Ed Leuthy would be the wheelman.

While I was at home preparing a liverwurst sandwich for my sister's dinner, the other five members of our team piled into the newly christened "Blackie" for a test drive. Ed took the wheel, his head barely reaching windshield level. When he backed the hearse into our driveway to pick me up, Mrs. Manno cried out from next door, Oh, Jackie, I'm so sorry.

A faint smell of flowers came from inset vases that Russ Spotz was using as ashtrays. Mark Donahue gave us all a start by shouting, What's that on the road? A head? Ed slammed on the brakes and we piled atop one another, giggling with the joy of riding in a motor vehicle that wasn't driven by our parents.

We settled down and peered out the S-shaped slits in the tonneau. Pedestrians covered their hearts. An old woman in a babushka crossed herself and reminded me of Nanny. A school crossing guard waved us through. Johnny Bucceroni said, How can we lose with fans like this?

In Manoa we beat a bunch of rich kids who wore ties and bowled with their pinkies extended. On the way home, Ed

Leuthy told off-color jokes. While the black hearse rocked, our choirboy Eddie Wales said, Mr. Leuthy, don't you know one joke that ain't dirty?

Yeah, Ed said. There was this Irish cocksuckers' party....

As we approached the Playhouse, we were followed by some cars with their lights on. Folks chase funerals, Ed explained.

Why? I asked.

I guess for the fun of it.

He parked the hearse around the corner and we piled out. One by one the trailing cars peeled off, but an old man in a Lincoln Phaeton rolled down his window and yelled, Who passed away?

Ed said, Oh, uh ... John Doe.

God rest his soul, the man said. He was a fine man.

Our Playhouse team won matches in Darby, Manayunk, and Frankfurt before Blackie broke an axle and put us out of business. I missed the free food almost as much as I missed the bowling. After each match, Ed would take us to a sandwich shop in Clifton Heights and order hoagies at the expense of Jack Robbins and the Playhouse. Hoagies sold for fifteen cents and a quarter. In those days the big model was so large that no one would think of ordering seconds.

One night Ed took us to a place in South Philly that served tomato pies, "direct from Naples." We watched as the cook twirled a blob of dough into a thin round pancake, brushed it with tomato paste, sprinkled on some herbs and slid it into a big oven.

As we drove away, Butch Bucceroni said, Let's stick wit' hoagies.

Yeah, said his little brother Sal. This tomato pie shit'll never catch on.[73]

---

73 This was in 1941 and local specialties like Philly cheese steaks were still unknown. The original Philadelphia hoagies were made with Italian bread, ham, pep-

19.

One day Daddy telephoned from town to announce that he'd
bought a second car for the family and would be driving it
home in the evening. I took off from Playhouse Bowl and hung
around the house so excited I could hardly talk. Mother said it
must be his idea of a joke. What a cruel thing to do, she said.
He barely sleeps here anymore. Why would he buy us a car?

I said, I heard him, Mother! Would Daddy lie?

We heard the car before we saw it. The old black sedan
bucked and lurched and backfired down Turner Avenue and
stalled halfway up our driveway. Daddy climbed out like an
Indy racer after the victory lap.

Whattaya thinka this baby, Sonny?

He told me it was a 1916 Hupmobile Runabout, the four-
cylinder model. He said, You're chief driver and mechanic. This
is what every kid wants.

Yes, I thought, but where'll I find leather gloves up to my
elbows? And goggles?

Mother asked how much the heap cost.

Ten bucks, Daddy said.

Mother said, Gee, another bargain.

For three days I spent every spare minute in my car. I would
buck and jerk along for fifteen or twenty feet to the end of our
driveway, stomp on the brake pedal, shift into neutral, and push
the car back to the starting point in lieu of learning how to go
into reverse gear. Then I would re-set the spark and magnetos.

Sis helped with the pushing, but Mother said that the constant backfires gave her headaches. An exposed spring gouged
out my rear end as I drove. Rain came through a leak in the

---

peroni, provolone, lettuce, onions, tomatoes, olive oil, salt, pepper, and oregano. I
tasted hundreds of "improved" versions through the years, some containing celery,
hot peppers, garlic, marjoram, and other spices and condiments. Some were delicious. But they weren't Philadelphia hoagies.

roof and sent a steady drip down my back. The horn made an old-fashioned *oooo-gah* except when I pressed the black button in the center of the steering wheel. The steering wheel itself had a tendency to fall off. The back seat and running boards were missing.

On the fourth day I heard a whoosh and caught a smell like the refineries down by the river in Essington. Blue flames darted from the hood openings. By the time I hooked up our garden hose, the fire was burning so hot that the side-mounted spare tire burst with a noise like a cherry bomb.

The fire department extinguished the blaze, and a wrecker hauled off the remains for twenty-five dollars. The Olsens had scored another bargain.

20.

In my senior year I began to notice a change in the style of humor at Upper Darby High, and it caught me by surprise, not unusual in matters of sophistication. In junior high, most of our jokes had been about bodily functions and nudity, and in the first years of high school we'd been preoccupied with the ins and outs of sex. Now the tone changed. Carter Harrison couldn't understand why I didn't laugh when he informed me that the Teddy van Axel ate at the Y. Dummy Davis talked about the Frenchman who fell asleep the minute his feet hit the pillow. Dummy claimed that he knew a queer midget who went up on people. Sal Bucceroni said his uncle drove a per-vertible: The top don't go down but the driver does. To the tune of "One O'Clock Jump," Homer Smith sang, Spread your legs, you're steaming my glasses, and Bobby Filmer followed with Spread your legs, you're crushing my straw hat. Billy Glossop's standard greeting became, The wind blows free. How much do you charge?

I laughed, but as usual I wasn't entirely sure what I was laughing about. My friends came out with remarks like, He eats it with a spoon .... He eats it with a straw.... Holy Smokes, I thought, eats what?

I mentioned the comedy trend to my pal Dudley Beyler and learned that he was also in the dark. All's I know, he told me, it has something to do with oriole sex.

I wondered why a bunch of teenage boys would joke about birds and decided to ask Ed Leuthy. He wasn't as worldly as my father, but he'd traveled all over eastern Pennsylvania.

Oh, he said, you mean eating pussy.

I couldn't believe my ears.

He said, It means sucking dick, too.

Before I could stop him, he was halfway through a tedious joke about three workmen: a coke-sacker, a cork-socker, and a sock-tucker. I listened politely, then made the mistake of smiling. Apparently the wizened little man had a vast repertoire of jokes about oriole sex and had been waiting for an audience.

Knock-knock, he said.

I said, Who's there?

Honeysuckle.

Honeysuckle who?

Honeysuckle little harder.

My embarrassed cackle only encouraged him. Hey, he said, didja hear that the Pope raised the height of the urinals in Rome?

I ducked out the side door. 1 thought, Better a little rudeness than eternity with scorpions.

When I encountered Ed touching up the alleys an hour later, he yelled, To keep the dagoes on their toes!

Butch Bucceroni stormed out of the pits and threatened to punch out his last few teeth if he didn't apologize on the spot.

Yeah, yeah, I'm sorry, Ed said. I meant Belgians.

21.

Two months before I was scheduled to graduate, Mother told me that Daddy had left and this time she didn't expect him back. He'd complained again that she was sullying his reputation by working, and when she told him we couldn't pay our bills without her income, he said, I got youse this far, didn't I? Where'd I find ya, Flo? In an alley? Then he sped off in his maroon Terraplane with the electric gearshift.

Sis and Mother didn't seem to care. Carolyn was growing into a beautiful and talented young woman. She sang lead roles in school musicals, and everyone expected her to win a scholarship to the Curtis Institute of Music on Locust Street. Daddy had always seemed annoyed at her social successes. He'd forbidden her to date after he saw her drinking a milkshake with classmates at the Hot Shoppes. He told her, I know what goes on in them sody places.

When she brought a boy home to rehearse a duet, Daddy asked him if he was Jewish. Timothy McGurk never returned.

Over the dinner table, Mother told us, Your father's been gone for years, Jackie. You should be used to it.

He'll be back, I said, rubbing my eyes.

Mother said, A bad penny never turns up.

I'll find him myself and bring him home.

How? On Sister's bike?

I slumped in my chair and we all fell silent. Then Mother said, Drexel Hill's too rich for our blood. We'll have to find a place in the city.

I did some quick arithmetic, never my long suit. Jack Robbins had just promoted me to morning clean-up man. I opened the Playhouse at seven with my own key, emptied ashtrays, collected bottles and cans, polished the metal, swept up, and cleaned the ladies' and gents' for ten dollars a week. Sometimes I filled in as evening manager, and I set pins on nights when we were shorthanded. Every week Jack slipped me an extra five or ten bucks for taking money from his fish, and I was winning a few side bets of my own. I hardly had time for schoolbooks and wobbled from classroom to classroom like a sleepwalker, but I had money in my pocket for the four basic food groups: Tastykakes, Welch's Fudge Bars, chocolate malts, and Hershey Bars.

I said, Mother, we can make it!

We sat at our kitchen table and roughed out a budget. She was earning thirty-five dollars at the Pink 'n' Blue Shop, which meant that the two of us brought home sixty or sixty-five a week. Our rent was sixty a month, utilities were six or eight, we had no car expense, and we knew how to skimp on food.

It's right here in black and white, I said. We'll be okay!

Mother chewed on her lower lip and was quiet for a while. Then Sis jumped in. I can work, she said.

I hated to hear it. She had too much talent to waste on some squirrely after-school job that might pay a quarter an hour and wear her out. She needed to concentrate on her career. When I argued, she said that she was fourteen now, still getting straight A's, and her childhood was over. She said she would babysit and clean houses, if necessary. Yeah, I said to myself, and you'll work on a road gang and outperform the men. And get the biggest piece of pie! Sis was born to win.

Mother stared out the kitchen window. I knew what she was thinking. Our persimmon tree was heavy with fruit, and Maiden's Blush rosebuds dotted the arbor. As usual she'd bleached our clothes so white that they resembled dogwood blossoms flapping on the line. Our lawn was clipped, my regular chore.

We'd lived in Upper Darby off and on for twelve years, and it was the first time in Mother's life that she could look out and see Gloriosa daisies the size of dinner plates, pale purple morning glories, snapdragons, and nasturtiums that she'd planted herself. I knew it would break her heart to leave.

We'll give it a try, she said. One day at a time.

I was relieved that we didn't have to move to the city, my oldest nightmare. I was almost seventeen now, six feet tall, 160 pounds, and filling out. I remembered when Mother had told me to act like the man of the house. Now I was. It was every boy's fantasy.

22.

"John Edward Olsen" graduated from Upper Darby High School in June, 1942. My name appeared on the list of college prep candidates even though there'd never been a chance that my family could afford the tuition even if we'd been able to find a school with subterranean admission standards.

The commencement ceremonies were held in the Tower Theater on 69th Street, a fancy moviehouse with its own version of the Eiffel Tower, a lobby with ivory-colored plaster statues and deep-pile carpeting, miles of swags, and curtains in plum-colored velvet, and a huge pipe organ.[74] Mother and Sis wore their Sunday outfits.

I kept scanning the crowd for Daddy. For all we knew, he was dead. I tried not to think about it.

Organist Dorothy Grotz, '38, patted down her billowing skirts and swung into "Vision" by Josef Rhineberger as the last guests settled in their seats. I perused my program. It seemed

---

74 "One of the largest organs in the world," according to the management. Billy Glossop observed that they'd never seen Dummy Davis in the boys' shower.

as though every other member of my class had won an achievement award or a scholarship. Billy G said, D'ya see my name?

What for? I said, achievement in smoking? I was closing in on my goal to be a wise guy.

Taylor Klein handed me his yearbook and a fountain pen. As I signed, he told me he hadn't made up his mind about the halls of academia, so to speak. He wanted to be Skull & Bones like his father, but the registrar at Yale kept insisting that he enroll first. Frank Videon was graduating two years late; he'd been the wittiest boy in the classes of '40, '41, and '42. I was happy to see that John T. Ramsay[75] was named outstanding athlete, since he was one of the few Big Men on Campus who treated me like a human. Butch Bucceroni and Russ Spotz were among the caps and gowns, but of all my cronies only Eddie Wales won an award, a $50 purchase order for Achievement in Bible Studies. I was pleased that Peggy Beecher took home a prize in Pittman Shorthand as she was already on my personal honors list for best legs. Amanda Rigi went unmentioned in the program and had to settle for having the biggest balcony even though Jack Nokes still insisted it came from her brother's sweatsocks. He admitted that he had no proof. I just know, he said.

My name didn't appear among the prizewinners, of course. Upper Darby High School awarded no prizes for blue-collar sports like bowling or for cheating at German or failing to master the multiplication tables or to learn how to draw a rectangle. In the lobby after the ceremonies, I ran into Mr. Kehl, my homeroom teacher, and he clucked and asked me how the young man with the highest IQ in his room had managed to graduate in the bottom three percent of his class.

I told him it was a long story.

---

[75] Later coach of the Philadelphia Seventy-sixers professional basketball team. As Dr. Jack Ramsay, he became a highly respected TV commentator and basketball guru.

23.

That summer of 1942, something unexpected was happening in the vacant lot next to Playhouse Bowl. A friend named Dickie Clark and I had begun throwing a baseball around when we weren't on duty, and I was finally showing signs of becoming a pitcher. Ever since Daddy had dressed me in my first uniform with spikes and a toe-plate, I'd considered myself a pitcher despite strong indications to the contrary. In an outing the previous summer for the misnamed Drexel Hill Stars, I'd been on the mound against a pickup team that was so incompetent we nicknamed it The Little Sisters of the Poor. After I gave up six or eight runs, our playing manager Dick Coffey called a conference at the mound:

Gimme the ball.

No.

You're finished.

Why?

The bases are loaded. Starkey's up. He doubled the last time.

It was a fluke.

You couldn't find the plate with a microscope.

I'm getting bad calls.

You walked Dath and Slaughter on eight pitches.

Eight bad calls.

That pitch over the backstop was a strike?

It caught the corner. The ump's blind in one eye ...

... and can't see outa the other. Yeah, yeah. Criminy, Jack, gimme the darn ball....

Earlier in the season an umpire had ejected me for my own safety. What'd I do? I whined.

Son, he said, I got boys of my own.

None of these humbling events had shaken my belief that I was a potential Detroit Tigers' hurler and the possessor of six finely honed pitches: fast ball, slow ball, curve, drop, screwball, and knuckleball. I had such an array that I had to teach our catcher extra signals. Catchers traditionally put down one finger for a fastball, two for a curve and three for a slow ball. I taught Buttsy O'Neal to signal my first five pitches with fingers and the sixth (my screwball) by scratching his crotch. Sometimes we crossed each other up, just as my father had crossed me up and broken my nose, but it was never a problem between me and Buttsy since most of my pitches came in at the same speed and didn't curve one way or the other except in my imagination. More often than not, my knuckleball bounced. Dick Coffey said it would be useful in mole control.

But now that I'd graduated, a miracle seemed to be in progress. Dickie Clark and I were having one of our afternoon catches in the vacant lot next to the Playhouse when he took off his glove and shook his hand. Hey, he said, where'd you get all that steam?

Dickie was wearing a fielder's glove and I hadn't realized how hard I was throwing. No more steam, I promised. I'll try my other stuff.

Lately my curve had been breaking so sharply that I would aim a few inches off the plate and watch it arc back over the middle. When Tommy Bridges threw that pitch, sportswriters like Jack Ryan called it a roundhouse. I would never be in the same league as Tommy Bridges, but at least I was playing the same game. A year and a half of lifting sixteen-pound bowling balls and five-pound pins had changed me from a pathetic little thrower to a pretty good pitcher for a kid.

After five or six hard curves Dickie shook his meat hand and told me he'd had enough. Tell you sumpin', he said. You got as much stuff as my brother.

I was surprised. His brother was Bobby Clark, star pitcher of the Upper Darby High baseball team. In 1940 Bobby had pitched a practice game against our Drexel Hill Stars and made us look like home econ majors. I struck out four times and was the happiest kid in Drexel Hill when I went back to the bench without any major fractures.

Thanks, Dickie, I said. But don't tell your brother. I might have to hit against him again.

24.

The military recruiting offices were luring our players, and the Drexel Hill Stars were just about to go out of business. Our left fielder Eddie Wales and right fielder Russ Colegrove had signed up for the Army, reducing us to one regular outfielder, and our second baseman Roger Kapps was headed for the Marines. I was still too young to enlist, but after I read in the *Philadelphia Daily News* that Francis "Gabby" Gabreski was the hottest fighter pilot in the European theater, I planned to fly P-38 Lightnings.[76]

The opponent for our final game was Drexel Manor, the toughest team in Upper Darby and a regular test of our survival instincts. The Manor regarded games with us as light workouts. Our two-year record against them was 0-11. I was the losing pitcher in three of the games, but I'd been showing steady improvement, giving up fourteen runs in my first loss of the season and only three in my last.

The game began on a warm summer evening with the feel of rain in the air and the sun peeping in and out, mostly out. I pitched because Dick Coffey had broken his arm sliding into first base in practice. He always ran the bases like Pepper Martin.

Enemy fans lined up along the foul lines, the men in their

---

76 Gabreski shot down 28 enemy planes in Europe and also became an ace in the Korean war. He made one-fourth of me proud.

undershirts and the women in shorts and frocks, swatting mosquitoes and ducking stubby-winged June bugs. The Manor players looked like pros in their fresh-laundered gray uniforms. The Stars played in street clothes. Catcher Buttsy O'Neal and I were the only Stars wearing spikes. Butts didn't even own a cup. If a pitch was in the dirt, he covered up his crotch and let the ball bounce off his chest protector or mask. The Drexel Hill Stars weren't finicky about equipment. We were so happy to be playing baseball that we'd have played in bare feet and jock straps.

It wasn't long before we began to get an inkling that history might be in the air. In the first inning we scored a run when Gene Weinert hit two batters and gave up two walks. That was the only way we ever scored on him since any hits he gave up were flukes. For the first time in history, the Drexel Hill Stars were leading Drexel Manor.

I didn't allow a base runner for four innings. My curve ball was catching the corners, leaving sluggers like Jack Miller and Bud Coneys enraged at being flamboozled by a pitcher who was so untalented that if he didn't show up for a game they would send a taxi. We were scheduled to play seven innings, and with three to go the Drexel Hill Stars clung to a 1-0 lead.

Then the umpire tore our hearts out. He was Joe Cimboli, a moustached fireplug who'd played sandlot ball in Philadelphia and knew the rulebook backwards. He wore glasses to keep a loose eye on course, but he was considered the best umpire in Upper Darby Township.

In the fifth inning, there was a hint that Mr. Cimboli might be having a rare off night. After Buttsy O'Neal hit a foul ball, he turned and asked, Was that pitch over the plate?

Mr. Cimboli nodded.

Buttsy shook his head about a quarter-inch.

Mr. Cimboli ripped off his mask, stuck his nose in Buttsy's

face and said, One more word and you're outa here!

Between innings, our wounded manager warned us, Don't aggravate the ump. We can win this game. He pointed to the covered scoreboard:

Visitors – 1

Home – 0

All we needed was a good thunderstorm.

With two innings to go, a black-edged cloud obscured the setting sun. Somehow our players took this as a sign that we should start playing like the Bloomer Girls. But so did the Manor. With one out and the bases loaded with my teammates, I hit an easy pop-up that their second baseman Billy Harshman kicked ten yards into right field. By the time Tubby Coneys threw the ball back in, our lead had doubled.

I was standing on first base congratulating myself on my awesome display of power when I heard Dick Coffey yell, Are you crazy?

Mr. Cimboli was standing on home plate and motioning our runners back. He'd called the infield fly rule, a technicality that meant I was out before I left the batter's box and our runners couldn't advance. We griped and bitched and pounded our chests like orangutans, but the call stood. Look it up! the ump yelled. Play ball!

Our rally ended when Brennan Stoknes struck out on a fastball around his ankles. He said he never saw the pitch.

In the bottom of the sixth I threw a weak-sister curve ball to the wrong corner of the plate and Jack Miller, their first baseman, cranked it over the fence. With one inning to play, we were tied at 1-1.

In the top half of the seventh, our dreamy left fielder Pat McGrady beat out a Baltimore chop for a single but got caught in the hidden ball play. Patty dragged his bones back to the bench and said, That's not fair!

Dummy Davis struck out on three pitches. Gene Weinert was throwing harder than he'd thrown in the first inning. He looked as though he could go seven more, or seventeen.[77]

I walked toward the plate swinging three bats. Before discarding two, I swung hard and almost fell down. It was Jersey City stickball all over again. The fans laughed at my coordination.

After the third strike blew by me I was relieved that I didn't have to run the bases. I'd never pitched more than five innings and now I was going out to start the seventh. That afternoon I'd bowled a dozen games. In Phillyspeak, I was "all pooed out."

How they hanging? Dick Coffey asked as I headed toward the mound.

Strong, I said.

How's the arm?

G-r-r-reat.

Daddy always drilled me that a gamer never admitted he was tired or hurt. You could be carried off the field on a stretcher, subjected to major surgery, and when you came out of the ether you were supposed to yell, Gimme the ball. C'mon, doc, gimme the ball! That was the way Christy Mathewson played the game, and Walter Johnson, "the Big Train." And Cy Young and Grover Cleveland Alexander, Lefty Grove, Bob Feller.

I was sure that Daddy had played the same way even if it wasn't for the Tigers. He would still be pitching if it wasn't for that darn injury. I wondered what he was doing tonight and where he was doing it. I couldn't think bad of Daddy. In fifty-two years, he never got a break. If God dumped me in Indianapolis with a vicious stepmother, I would turn out a whole lot worse. At least Daddy kept trying.

I took the mound for the last inning under a purple sky.

---

77   He pitched hundreds of more innings in the minor leagues before spending 42 years as an engineer with General Electric.

The best we could get was a tie, but a tie against Drexel Manor would be like whipping the Yankees.

I'd been pitching for nearly two hours. I could bowl and set pins all day and half the night, but pitching always drained my energy. I threw a couple of warm-ups to Buttsy and wondered what happened to the feeling in my arm.

The first batter was Johnny Cutts, a chunky lefthander who had a big rusty-gate swing and often struck out. After Buttsy O'Neal put down two fingers, I reared back and cocked my wrist. The ball squirted from my hand and dribbled to our second baseman. A laugh went up from the fans, and the Manor cheerleader led a song to the tune of the bugle call Assembly:

There's a pitcher in the box
With a head like an ox
Take him out, take him out
Take him out, take him out.

I realized that I had to lay the ball right down Broad Street and hope for the best. I'd seen tired major leaguers in the same fix. They had nothing left, so they just pitched and prayed. Sometimes it worked.

Johnny Cutts swung from the soles of his spikes and sent my first pitch ten feet over the right field fence. I felt pole-axed. A few years back his homer would have been a loud out, but "over the fence is out" was no longer the rule.

The Manor fans screamed and yelled and jumped up and down as I dragged my tired bones toward our bench. I still had to set pins for the late league. I was hoping someone would give me a lift to the Playhouse, four blocks away. Then I heard the boos.

Go back! Dick Coffey was yelling. His splinted arm flapped against his side as he gestured at me with the other. The fans were booing. I didn't understand. Their team had won the game. What the heck did they want?

I turned and saw Mr. Cimboli standing on the third base line with his arms crossed. As Johnny Cutts jogged down the line, the ump pointed at him with his index finger and then jerked his thumb straight up. Johnny was out. In the excitement of hitting the game winner, he'd carried his bat past first base, a violation of one of the oldest rules in kid baseball.

A banshee argument and several death threats at the plate didn't help my composure. After Joe Cimboli broke the Manor cheerleader's megaphone over their bench, I still needed two more outs to earn a tie.

I threw four straight balls to Ducky Miedwig, not one missing the plate by more than an inch or two. In the gloaming, the ump was calling balls and strikes as tough as ever.

Larry Bloke stepped into the left-handed batter's box. He usually treated me like his personal batting-practice pitcher. There was nothing on my first pitch except the Spalding label, but it caught the low outside corner of the plate where Larry couldn't pull it over the fence.

Mr. Cimboli barked, Ball!

I was trying to read Buttsy's sign when I heard someone yell, Hey, ump, you're missing a great game!

I wondered who had the guts to criticize the toughest umpire in Delaware County.

Joe Cimboli had been known to throw hecklers out of the ballpark. Bodily.

My second pitch was outside. Ball two. No argument.

The foghorn voice shouted, Clean your specs, ump!

Mr. Cimboli was sensitive about his eyesight and I expected him to blow up. He glanced toward the sound as he dusted the plate. I wished the loudmouth would shut up. He wasn't helping anybody's concentration, least of all mine. I didn't need some fool to make an angry ump angrier.

I ended up walking Larry Bloke. Now the Manor had men

on first and second with one out. A hit could win the game.

I started Tubby Coneys with a fat pitch that he missed by a foot. The shadows were tough on everybody. No more free passes, I told myself. Make 'em hit their way on base. God and the law of averages might save my backside.

I laid a slow ball right down Broad Street, and Coneys took it for a strike. Then I threw three straight balls that weren't even close. With the count three and two, I shut my eyes and snapped off the last hard curve my arm had left.

It headed straight for Tubby's shoulders, then dropped and twisted over the heart of the plate.

Joe Cimboli yelled, Ball four!

I was stunned. How could he miss that pitch? Now the bases were loaded, and the Manor fans were singing:

The pitcher's in the air
The catcher needs a chair.
Take him out, take him out
Take him out, take him out.

When the racket subsided, the same loud heckler yelled, Hey, four-eyes, be fair! These is just kids! I looked toward third base and spotted a dim figure in the shadows. As I watched, the man held his hands to his mouth and bellowed, Get a tin cup, for Chrissakes! Mr. Cimboli took off his mask and headed for the sound in a pigeon-toed walk. The man called out, I ain't going nowhere, dago!

I recognized the voice.

I put my hands on my knees, shut my eyes, and tried to will myself onto the observation deck of the Blue Comet, drinking an RC Cola. My eyes were still closed when I heard the ump shout, Play ball!

I said, Huh?

Somebody said, They're gonna fight it out after the game.

It was Dick Coffey. He'd come to the mound to settle me

down.

Daddy in a fistfight. I thought, Oh, my God, I can't let this happen. Mr. Cimboli's a tough guy and Daddy's an old man with a truss. He can't even run away.

I walked Jack Miller on four pitches. Ducky Miedwig was forced in from third and the game was over. I watched as Mr. Cimboli undid his mask and chest protector, laid them in the grass, and headed for the crowd behind third base.

I started toward the action. When I reached the sidelines I heard loud laughter. The crowd parted, and Mr. Cimboli and Daddy were standing face to face, shaking hands. All I heard was, Just a game, Joe.... Sticking up for your kid, Swede....

I turned toward our bench to collect my Paul Waner model bat. Dick Coffey smacked me on the back with his good arm and said, You pitched the greatest game we ever lost. Players from both teams congratulated me, but I hardly noticed.

I saw Daddy heading my way, skipping over the foul line as usual. Gotta get a move on, he called out. I'm running late.

I said, Wait, Daddy. I'll walk you.

He needed a shave, and his wavy hair was tousled. He seemed surprised that I was glad to see him. He said, How ya was, Sonny boy?

I'm all in, Daddy. Could you gimme a ride to the Playhouse?

I wish I could, Son, but I'm, uh ... I'm late.

After all these years he'd found out that his kid could pitch a little. Why rush off?

Sorry we lost, I said as we left the field side by side.

Nobody's fault, he said. When you threw that curve? To their first baseman?

The home run?

Yeah. You hit the wrong corner.

I was trying ...

You dropped your shoulder.

I didn't want to discuss the game. I wanted to say how much I missed him. I wanted to tell him that Sis and Mother and I had jobs and if he came back home we'd have enough money to eat Hap's ice cream and watch him knock over the metal bottles at Woodside Park and see some games at Shibe Park and Baker Bowl.

He stepped up his pace and I could hear his breathing. Gotta go now, he repeated. Be seeing ya, Son.

When?

I'm working on something hot. I'll write.

I should have been surprised, but I wasn't. Daddy was always working on something hot. Mother said that his biggest problem was that he could never walk past a racehorse or a crap game.

He patted me on the arm and said, You got a nice little curve ball. Then he walked off. Something told me he was gone for good.

I love you, Daddy.

I said the words, but not out loud.

It was dark by the time I reached Playhouse Bowl. A lightning bug blinked in my face and spring peepers whistled in the grass. As I started up the steps, I heard the pins fall from the early league's final frames.

A car eased from a parking spot under a big maple across Garrett Road. I barely made out the silhouettes of a man and a woman. As the car picked up speed and headed toward the city, I heard the metallic clank of an electric gearshift.

I told myself, I'm seventeen now. I'll get over it. They can kill you but they can't eat you.

The rest of my life will be easy.

Author's Note

A few of the incidents in *The Pitcher's Kid* were recounted in my earlier work, *Over the Fence Is Out* (Holt, Rinehart & Winston, 1961). At that time my father was alive, and to spare him any discomfort (not to mention arrest and incarceration), I wrote under the pseudonym "Jonathan Rhoades." My mother and sister advised that this was unnecessary as my father never read anything except the sport pages and would have welcomed the publicity, even the parts that made him look foolish. Perhaps he is reading this somewhere and will find a way to tell me what he thinks of my work. He might claim that this isn't the way it happened, but this is the way I remember it.

Please note also that I have changed some names to avoid invading privacy. Many of the characters are dead or in their final years. In cases where there was the slightest possibility of libel or where the character may still be alive, I have changed the name.

About the author

Born June 7, 1925, Jack Olsen was the award-winning author of 33 books published in 15 countries and 11 languages. A former *Time* bureau chief, Olsen wrote for *Vanity Fair, People, Paris Match, Readers Digest, Playboy, Life, Sports Illustrated, Fortune, New York Times Book Review* and others. His books included *The Misbegotten Son, The Bridge at Chappaquiddick,* the eco-thriller *Night of the Grizzlies,* and his monumental study of a Nazi massacre in Italy, *Silence on Monte Sole.* Three of his works were adapted for the screen, including *Have You Seen My Son?* on ABC. The *Philadelphia Inquirer* described him as "an American treasure."

The Pitcher's Kid is Jack Olsen's memoir of the first 17 years of his life, years that formed his voice, his ear, and his passionate concern for the underdog. It is a story of a young boy's desperate yearning for a father during a time of extreme poverty and confusion. The book has been compared to the work of Frank McCourt for its depiction of deprivation, of Geoffrey Wolff for its depiction of a deceptive father, and of David Sedaris for its tragicomic depiction of childhood.

Jack Olsen passed away on July 18, 2002.

A information can be obtained at www.ICGtesting.com
in the USA
1527271011
3V00001B/1/P